The Germans from Lithuania of Cleveland

A collection of genealogies
of the *Deutsche aus Litauen* in Cleveland, Ohio,
their children and grandchildren.

Compiled by
Owen M. McCafferty II

Edited by
Cynthia Spurgat Jacobson

Published by

The International Association of Germans from Lithuania

The Germans from Lithuania of Cleveland: A Collection of Genealogies
© 2025 International Association of Germans from Lithuania

All rights reserved. No part of this book may be reproduced or transmitted in any form or by any means, electronic or mechanical, including photocopying or recording, or by any information storage and retrieval system, without permission in writing from the publisher.

Library of Congress Control Number: 2025947371
ISBN: 979-8-218-78459-1

Published by International Association of Germans from Lithuania, LLC
Printed in the United States of America

On the cover: background—Terminal Tower – East 3rd Street View, 1929. Reproduced with permission from Cleveland State University.

Dedicated to my great-great-grandparents:

Johann Andreas Heinrich Saleker
and
Emilie Wiemert

and all the other brave immigrants of past generations who traversed treacherous waters and made Cleveland their home.

Table of Contents

Table of Contents 4

Acknowledgements 11

Foreword 13

Introduction 15

Map: Lithuania, Poland and the Kalinigrad Oblast 20

ACKERMANN 27

ALBRECHT 31

ANDECHSER / ANDEXEL/ ANDEXLER / ANDEXEN 33

AUGUSTAT / AUGUSTAITIS 37

AUKSCHUN 39

BALTRUNAT / BALTRONAT 41

BARANOWICZ / BARANOWITZ / BARANOWITSCH / BAUER ... 43

BASENAU / BAZENAU / BOSSMAN / BOZMAN 44

BASCHAR 49

BATKE 50

BAUMANN 51

BENDER 53

BERWING 54

BIRKOBEN / BERKOBEIN / BERKENBEIN 57

BLUM / BLUHM / BLOOM 58

BOMBLIS / BUMBLIS 59

BORCHERT 63

BRAUER 64

BUDNIK 65

BUKNAT / BUKNAITIS / BOKNAT 66

BURKE 67

BUSCHAR / BUSCHER 69

DANGELAT / DANGELEIT	70
DIKHEISER / DYKHEYSER	71
DIKSCHAT / DUKSCHAT / DICK	74
DILL / DILEWSKI / DYLEWSKI	75
DINGFELD / DINGFELDT	80
DOCZKIS / DOCZKAT / DUTCHCOT	81
DORN	83
ECKERT	85
EICHELBERGER	87
ELMENTHALER	88
ERNST	89
ERZTHALER / STAYLER	90
ESSEL	91
FILIER / FILLER / FIEHLER	95
FISCHER	96
FRANULEWITZ / FRANULEWICZ / FRANLEY	97
FRENKEL	99
FRIEDKE / FRETKE	100
FRIEDRICH	101
GERULAT / GERULAITIS / GERLAT	104
GESCHWANDTNER	105
GLEICHFORSCH	106
GLEID / GLEIDT	107
GÜNTHER / GINTER	108
GRIGAT / GRIGAITIS	110
GRÜBNER / GRIBNER	112
GUDAT / GUDAITIS	113
GUTMANN	115

HAASE / HASE / HAZE	116
HABERSAT	118
HARTIG	119
HASENHEIT	120
HAUSRATH	121
HEIMERT	125
HEIN	126
HEINRICH / HENRY	131
HEMPEL	135
HERR	136
HESS	137
HIRSCH	138
HUBERT	140
JESSAT / JESSET / JANZAT / JANSZAT	141
JONAT / JONAITIS / JONATH	142
JURGELEIT / YURGELEIT / URGELEIT	143
JURGELEWICZ / JURGELEWITZ	145
JURKSCHAT / YURKSCHAT / JURKSCHAITIS / URKSCHAT	146
KALCHERT	148
KALWEIT / KALLWEIT / KALWAITIS	149
KAPTEIN	150
KAUSCH	152
KELLER	153
KEMERAIT / KEMMERAIT / KEMERAITIS	154
KIESLING / KIZLING	155
KINAT / KINAITIS / KENAT	156
KIRSCHNER / KROSCHNEWSKI	162
KLAUS	165

KLESS / KLEES / KLÖS / KLOSS / KLASS	166
KLEIN	169
KLOTZHOBER / GLOTZOBER	170
KOKOSCHKA / KOKOSKY / KOKOSKI	171
KONRAD / CONRAD	172
KRAMER / KRÄMER	173
LACKNER / LACHNER / LOCKNER	174
LANG / LANGE	175
LAUKS	180
LEHMANN	181
LEICHERT	183
LIER / LEAR	184
LINDHAMMER	186
LOGIES	187
LUKAT	189
MAI / MAY	191
MAURUSCHAT / NAURUSCHAT / NAURUSCHAITIS	193
METT	194
METZDORF	195
MÜLLERSZOWSKI / MILLERSKOWSKI / MILLERSKOFSKI / MILLER	196
MISSUN	198
MITTAG	199
MURANKO / MURANKE / MURANKI	200
MUSCHINSKI	201
NAUSNER / NOS	203
NEITZEL / NETZEL / NECEL	207
NEUBACHER	209
NEUMANN / NEIMANN / NIEMANN	211

NIEDERSTRASS / NIEDERSTRASSE / NIEDER	214
NIESS / NEISS	216
NOWIAK / NAUJOK / NOWJACK	218
PASEKEL	222
PAMPUS / PEMPUS	223
PERREY / PERRY / PERREI / PERREJ / BAREIG	224
PETER / PETERS	229
PODZIS / PODGIS / PODGIES	233
POLLAK / PAULAK	234
PUDIMAT / PUDIM / PUDIMAITIS	235
PUSHKAT / PUSKAT	237
PUTNAT / PUTNOT / PUTNAITIS	238
REBNER	239
REDER / RÄDER	240
REICHEL / REJCHEL	241
REINECKER	242
REINKE / RENKE / RENK	243
REITER	246
ROMANOWSKI	248
ROSEKEIT	249
SALEKER / SALECKER	250
SCHAAK / SZAK / SCHACK	253
SCHARFETTER	254
SCHILLER	255
SCHMIDT / SZMIDT	256
SCHNEIDER	258
SCHNELL	260
SCHÖNRANK / SCHÖNRANG	261

SCHRÖDER	262
SCHULZ / SCHULTZ / SCHÜTZ / SCHITZ	264
SCHWANDT / SCHWAND	267
SCHWED / SZWED / SCHWEDAS	268
SCHWELGIN	272
SCHWENTER / SCHWENTOR	274
SEMLER	275
SIMON / SIEMON / SEAMAN / SEAMON / SIMONAT / SIMONEIT	276
SOKOLEK / SOKOLIK	277
SPEI	278
SPURGAT / SPORGAT	279
STASSUN / STASUN / STOSSUN	280
TENNEBOR / TENNEBAR	282
TETMEIER / TETMEYER / TETTMEIER	285
TIEDMANN	287
TIESLAU / TISLAU / TIESLAUK / TISLAUK / TISLAK / DYSLAK / TISCHLER	293
UNTERBERGER	296
WACHHAUS	298
WALINSKI / WOLINSKE	299
WEGNER / WAGNER	300
WEIER / WIEHER	301
WEINSCHRÖDER / WEINSCHREIDER	302
WIEMERT	304
WILK / WILCZINSKI / WOLF	306
WISGIN	308
WORM / WURM	309
APPENDIX A – CLEVELAND LUTHERAN CEMETERY	311
APPENDIX B – PHOTOGRAPHS OF LUTHERAN CEMETERY	314

APPENDIX C – WORKS CONSULTED 345

INDEX OF IMMIGRANTS 347

INDEX OF PLACES WHERE IMMIGRANTS WERE BORN 362

INDEX OF *DEUTSCHE AUS LITAUEN* INTERRED AT LUTHERAN CEMETERY 372

Acknowledgements

I would like to thank the editor in chief of *Die Weite*, Cynthia Spurgat Jacobson, for her editing and expertise as well as for writing the Foreword to this book. Her constant support and encouragement drive me to do projects like this.

Thanks also to Amy Wicks of the Lutheran Cemetery Association for her help in locating many graves that I could not find on my own.

I also extend my gratitude to Deborah of Zion Evangelical Lutheran Church, who provided me with digital copies of church records that have aided in my research of the *Deutsche aus Litauen* for almost a decade. This book would not have been possible without her help in accessing the records.

Finally, to the IAGL community members and supporters who either directly or indirectly aided me with this work.

Foreword

Cynthia Spurgat Jacobson

The reader is struck by the following notable inclusions.

Most dates of immigration cover a 60-year range. The earliest documented immigrant arriving in Cleveland was Karl Andechser (nr. 264; 1864-1911) who immigrated in 1888. The majority of the *Deutsche aus Litauen* immigrated to Cleveland after 1890. Some even came after WWII. One traveled by automobile via a bridge and a tunnel. A few even came by air.

The reader will also be impressed with the variety of locations: So many were baptized and confirmed in the Marijampolė Evangelical Lutheran Church. The origins of this congregation date to 1819. Between 1874 and 1894 there were 3,099 members. Three more churches – Kalvarija, Seirijai and Vilkaviškis – belonged to Marijampolė Evangelical Lutheran Congregation, are also well represented in these pages.

Sometimes the reader may be disappointed with the lack of specific information. What ship? What parish? What month and date of birth, confirmation, marriage, or immigration occur? One need only to be reminded of the exhaustive research behind the extensive inventory (117,388 at the time of publication) on the Germans from Lithuania website **www.germnansfromlithuania.org** to realize that the status of some of these records is "lost/unknown." Occasionally, information on missing records can be replaced with precious family artifacts or located on American church records which may have been recorded by an overly attentive German Lutheran pastor.

One cannot help but notice the variety of surnames:

Some are classic "German" names like Bauer and Weber. They may have been Swabians or Franconians from southwestern Germany before their ancestors emigrated to East Prussia, where almost all the *Deutsche aus Litauen* originated before migrating farther east.

Others are Salzburgers, like Saleker and Wiemert, Protestants exiled by the Archbishop of Salzburg, Austria, in 1731 only to find a home in East Prussia offered by Friedrich Wilhelm I in 1732. Some Salzberger descendants migrated to *NeuOstPreussen* (New East Prussia), Prussian territory only from 1795 to 1807 and after the 1815 Congress of Vienna, a protectorate of the Russian Empire until 1918. It was during the first half of this 100-year era that most of our ancestors lived for two or three generations in what became southwest Lithuania after WWI.

Some names are Prussian-Lithuanian like Baltrunat with the truncated "-at," instead of the Lithuanian "-aitis" or Simoneit with the "-eit" ending. Over the centuries, native Lithuanians and Prussians inhabited the eastern half of the province of East Prussia in what became known as the Gumbinnen Administrative District, today the eastern part of the Kalinigrad Oblast of Russia.

Others have Slavic origins like "-ski" in Muschinski or "-wicz" in Franulewicz. Perhaps these *Deutsche aus Litauen* were "Germanized" as Prussian rulers acquired Polish lands over the centuries and/or married into the *Evangelische* church.

Perhaps most notable is the passion with which the author completed this project. It is most evident in the listing of places Appendix A and the photographs in Appendix B from Cleveland's Lutheran Cemetery.

Introduction

And whoever observes the factories, whoever passes down commercial streets and seeks after the names of the owners of businesses, he will discover uncommonly many German names, which would be proof that Germans have been most deeply involved in the building of the city and that German energy and entrepreneurial spirit has done the most to make Cleveland what it is today.

Cleveland and its Germans, 1907

Although Lithuanian colonies were established in other industrial centers in Ohio, such as Akron, Dayton, Youngstown, and several more, nevertheless, Cleveland was the center for Lithuanians in Ohio.

Lithuanian Americans and their Communities of Cleveland
John Cadzow

Growing up, I was raised with the Irish traditions and customs from my father's side of the family. As a child on the west side of Cleveland, I was surrounded by other Irish families. During the 1990s on Lydian Avenue in West Park (a Cleveland suburb), it seemed like everyone on our street was Irish. We went to an Irish Catholic church, and I started my early education at an Irish Catholic school. As a result, I had never viewed Cleveland as a 'German city,' and certainly not as a 'Lithuanian' one. Fellow Clevelanders will understand this geographic divide — communities split between the mighty Cuyahoga River, the East Side and the West Side.

Imagine my surprise when, during the earliest days of my genealogical research, I discovered my maternal family were not just Germans or Prussians but *Deutsche aus Litauen*. Why would they choose Cleveland as home? Were there Lithuanians here, too?

Indeed, there were — Cleveland boasts a large and vibrant Lithuanian community that once centered itself just east of Downtown Cleveland around Hamilton Avenue and the east 60s and 70s. Later, Lithuanian immigrant families moved to Euclid and Collinwood, both farther eastern suburbs of Cleveland. Today, the Cleveland Lithuanian Club is still thriving in Euclid, and some families have even made it to the West Side of the city.

For many years I assumed, quite incorrectly, that my Saleker and Wiemert ancestors (who hailed from Liukiai and Kalvarija respectively) were only one of a tiny handful of German Lithuanians who settled in Cleveland. It was not until I began to search through the church books of the Zion Evangelical Lutheran Church on East 30th and Prospect Streets in Downtown Cleveland that I understood just how large the *Deutsche aus Litauen* community was in northeast Ohio. Cleveland was not just home to 'ethnic' Lithuanians — it was home to German Lithuanians as well and not just those of my own family.

Initially, I only expected to publish a small booklet of names — a hundred or so — but as the weeks and months passed, that tiny booklet grew into a book of over 1,500. Unsurprisingly, the *Deutsche aus Litauen* community in Cleveland was tight-knit. You will notice many families intermarrying, proving that there was a network of compatriots from the *Heimat* that socialized, lived, and worshipped together.

It is my hope that this work aids genealogists and family historians both in the US and Europe with their research — to make lost connections between those who immigrated here and those who stayed in Europe. It is also my hope that this book helps to establish the relevancy of our community and our ancestors' origins. Cleveland truly was a hub for our diaspora, and I am immensely proud that I was born and raised here.

I encourage anyone with familial roots here to visit — come and stroll among the headstones of the many *Deutsche aus Litauen* families in the Lutheran Cemetery on Pearl Road and Knollwood Cemetery on SOM Center Road. You will find many recognizable names and many German words and phrases which adorn the centuries old headstones. Of note is the Zion Evangelical Lutheran Church which boasts a beautiful interior and a hand-carved altar brought from Germany in the 19th century.

I only have one piece of advice before you visit: don't come in the winter!

Owen M. McCafferty II
Cleveland, October 2025

Research Methodology

It is important for the reader to know that this collection of names and genealogies is by no means complete. I have missed or omitted individuals for a variety of reasons – often because of a lack of information, particularly those who came to Cleveland from Europe directly following WWII.

Various sources were used to identify individuals who belonged to the *Deutsche aus Litauen* minority and who resided in northeast Ohio. The decision to include those individuals was based on a variety of factors and was made at my own discretion.

Most importantly, only individuals who were born in what is today southwest Lithuania and northeast Poland – both of which were part of the Russian Empire from 1815-1914/1918 as the Suwałki Governorate – were included. The word "Governorate" is a translation of the Russian word *gubérniya* (губéрния) or *gubernia* meaning an administrative division or province which is ruled by a Governor (Russian: *gubernator*.)

To substantiate the place of birth, only individuals whose records could be found in Lithuania — from records of the various Evangelical Lutheran Churches in the Suwałki Governorate — were included. Indeed, there were some who, though certainly born there, were excluded due to the inability to find a birth record in the Suwałki Governorate. There are some rare exceptions when other overwhelming evidence existed to support a place of birth.

Individuals did not need to live exclusively in the city of Cleveland to be listed. Those who lived in northeast Ohio and, as far west from Cleveland as Sandusky and Toledo, are also listed. In most cases, I included individuals who lived a significant amount of their lives in northeast Ohio — many retired to other locations in the US. Generally, I did not include individuals who emigrated *back* to Europe or who appeared to only live in northeast Ohio for less than a year.

Information about places of birth, baptism, and confirmation (and marriage in the cases of individuals who married before emigrating to the US) came from records of Lutheran churches in the Suwałki Governorate for most individuals. The IAGL online index was the major source for these records, and readers can find these individuals in that index. Readers should note that if a baptism, confirmation, or marriage place is listed, I was able to locate the record to substantiate the claim. Individual citations for each piece of data are not included.

Although the primary interest for most readers is for individuals who emigrated to Cleveland from the Suwałki Governorate, three generations of families are included: the 'primary immigrant' who was born there, their children, and their grandchildren. Children who were born there also have their children and grandchildren listed. The level of detail included for each generation lessens between the primary immigrant, their child, and the grandchild of the primary immigrant.

Other sources of information include those typical in American genealogical research such as federal census records, the Social Security Death Index, civil birth, marriage, and death records. A general list of works consulted is available in Appendix C.

Of particular usefulness were the various church records of several Evangelical Lutheran Churches in northeast Ohio which featured a significant population of *Deutsche aus Litauen* including Zion Evangelical Lutheran Church, St. Paul's Evangelical Lutheran Church, Schifflein Christi Evangelical Lutheran Church, and others. The marriage records of Zion Evangelical at E 30th and Payne Avenue provided important details as the person who recorded the information also included the names of towns and villages of births for the bride and the groom during the late 19th and early 20th centuries.

The reader should be warned that information concerning individuals born less than 100 years ago is sparse — this is especially evident in the listing of primary immigrant's grandchildren. In some cases, the names of these children were taken from obituaries or other sources and may not be complete or entirely correct.

Alternate Surnames

The genealogical researcher often encounters alternate spellings or a complete 'reinvention' of a surname – usually a transliteration into English, German, Polish, Russian, etc.

Changes happened for various reasons. Typically, immigrants simplified their names to make them more phonetically compatible with the English speakers. In other cases, the transliteration of the original Germanic surname into Polish or Russian, the languages used in recording birth records in the Suwałki Governorate (until Lithuanian independence), also affected how the name was spelled.

Immigrants to the US did not have their names changed by officials at the port of entry (i.e. Castle Garden, Ellis Island, Baltimore, etc.) against their will. First, the recording of an immigrant's name on a ship manifest *does not* constitute an official recording of the name (as a social security application or birth certificate). Second, the names on the manifest were usually recorded at the port of *departure* — not at the port of arrival.

Several formatting methods are used. For example, the title of each surname includes common versions separated by a stroke:

FILIER / FILLER / FIEHLER

Name variations are also included within the entry itself. For example, Wilhelmine Filier married Jakob Tieslauk, and so she became Wilhelmine Tieslauk. However, in the US, Jakob Tieslauk used the surname "Tischler" instead as it was easier for many English speakers to pronounce because it was a common German surname in America.

To account for these different spellings, the first entry always includes the birth name of the individual:

Wilhelmine **FILIER**

Her married name is bolded and capitalized in parenthesis, using the birth name of her spouse:

Wilhelmine **FILIER (TIESLAUK)**

To account for the variation of Tieslauk into Tischler, the alternate name is *italicized* to denote that it is a variation of the surname Tieslauk:

Wilhelmine **FILIER (TIESLAUK)** (*TISCHLER*)

Alternate spellings of spouses may also appear within the body of the immigrant's entry. For example:

iii. Gustav Saleker b. 1 Sep. 1897. d. 22 Nov. 1965. m. Julianna **Dauksza** (*Dickson*) 1901-1929.

Note that the alternate spelling of Julianna's birth name is in parenthesis, bolded, and italicized. This may occur with other individuals within the body of the entries, including parents.

Place Names of Birth, Marriages, and Confirmations

The borders of modern Lithuania, Poland, and the Kaliningrad Oblast are shown in the IGGL Map, "Lithuania, Poland and the Kalinigrad Oblast." See Figure 1. These modern borders replace the former German province of East Prussia and are vastly different than they were when most immigrants in this book were born. These shifting borders were the results of three major partitions (1772-1795) between the ruling empires in Europe at the time: Prussia, Austria-Hungry, and Russia. Most of what is today known as Lithuania and northeast Poland fell under the control of the Russian Empire from 1815 until Lithuanian independence in 1918. I provide the reader with information to understand the geographic context as it relates to the genealogical information.

Map: Lithuania, Poland and the Kalinigrad Oblast

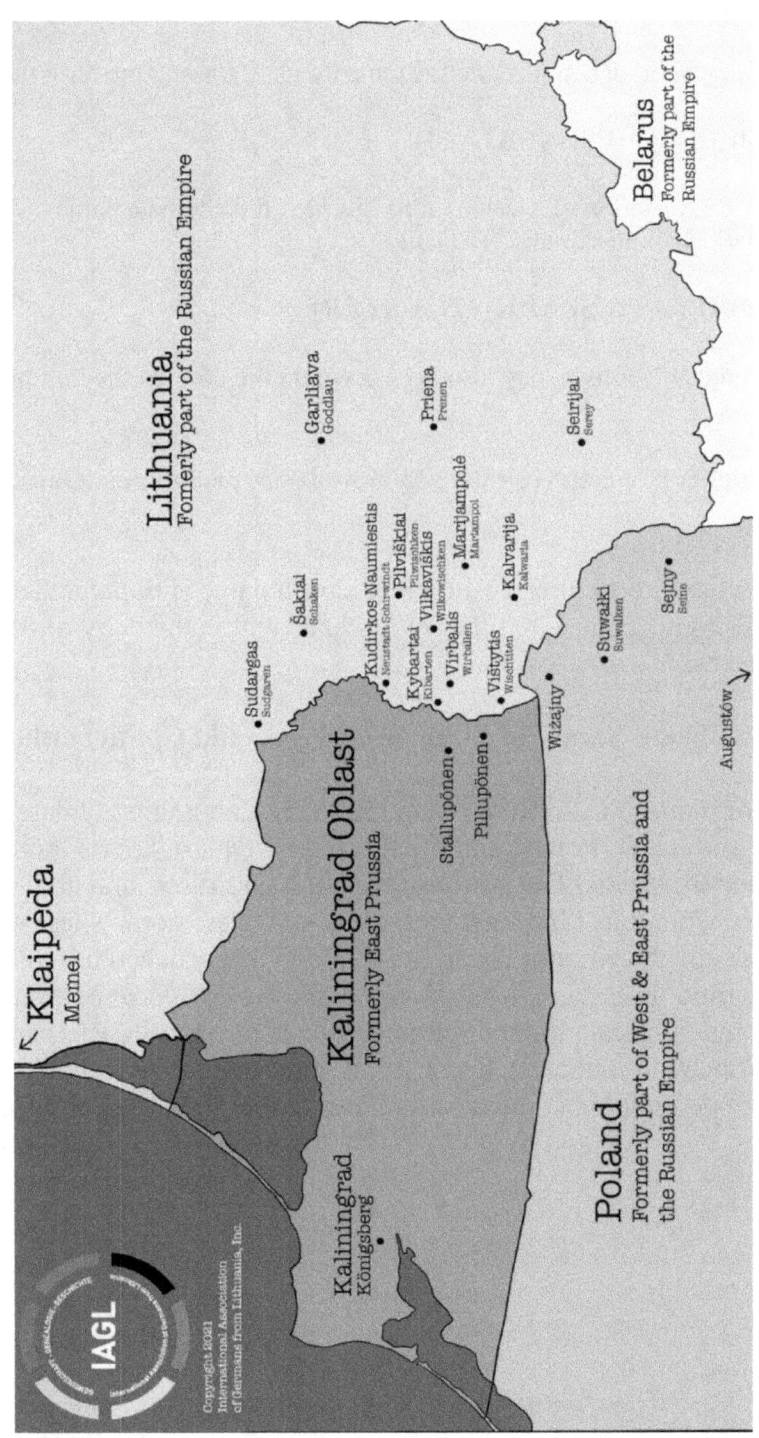

Figure 1 This map features the locations of Evangelical Lutheran Churches in southwest Lithuania and northeast Poland. All of the individuals listed in this book born in Lithuania or in what is today northeast Poland lived in or near these towns.

For example, the reader may come across the following entry:

August **BARANOWICZ (BAUER)** born 11 Oct 1882 near Wiżajny (Poland). Son of Friedrich Baranowicz (1857-????) and Anna **Rabenstein** (1861-????).

Note that the place of birth is listed as near Wiżajny **(Poland)**. The country is in parenthesis because today the town of Wiżajny is located in Poland. However, at the time of August Baranowicz' birth, it was still part of the Suwałki Governorate of the Russian Empire. The current border of Lithuania-Poland near this area did not exist in 1882, and as a result, many families who lived in what is today Lithuania, attended church in what is today Poland — and vice versa!

When an individual is born in independent Lithuania, the current Lithuanian name of the place of birth is noted. In the case below, it is the village of Mikabaliai. For example,

Adolf Franz **ACKERMANN** born 1856 in Mikabaliai. Son of Friedrich Ackermann and Wilhelmine **Hartig**.

Many small villages in Lithuania and northeast Poland no longer exist. While they are on historical maps and gazetteers of the area before WWII, they are not on modern maps. In this case, the former Polish name of the village or town is provided, along with a notation of nearby towns in their Lithuanian names to give the reader some geographic context.

The reason for the Polish spelling of the town is a result of the aforementioned Partitions of Poland (1772 to 1795). Because what is today southwest Lithuania belonged to the Russian Empire (specifically, this partition belonged to "Congress Poland", a territory of the Russian Empire from 1815 to 1918, the official name of the towns was Polish (until the mid-to-late 1860s) or Russian (until WWI). This spelling appears on older maps, so the reader is provided with the former Polish name to aid in finding the location on historical maps.

For example, Emilie Baumann was born in Puszogród which has since disappeared from the map but was located between Panemunė and Pakuonis today.

Emilie **BAUMANN (SCHWED)** born in 1892 in Puszogród (no longer exists; was located somewhere between Panemunė and Pakuonis). Daughter of Karl Baumann and Karoline **Nibergala**.

Many of these small villages that have disappeared were once dominated by Germans. After WWII, when nearly all of the Germans of Lithuania fled to Western Europe, they were deserted or so sparsely populated, that they lost their designations as a village or town.

Entries for immigrants also include the place of baptism, marriage, and sometimes confirmation. When these events took place in what is today Lithuania or northeast Poland, the German name of the parish is noted. In the example below, Adolf Franz Ackermann was born in the village of Mikabaliai (the Lithuanian name of the village) and was baptized at Serey Reformed Lutheran Church. The Lithuanian spelling of "Serey" is *Serijai*. It also notes that his marriage to Emilie Nauser took place at Prenen Evangelical Lutheran Church. The Lithuanian spelling of Prenen is *Prienai*.

Adolf Franz **ACKERMANN** born 1856 in Mikabaliai. Son of Friedrich Ackermann and Wilhelmine **Hartig**. Baptized at Serey Reformed Lutheran Church. Married Emilie **Nausner** (1859-1942) at Prenen Evangelical Lutheran Church in 1882.

Living Individuals

When an individual listed is either living or assumed living, the year of death is, naturally, not listed. For example:
 Owen M. McCafferty II 1991-
Again, the reader should be cautioned that verifiable information about individuals who are living or assumed living, may be inaccurate as a result of research difficulties with more recent generations, or privacy concerns.

Unknown Years

The reader may come across entries with years of birth or death noted with four question marks (????). This signifies that the year of birth and/or death could not be substantiated. For example, the years of birth for the parents of August Baranowicz could be substantiated, but their year of death could not:

August **BARANOWICZ (BAUER)** born 11 Oct 1882 near Wiżajny (Poland). Son of Friedrich Baranowicz (1857-????) and Anna **Rabenstein** (1861-????).

Names and Details of Spouses and Second Marriages

In most cases, the birth name of the spouse (in the case of males) or the surname of the spouse (in the case of females) is noted. However, especially in listings of the 2nd generation, the first name or last name of the spouse may not have been substantiated. In this case, a (?) may appear following the first name.

The level of detail regarding the marriage is dependent on what information was available when researching the couple. In many cases, the date and place of marriage, such as the church, was found. In other cases, varying levels of details could not be substantiated.

Information on Children and Grandchildren

The most detailed information in this book is about the immigrant — the individual(s) who were born in the Suwałki Governorate and settled in northeast Ohio. If their children may have also been born there, those children have detailed listings. The amount of information about the children or grandchildren who were born in the US, lessens.

Of particular note are the names of grandchildren of immigrants. Because these are the most recent generation, the information is limited. Some listings do not include all the names of grandchildren.

For example, Charles Andexler had four children, but only three are listed:

ii. Charles Andexler b. 14 Feb 1898 d. 31 Mar 1956. m. Stella **Clay** 1905-1953.
    4 children:
        Alverna Mae 1922-1995
        Bette Jane 1924-1926
        Donald 1931-1990

The name of the 4th child could not be verified.

If the individual had children with more than once spouse, the names of the children may not necessarily be in birth order or by spouse.

Churches

Like cemeteries, if the church(es) mentioned in the entry does/do not include a city, then the church is/was located in Cleveland. Churches include:

Bethlehem Evangelical Lutheran Church
Immanuel Lutheran Church
St. John Lutheran Church
St. Paul Lutheran Church
St. Paul's Evangelical Independent Church
St. Peter Lutheran Church
St. Procop Catholic Church
St. Stephen Catholic Church
St. Theodosius Russian Orthodox Church
Third Reformed [Lutheran] Church
Zion Evangelical Lutheran Church

Cemeteries

Many immigrants were laid to rest at the Lutheran Cemetery in Cleveland, Ohio — specifically in the Old Brooklyn neighborhood of the city. There were other cemeteries in the city limits where families buried their deceased. If the cemetery was within the city limits of Cleveland, the city name is not provided. If the cemetery was located outside the city limits, the cemetery and the city are listed. See Figure 2. a map of the *Deutsche aus Litauen* Cemeteries of Cleveland on the next page.

Map of *Deutche aus Litauen* Cemeteries in Cleveland, Ohio

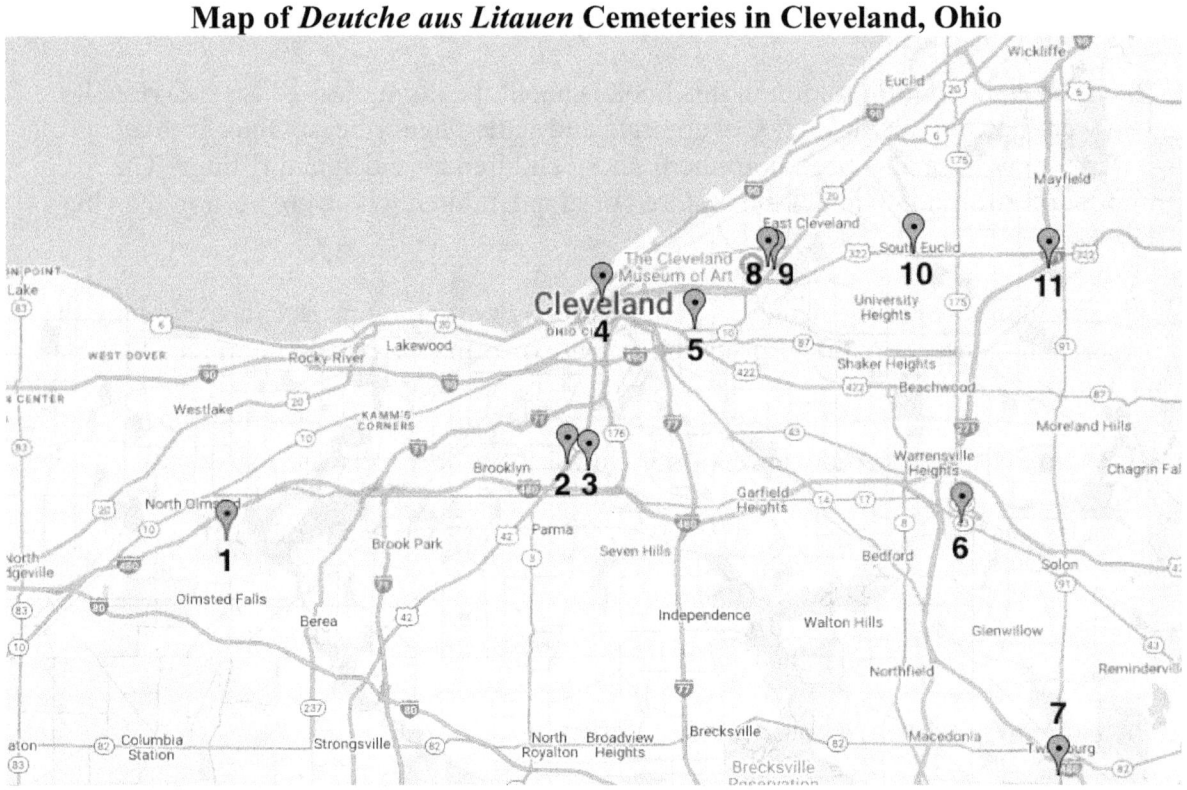

Figure 2

Map Key

1. Sunset Memorial Park
2. Lutheran Cemetery
3. Brooklyn Heights Cemetery
4. Downtown Cleveland (for reference)
5. Woodland Cemetery
6. Hillcrest Cemetery
7. Crown Hill Cemetery
8. East Cleveland Township Cemetery
9. Lake View Cemetery
10. St. John's Lutheran Cemetery
11. Knollwood Cemetery

How the Book is Organized

Individuals are listed alphabetically by surname. The formatting highlights the primary immigrant, listing their genealogical information. Their spouse, marriage date and place, date and place of death, and place of interment, if applicable, follows. If the spouse of the primary immigrant was also born in the Suwałki Governorate, that person is also a primary immigrant and has their own listing under their surname (i.e. birth name in the case of married women). This is also the case with children who were immigrants. Their information is located under the primary immigrant's listing as well as in their own listing (usually with more detail). Individuals born in the Suwałki Governorate and their children all have their own unique identifying number in chronological order when the individual was entered into this book — not numerically ascending or descending based on date of birth or other data. Children of these immigrants (even those born outside of the Suwałki Governorate) were also given a unique number. The reader will find this numbering system helpful especially when an individual (a spouse or child) is listed more than once in the book. In the next page is an explanation of how the book is organized:

A Note from the Author

It is my intention to continue to publish new editions of this publication as more information is uncovered.

Should the reader find any omissions or corrigenda in this edition, please contact the International Association of Germans from Lithuania (IAGL). Include the source of any information submitted.

Contact details for the IAGL can be found at **www.GermansFromLithuania.org**

SALEKER / SALECKER

> He is given an individual number because he was born in Lithuania.

> The names of Evangelical Lutheran Churches are listed in their German equivalents.

1. Johann Andreas "Heinrich" **SALEKER** born 4 June 1866 in Liukiai. Baptized and confirmed at Wischtiten Evangelical Lutheran Church. Son of Andreas Saleker and Marie Renkiewicz. Married Emilie **Wiemert**[21] 21 May 1893 at Zion Evangelical Lutheran Church. Died 7 Feb 1945. Interment at Lutheran Cemetery. Great-great-grandfather of IAGL co-founder Owen M. McCafferty II.

> Cemeteries in the Cleveland city limits do not have "Cleveland" listed.

   2.   i. Friedrich "Fred" Heinrich Saleker b. 28 Apr. 1894. **Peterson** 1902-1921.

> Note that spouses' names are in bold.

        1 child:
           Edmond Raymond 1920-2002

> Children of immigrants are also assigned a number, even if they did not immigrate or were not born in Lithuania. If they were born in Lithuania, they also have their own primary listing.

   3.   ii. ...ker b. 5 Jul. 1896. d. 5 Jul 1...

> The names of other individuals listed in the immigrant's listing are also assigned a number. Assuming there is documentation to support their births in Lithuania, they have their own listing. In this case, the reader can find Emilie listed under "Wiemert" and is listed as number 21.

   4.   iii. Gustav Saleker b. 1 Sep. 1897. d. 22 No... ...za (*Dickson*) 1901-1929.

        4 children:
           Richard 1921-1993
           Mary Julia 1923-2001
           Henry Edward 1924-1967
           ...er Allen **Schultz** 1927-1974

> Grandchildren of the primary immigrants are not assigned a number unless they were also born in Lithuania.

ACKERMANN

188. Adolf Franz **ACKERMANN** born 1856 in Mikabaliai. Son of Friedrich Ackermann and Wilhelmine **Hartig**. Baptized at Serey Reformed Lutheran Church. Married Emilie **Nausner** (1859-1942) at Prenen Evangelical Lutheran Church in 1882. Immigrated in August 1902 via Baltimore aboard the S.S. *Breslau*. Died 13 March 1931. Interment at Lake View Cemetery.

    189.   i. Berta Ackermann b. 1883. d. 1 Jan 1967. m. Paul Otto **Moebius** 1881-1964.
        2 children:
            Gordon William 1904-1957
            Eugene 1909-2003

    190.   ii. Leokadia Emilie "Catherine" Ackermann b. 1885. d. 21 Jun 1936. m. Julius **Tiedmann**[421] 1883-1944.
        9 children:
            Mathilde 1905-1990[433]
            William 1907-1985[434]
            Julius 1909-1980[435]
            Ruth 1911-2002[436]
            Helen L. 1912-1999[437]
            Irene 1915-2006[438]
            Arnold 1916-1999[439]
            Earl Howard 1919-2008[440]
            Evelyn 1912-2014[441]

    191.   iii. Emilie Ackermann b. 1887. d. 1894.

    192.   iv. Albin Ackermann b. 1889. d. 1890.

    193.   v. Edmund Eduard Ackermann b. 1891. d. May 1966.

    194.   vi. Heinrich Ackermann b. 1893. d. 12 Feb 1945. m. Winifred Helene **Maher** 1900-1984.
        2 children:
            Richard Edward 1925-1987
            Robert 1922-1985

    195.   vii. Natalie Ackermann b. 1895 d. 1896.

    196.   viii. Angelina Ackermann b. 1897.- d. 28 May 1963. m. Frank **Conrad** 1887-1952.
        2 children:
            Norman 1921-2013

Arleen 1922-1998

197.   ix. Lydia Ackermann b. 1899. d. 28 Oct 1970. m. Elmer Martin **Francis**.
3 children:
George 1919-1958
Edna 1921-1939
Betty May 1925-2002

198.   Albin "James" Ackermann b. 1902 d. 6 Feb 1961. m. Eunice **Neely** 1909-1968.
2 children:
James 1932-2021
Arthur 1934-2015

189. Berta **ACKERMANN (MOEBIUS)** born 1883 in Balbieriškis. Daughter of Adolf Franz Ackermann[188] (1856-1931) and Emilie **Nausner**[199] (1859-1942). Baptized at Prenen Evangelical Lutheran Church. Immigrated circa 1897. Married Otto **Moebius** (1881-1964) 18 Apr 1903 at Zion Evangelical Lutheran Church. Died 1 Jan 1967 in Maple Heights. Interment unknown.

200.   i. Gordon William Moebius b. 7 Dec 1904. d. 16 Sep 1938. m. Edith M. **Wells** 1905-1973.
1 child:
Jean 1924-2013

201.   ii. Eugene Moebius b. 13 Mar 1909. d. 27 Aug 2003. m. Eva **Fontana** 1920-2005.
4 children:
Gordon
Muriel
Allen
Eugene

190. Leokadia Emilie „Catherine" **ACKERMANN (TIEDMAN)** born 1885 Balbieriškis. Daughter of Adolf Franz Ackermann[188] (1856-1931) and Emilie **Nausner**[199] (1859-1942). Baptized at Prenen Evangelical Lutheran Church. Immigrated August 1902 via Baltimore aboard the S.S. *Breslau*. Married Julius **Tiedmann**[421] (1883-1944) 23 Jan 1904 at Zion Evangelical Lutheran Church. Died 21 Jun 1936. Interment at Lake View Cemetery. For list of children, see husband Julius Tiedman.

193. Edmund Eduard **ACKERMANN** born 1891 in Miroslavas. Son of Adolf Franz Ackermann[188] (1856-1931) and Emilie **Nausner**[199] (1859-1942). Baptized at Serey Reformed Lutheran Church. Immigrated August 1902 via Baltimore aboard the S.S. *Breslau*. Died May 1966. Interment unknown.

194. Heinrich **ACKERMANN** born 1893 in Balbieriškis. Son of Adolf Franz Ackermann[188] (1856-1931) and Emilie **Nausner**[199] (1859-1942). Baptized at Prenen Evangelical Lutheran Church. Immigrated August 1902 via Baltimore aboard the S.S. *Breslau*. U.S. WWI veteran, served in France and saw active combat. Married Winifred Helene **Maher** (1900-1984) 7 Sep 1920 at St. Joseph's Catholic Church in Collinwood, Ohio. Died 12 Feb 1945. Interment at St Paul's Catholic Cemetery, Euclid, Ohio.

- 202. i. Richard Edward Ackerman b. 14 Dec 1925. d. 10 Jun 1987. m. Alice M. **Kushan** 1926-2017.
  - 3 children:
    - Dennis Richard 1949-2013
    - Thomas J. 1951-2012
    - Gregory D. 1954-1954
    - Pamela A.
    - Christine M.

- 203. ii. Robert Ackerman b. 1922. d. 26 Jul 1985. m. Margaret M. **Sweeny** 1920-2018.
  - 3 children:
    - Patricia
    - Mary Ellen
    - Michael

196. Angelina **ACKERMANN (CONRAD)** born 1897 in Balbieriškis. Daughter of Adolf Franz Ackermann[188] (1856-1931) and Emilie **Nausner**[199] (1859-1942). Baptized at Prenen Evangelical Lutheran Church. Immigrated August 1902 via Baltimore aboard the S.S. *Breslau*. Married Frank C. **Conrad** (1887-1952) 7 August 1919 at Bethlehem Lutheran Church. Died 28 May 1963. Interment at Lutheran Cemetery.

- 204. i. Norman Carl Conrad b. 21 Oct 1921. d. Mar 1985. m. Betty **McCready** 1923-????. m. Anne Teresa ? 1925-????.
  - 4 children:
    - Norman Jr.
    - Dale
    - Darlene
    - Debra

- 205. i. Arlene Emma Conrad b. 27 Jan 1922. d. 12 Jan 1998. m. ? **Putrich**.

197. Lydia **ACKERMANN (FRANCIS)** born 1899 in Balbieriškis. Daughter of Adolf Franz Ackermann[188] (1856-1931) and Emilie **Nausner**[199] (1859-1942). Baptized at Prenen Evangelical Lutheran Church. Immigrated August 1902 via Baltimore aboard the S.S. *Breslau*. Married Elmer M. **Francis** 25 May 1918 in Cleveland by a Justice of the Peace. Died 28 October 1970. Interment at Lutheran Cemetery.

    206.   i. George Francis b. 1 Apr 1919. d. 30 May 1958. m. Juanita **Vann** 1919-2004.
        1 child:
            Craig Allen 1946-1999

    207.   ii. Edna Francis b. 23 Aug 1921. d. 1 Mar 1939.

    208.   iii. Betty May Francis b. 12 Aug 1924. d. 21 Feb 2002. m. John Paul **Haas** 1920-2000.
        2 children:
            Betty Jean
            Wayne P.

198. Albin "James" **ACKERMANN** born 1902 in Balbieriškis. Son of Adolf Franz Ackermann[188] (1856-1931) and Emilie **Nausner**[199] (1859-1942). Baptized at Prenen Evangelical Lutheran Church. Immigrated August 1902 via Baltimore aboard the S.S. *Breslau*. Married Eunice Margaret **Neely** (1909-1968) 24 August 1929 at St. Aloysius Catholic Church. Died 6 Feb 1961. Interment at All Souls Cemetery in Chardon, Ohio.

    209.   i. James Ackerman Jr. b. 5 Jun 1932. d. 30 Nov 2021. m. Doris Ann **Fike** 1934-2022.
        2 children:
            Cindy
            Kelly

    210.   ii. Arthur Ackerman b. 4 Mar 1934. d. 10 Mar 2015. m. Marian **Piliniak** 1935-1988.
        3 children:
            Gregory
            Therese
            Michael

ALBRECHT

1267. Gustav **ALBRECHT** born 12 Aug 1882 in Powosyje (no longer exists; near Griškabūdis). Son of Friedrich Albrecht and Bertha **Grigat**. Baptized and confirmed at Neustadt Evangelical Lutheran Church. Married Eva **Martin** (1885-????) November 1903 in Wilkes-Barre, Pennsylvania. Married Anna **Zygender** (1893-????) 28 Apr 1923 at St. Paul's Evangelical Lutheran Church. Died 5 Mar 1939. Interment at Lutheran Cemetery.

    1268.   i. Anna B. Albrecht b. 2 Nov 1904. d. 19 Dec 1989. m. Elmer Carl **Weber** 1898-1978.
        3 children:
            Florence 1925-????
            Raymond Carl 1927-1997
            Robert 1930-

    1269.   ii. Martha Albrecht b. 29 Apr 1906. d. 31 May 1980. m. Gustav **Blum**[1270] 1890-1967.
        2 children:
            Richard H.[1271] 1925-2006
            Emma D.[1272] 1926-1978

    1273.   iii. Lena Albrecht b. 14 Mar 1908. d. 22 Oct 1988. m. Millard A. **Young** 1905-1988. m. Wayne W. **Berry** 1915-1960.
        2 children:
            Lois Jean 1932-2001
            Barbara

    1274.   iv. William A. Albrecht b. 14 Jan 1911. d. 5 Jan 1977. m. Pauline Frances **Hochevar** 1913-1996.

    1275.   v. Frederick Walter Albrecht b. 18 Jun 1913. d. 4 Jun 1984. m. Lucy Louise **Sandella** 1917-1989.
        1 child:
            Fred William 1938-

    1276.   vi. Edward Albrecht b. 21 Mar 1917. d. 15 Jan 2000. m. Dorothy Mae **Lennon** 1919-2016.
        3 children:
            Susan E.
            Donald Richard 1942-2003
            Dean (Jean?) J. 1943-

1277. vii. Richard Gustav Albrecht.b. 2 May 1921. d. 19 Nov 1992. m. Erma **Platt** 1921-2003. m. Margaret **Fasola** 1917-1999.
2 children:
Grace 1939-1998
Dorlene Elise 1943-

ANDECHSER / ANDEXEL/ ANDEXLER / ANDEXEN

264. Karl **ANDECHSER** (*ANDEXLER*) born 1864 in Varnupiai. Son of Jakob Andechser and Hedwig **Certor**. Baptized and confirmed at Mariampol Evangelical Lutheran Church. Married Emilie **Berwing**[263] (1869-1932) 1886 at Mariampol Evangelical Lutheran Church. Immigrated September 1888 via New York aboard S.S. *Kaffraria*. Died September 1911. Interment first at Harvard Grove Cemetery. Reinterred at Lutheran Cemetery in 1913.

265. i. Edward Adolph Andexler b. 26 Aug 1894. d. 4 Jun 1929. m. Erma M **Dentz** 1901-1894.
    3 children:
    Edward 1923-2000
    George 1924-2008
    William 1929-2005

266. ii. Charles Andexler b. 14 Feb 1898. d. 31 Mar 1956. m. Stella **Clay** 1905-1953.
    4 children:
    Alverna Mae 1922-1995
    Bette Jane 1924-1926
    Donald 1931-1990

267. iii. Emma Andexler b. 6 Mar 1902. d. 7 Jul 1994. m. Albert **Hook** 1901-1987.
    3 children:
    Albert Jr. 1929-1997
    Jane Eileen 1931-2006
    Kenneth J. 1935-2007

268. iv. Lillian Andexler b. 23 Oct 1906. d. 18 Dec 1964. m. Wesley Everett **Stine** 1904-1982.
    3 children:
    Wesley David 1928-2003

269 v. Herman Andexler b. 14 Apr 1910. d. 26 Jun 1977. m. Louise ????-2007.
    2 children:
    Sharon 1939-

271. August **ANDECHSER** (*ANDEXLER*) born about 1861 in Ludvinavas. Son of Jakob Andechser and Hedwig **Certor**. Confirmed at Mariampol Evangelical Lutheran Church. Married Henriette **Zinkewitz** (1860-1923) likely at Mariampol Evangelical Lutheran Church between 1882-1883. Married Anna **Berow** (1876-1925.) Died 18 Oct 1933. Interment at Lutheran Cemetery.

    272.   i. Gustav Andexler b. 1883. d. 15 Mar 1939. m. Adelaide **Walsh** 1885-1945.
> 5 children:
> > Howard F. 1906-1980
> > Adeline 1909-1986
> > Roland Gustave 1911-1994
> > Kenneth Charles 1913-1959
> > Betty Eileen 1923-1992

    273.   ii. Anna Andexler b.1885. d. 12 Apr 1964. m. George **Abbey** 1882-????.
> 2 children:
> > Anna
> > Ruth 1905-1995

    274.   iii. Emma Andexler b. 1890. d. 17 Aug 1971. m. Patrick John **Fee** 1888-1929. m. Warren C **Russ** 1885-1951.
> 1 child:
> > William 1910-????.

    275.   iv. Charles Andexler b. 17 Jun 1894. d. 18 Jun 1965. m. Mabel **McGary** 1897-1944. m. Olga **Bawolak**.
> 3 children:
> > Bette Jane 1924-1926

    276.   v. Lydia Andexler b. 28 Aug 1897. d. 17 Jun 1986. m. Arthur E. **Lewis** 1895-????.
> 6 children:
> > Earl Arthur 1918-2005
> > Ruth 1922-
> > Rita 1924-
> > Clair 1928-
> > Carol 1930-
> > Elaine Ann 1933-1990

    277.   vi. August Andexler

274. Emma **ANDECHSER** (**FEE**) (**RUSS**) born 1890 in Marijampolė. Daughter of August Andechser[271] (1861-1933) and Henriette **Zinkiewicz** (1860-1923). Confirmed at Mariampol Evangelical Lutheran Church. Married Patrick John **Fee** (1888-1929) 16 Apr 1914 by a Justice of the Peace. Divorced 24 May 1922. Married Warren C. **Russ** (1885-1951) 9 August 1923 by a Justice of the Peace. Died 17 Aug 1971 in Warrensville Heights, Ohio. Interment unknown.

    278.   i. William Fee Andexler b. 4 Jun 1909. d. 11 Apr 1990. m. Violet A. **Bican** (**Bitzan**) 1913-????.
        2 children:
            Henriette 1933-
            Donna J. 1934-

864. Friedrich **ANDECHSER** (*ANDEXLER*) born about 1875 in Liudvinavas. Son of Jakob Andechser and Hedwig **Certor**. Likely baptized at Mariampol Evangelical Lutheran Church. Married Auguste **Romonat** (1880-1974) 1889 at Mariampol Evangelical Lutheran Church. Immigrated August 1899 via Baltimore aboard the S.S. *Hanover*. Died 29 Jan 1945. Interment at Crown Hill Cemetery and Mausoleum in Twinsburg, Ohio.

    865.   i. Ewald O Andexler b. 5 Aug 1905. d. 25 Aug 1968. m. Violet **Priebe** 1908-1960.
        8 children:
            Donald Arthur 1927-2008
            Allen Ewald 1929-1999
            Kenneth Ralph 1930-2009
            Dorothy Lorene 1931-2004
            Virginia C. 1932-1992
            Joanne Marie 1935-2015
            Robert 1939-
            Joyce E. 1941-2020

    866.   ii. Otto Leonard Andexler b. 27 Feb 1907. d. 31 Mar 1948. m. Lucy **Zilcosky** 1906-1990.
        2 children:
            Ronald R. 1932-
            Nancy L. 1935-

    867.   iii. Olga E. Andexler b. 1 Oct 1909. d. 16 Sep 1910.

    868.   iv. Emma P. Andexler b. 9 Jun 1911. d. 22 Jul 1998. m. Wilber **Jagusch** 1909-1995.
        1 child:
            Wilmer Edward 1935-2009

869.   v. Ida Augusta Andexler b. 20 Nov 1912. d. 13 Jul 1948. m. Andrew S. **Plezia** 1909-1972.
>   2 children:
>> Baby girl 1946-1946
>> Baby girl 1948-1948

870.   vi. Edith A. Andexler b. ????. d. ????. m. ????.

871.   vii. Edward Frederick Andexler b. 29 Dec 1914. d. 14 Feb 2001. m. Eleanor L. **Ritter** 1920-1975.
>   3 children:
>> Richard E. 1941-
>> Carol A. 1945-
>> Janice L. 1950-

872.   viii. Carl Joseph Andexler b. 29 Jul 1917. d. 10 Mar 1988. m. Clara Alma **Jantz** 1920-1991. m. Irene Barbara **Kolakowski** 1925-2001.
>   1 child:
>> Gary Fred 1955-2010

873.   ix. Leonard Elmer Andexler b. 28 Feb 1920. d. 9 May 1994. m. Anna **Hawrylak** 1920-1993.
>   2 children:
>> Dennis 1943-
>> Diane 1947-

874. Anna **ANDECHSER (JESSAT)** born about 1865 in Liudvinavas. Daughter of Jakob Andechser and Hedwig **Certor**. Baptized and confirmed at Mariampol Evangelical Lutheran Church. Married Gustav August **Jessat**[875] (1869-1936) 1889 at Mariampol Evangelical Lutheran Church. Died 2 Jan 1957. Interment at Highland Park Cemetery, Highland Hills, Ohio. For list of children, see husband Gustav August Jessat.

AUGUSTAT / AUGUSTAITIS

526. Josef **AUGUSTAT** (Sr.) born 1853 in Kamičiai (Vilkaviškis). Son of Josef Augustat and Karoline **Müller**. Baptized at Kalwaria Evangelical Lutheran Church. Married Karoline **Anderkeit** (1855-1937) 1874 at Kalwaria Evangelical Lutheran Church. Died 15 Oct 1929. Interment at Bedford Cemetery, Bedford, Ohio.

    527.   i. Georg Augustat b. 1877. d. ????.

    528.   ii. Anna Augustat b. 1881. d. 23 Mar 1978. m. William W. **Furst** 1872-1956.
        5 children:
           Thelma Ruth[532] 1909-1985
           Emily Grace[533] 1911-1913
           George William[534] 1913-1968
           Viola L.[535] 1916-1987
           Eugene Arthur[536] 1920-2007

    529.   iii. Marie Augustat b. 1883 d. ????.

    530.   iv. Josef Augustat b. abt. 1885. d. 5 May 1908. m. Natalie **Kenat**[498] 1885-1955.
        1 child:
           Joseph Adolf Hugh 1908-1980

    531.   v. Edna C. Augustat b. 17 Dec 1894. d. 10 Jul 1957. m. Joseph Hermann **Imars** 1882-1950.
        1 child:
           Joseph M. 1923-2005

528. Anna **AUGUSTAT (FURST)** born 1881 in Kalvarija. Daughter of Josef Augustat[526] (1853-1929) and Karoline **Anderkeit** (1855-1937). Baptized at Kalwaria Evangelical Lutheran Church. Married William W. **Furst** (1872-1956) 16 Oct 1907 at St. John's Lutheran Church, Garfield Heights, Ohio. Died 23 Mar 1978 in Floral City, Florida. Interment at Bedford Cemetery, Bedford, Ohio.

    532.   i. Thelma Ruth Furst b. 21 Jul 1909. d. 22 Jan 1985. m. Frank Evans **Tomko** 1897-1980. m. Emmett James **Markley** 1895-1963.

    533.   ii. Emily Grace Furst b. 18 Jul 1911. d. 26 Aug 1913.

    534.   iii. George William Furst b. 10 Dec 1913. d. 3 Jul 1968. m. Geraldine **?** 1917-????.

        1 child:
            Darlyn D. 1942-

535.   iv. Viola L. Furst b. 17 Apr 1916. d. 26 Jun 1987. m. Forrest Homer **Bales** 1912-1989.
        1 child:
            Keith Forrest 1944-1968

536.   v. Eugene Arthur Furst b. 30 Apr 1920. d. 19 Feb 2007. m. Pearl Elsie **Olsen** 1919-????.
        2 children:
            William G. 1946-
            Sally G. 1949-

AUKSCHUN

211. Leopold **AUKSCHUN** born 1871 in Bartninkai. Son of Karl Aukschun (1845-????) and Marie **Geschwantner** (1850-????). Baptized and confirmed at Mariampol Evangelical Lutheran Church. Married Auguste **Baschar**[223] (1877-1931) at Mariampol Evangelical Lutheran Church in 1897. Immigrated October 1900 via New York aboard the S.S. *Bonn*. Died 19 Apr 1919. Interment at Lutheran Cemetery.

    212.   i. Oskar Aukschun b. 1898. d. 17 Feb 1945. m. Alma **Missun** 1909-2002.
        3 children:
            Loretta Jean 1931-2006
            Virginia Joan 1939-2017
            Richard 1933-

    213.   ii. Rudolf Aukschun b. 1900. d. ????. m. Rose **Riley** 1905-1979.
        1 child:
            Rudolph Jr. 1937-

    214.   iii. Gustav Leopold Aukschun b. 30 Jul 1903. d. 9 Nov 1977. m. Ruth E. **Miller** 1913-2007.
        2 children:
            Judith 1941-
            Robert 1944-1993

    215.   iv. Martha Aukschun b. 24 Nov 1904. d. 5 Sep 1978. m. Charles **Nemec**. m. Harry **Evenden** 1898-1976.
        1 child:
            Richard 1925-1986

    216.   v. Emma "Sister Nora" Aukschun b. 14 Feb 1908. d. 10 Nov 1979.

    217.   vi. Adeline Aukschun b. 10 Aug 1911. d. 30 Oct 2003. m. Carl L. **Runkle** 1902-1955.
        1 child:
            Carol 1938-

212. Oskar **AUKSCHUN** born 23 Nov 1898 in Degučiai. Son of Leopold Aukschun[211] (1871-1919) and Auguste **Baschar**[223] (1877-1931). Baptized at Mariampol Evangelical Lutheran Church. Immigrated October 1900 via New York aboard the S.S. *Bonn*. Married Alma **Missun** (1909-2002) 16 Jul 1930 at Zion Evangelical Lutheran Church. Died 17 Feb 1945 in Avon, Ohio. Interment at St. Paul Lutheran Cemetery, Westlake, Ohio.

218.   i. Loretta Jean Aukschun b. 9 Aug 1931. d. 10 Jan 2006
219.   ii. Richard L. Aukschun b. 24 Apr 1933.
220.   iii. Virginia Joan Aukschun b. 29 Oct 1939. d. 13 May 2017. m. David Francis **Bruening** 1939-2012.
    4 children:
      Mark 1961-1961
      David
      Michael
      Lisa

213. Rudolf **AUKSCHUN** born 17 Aug 1900 in Degučiai. Son of Leopold Aukschun[211] (1871-1919) and Auguste **Baschar**[223] (1877-1931). Baptized at Mariampol Evangelical Lutheran Church. Immigrated October 1900 via New York aboard the S.S. *Bonn*. Married Rose **Reily** (1905-1979) 17 Sep 1935 in Manhattan, New York. Map draftsman and cartographer for the U.S. government. Death date, location, and interment unknown.

  221.   i. Rudolph Aukschun Jr. b. 1937.

214. Gustav Leopold **AUKSCHUN** born 30 Jul 1903 in Degučiai. Son of Leopold Aukschun[211] (1871-1919) and Auguste **Baschar**[223] (1877-1931). Baptized at Mariampol Evangelical Lutheran Church. Immigrated October 1900 via New York aboard the S.S. *Bonn*. Married Ruth E. **Miller** (1913-2007) 28 Dec 1938 at Hope Lutheran Church. Died 9 Nov 1977 in California. Interment at Cedar Lawn Memorial Park, Fremont, California.

  222.   i. Judith A. Aukschun b. 29 Mar 1941. m. ? **Hornak.**

  223.   ii. Robert A. Aukschun b. 15 Apr 1944. d. 27 Jul 1993.

215. Martha **AUKSCHUN (NEMEO) (EVENDEN)** born 24 Nov 1904 in Degučiai. Daughter of Leopold Aukschun[211] (1871-1919) and Auguste **Baschar**[223] (1877-1931). Baptized at Mariampol Evangelical Lutheran Church. Immigrated October 1900 via New York aboard the S.S. *Bonn*. Married Charles **Nemec** 8 Aug 1923 at Bethlehem Evangelical Lutheran Church. Divorced. Married Harry M. **Evenden** (1898-1976) 44 August 1937 at Broadway Christian Church. Died 5 Sep 1978. Interment at Crown Hill Cemetery and Mausoleum in Twinsburg, Ohio.

1302. Adolf **AUKSCHUN** born 4 Mar 1898 in Pilviškiai. Son of Johann Aukschun and Anna Müller. Baptized at Mariampol Evangelical Lutheran Church. Immigrated August 1914 via New York aboard the S.S. *Pennsylvania*. Married Antoinette **Slauta** (1909-1957) 18 Oct 1924 in Washington, Pennsylvania, by a Justice of the Peace. Died 19 Oct 1948. Interment at Calvary Cemetery.

BALTRUNAT / BALTRONAT

779. Karl **BALTRONAT** born 1871 in Vilkabaliai. Son of Christof Baltronat and Karoline **Stalgies**. Baptized at Kalwaria Evangelical Lutheran Church. Married Magdalene Helene **Leichert**[788] (1872-1941) 1896 at Mariampol Evangelical Lutheran Church. Immigrated November 1902 via Baltimore abord the S.S. *Neckar*. Died 19 Jun 1943. Interment at Lutheran Cemetery.

    780.   i. Auguste Baltrunat b. 1897. d. bef. 1903.

    781.   ii. Helene Bertha Baltrunat b. 1899. d. 28 Apr 1985. m. Henry Hermann **Buehrmann** 1900-1975.
        1 child:
           Leona 1933-

    782.   iii. Karl Wilhelm Baltronat b. 1902. d. 20 Feb 1903.

    783.   iv. Maria Lydia Baltrunat b. 26 Mar 1904. d. 21 Oct 1986. m. Matthew **Brinz** 1905-1980.
        1 child:
           Dolores 1931-

    784.   v. Emma Baltrunat b. 31 Jan 1907. d. 25 Mar 1994. m. Walter Emil **Tancre** 1908-1976.
        1 child:
           Lesley M. 1938-

    785.   vi. Adolph Gustave Baltrunat b. 5 Sep 1908. d. 6 Jun 1986. m. Adeline **Derschau** 1909-1998.
        3 children:
           Bernard
           Barbara 1948-
           Paul A. 1951-1969

    786.   vii. Harold August Baltrunat b. 9 Aug 1910. d. 16 Aug 1986. m. Katherine **Jurissen** 1910-1983.
        1 child:
           Susan Helene 1946-

781. Helene Bertha **BALTRUNAT (BUEHRMANN)** born 1899 in Kalvarija. Daughter of Karl Baltronat[788] (1871-1943) and Magdalene Helene **Leichert**[787] (1872-1941). Baptized at Kalwaria Evangelical Lutheran Church. Immigrated November 1902 via Baltimore aboard the S.S. *Neckar*. Married Heinrich Hermann **Buehrmann** 22 July 1931 at Zion Evangelical Lutheran Church. Died 28 Apr 1985 in Volusia, Florida. Interment at Coral Ridge Cemetery, Cape Coral, Florida.

> 787. i. Leona Buehrmann b. 1933. m. Essell Everette **Lowery** 1919-1986. m. John W. Riley 1906-????.

782. Karl Wilhelm **BALTRUNAT** born 1902 in Kalvarija. Son of Karl Baltronat[779] (1871-1943) and Magdalene Helene **Leichert**[788] (1872-1941). Baptized at Kalwaria Evangelical Lutheran Church. Immigrated November 1902 via Baltimore aboard the S.S. *Neckar*. Died 20 Feb 1903. Interment at Woodland Cemetery.

798. Auguste **BALTRUNAT (NEUBACHER)** born 1880 in Kalvarija. Daughter of Christof Baltrunat and Marie **Dorn**. Baptized at Kalwaria Evangelical Lutheran Church. Married Johann **Neubacher**[799] (1881-1957) 2 Nov 1904 at Zion Evangelical Lutheran Church. Died 8 Nov 1915. Interment at Lutheran Cemetery. For list of children, see husband Johann Neubacher.

1369. Helene **BALTRONAT (SCHWELGIN)** born 1885 on the Kalvarija manor farm. Daughter of Christof Baltrunat and Marie **Dorn**. Baptized and confirmed at Kalwaria Evangelical Lutheran Church. Married Johann **Schwelgin**[1368] (1876-1936) 18 Feb 1906 at Zion Evangelical Lutheran Church. Died 27 Jul 1942. Interment at Lutheran Cemetery. For list of children, see husband Johann Schwelgin.

BARANOWICZ / BARANOWITZ / BARANOWITSCH / BAUER

1082. August **BARANOWICZ** *(BAUER)* born 11 Oct 1882 near Wiżajny (Poland). Son of Friedrich Baranowicz (1857-????) and Anna **Rabenstein** (1861-????). Baptized at Wischainy Evangelical Lutheran Church. Immigrated August 1901 via New York. Married Emilie **Wilk**[1083] (1884-1978) 7 Apr 1907 at Zion Evangelical Lutheran Church. Died 15 Sep 1953. Interment at Lutheran Cemetery.

    1084. i. Elmer Bauer b. 31 Jan 1908. d. 6 Sep 1972. m. Adeline **Hastman** 1914-2003.
           2 children:
                Dennis Frederick 1939-2001
                Madelyn Marie 1941-2006

    1085. ii. Walter Bauer b. 9 Jun 1909. d. 23 May 1978. m. Julia **Novak** 1911-????.
           3 children:
                Lillian 1934-
                Judith 1944-
                Ruth 1937-

    1086. iii. Arthur Bauer b. 31 Mar 1913. d. 22 Jul 1991. m. Eva **?** 1912-????.

    1087. iv. Roy Frederick Bauer b. 14 Sep 1916. d. 15 Nov 1993. m. Irma **Baloga** 1915-1997.
           2 children:
                Timothy R. 1941-
                Caren L. 1943-

    1088. v. Leonard Carl Bauer b. 24 Apr 1918. d. 15 Dec 2002. m. Mildred Lorna **Zugovitz** 1918-2004.
           2 children:
                Ronald Karl 1949-2018
                Barbara 1951-1978

    1089. vi. Eleanor Bauer b. 23 Aug 1925. d. 17 Oct 2014. m. Walter Gustave **Burke**[1080] 1919-2017.

BASENAU / BAZENAU / BOSSMAN / BOZMAN

606. Karl **BASENAU** (*BOSSMAN*) born 1866 in Paužiškiai. Son of Karl Basenau and Elizabeth **Büscher**. Baptized and confirmed at Mariampol Evangelical Lutheran Church. Married Pauline **Jurkschatt**[645] (1865-1924) in 1887 at Mariampol Evangelical Lutheran Church. Immigrated March 1907 via Baltimore aboard the S.S. *Bremen*. Married Anna **Jurkschat**[646] (1874-1944) 10 Jan 1925 at St. John's Lutheran Church. Died 16 Jun 1925. Interment at Lutheran Cemetery.

607.   i. Adeline Basenau b. 06 Jan 1888. d. 1 Jul 1936. m. Christ **Jurgeleit**[597] 1881-1949.
       7 children:
            John[598] 1907-1965
            Edith[599] 1910-2005
            Leonard Christian[600] 1912-1987
            Mildred[601] 1920-1978
            Charlotte[602] 1923-2003
            Lois Pauline[603] 1926-1995
            Lloyd Carl[604] 1926-2014

608.   ii. Johann Basenau b. 11 Dec 1889. d. 22 Mar 1947. m. Emma **Günther**[626] 1892-1970.
       4 children:
            Arthur A.[631] 1912-1988
            John[632] 1914-1972
            Charles[633] 1915-1990
            Emma Martha[634] 1920-1993

609.   iii. Amelia "Mollie" Basenau b. 7 Mar 1891. d. 15 May 1937. m. Martin **Wurm**[614] 1881-1949. m. Martin F. **Love** 1881-????.
       5 children:
            Florence[615] 1911-1967
            Edna[616] 1913-1914
            Ruth[617] 1917-2000
            Walter[618] 1918-1980
            Bettie[619] 1921-1976

610.   iv. Adam "Edward" Basenau b. 1894. d. 27 Mar 1952. m. Elizabeth **Heitenbach** 1901-1984.

611.   v. Eva „Evelyn" Basenau b. 1900. d. 28 Jan 1976. m. Walter J. **Ortman** 1899-1932. m. James Edward **Horacek** 1888-1960.
       12 children:

                        Russell A. 1922-1983
                        Walter John 1923-2008
                        Robert R. 1924-2004
                        William Roy 1926-1991
                        Grace J. 1927-2005
                        Arlene Pauline 1928-2014
                        Dorothy L. 1930-2005
                        Richard E. 1930-2005
                        Charlotte 1932-????
                        Ronald E.
                        Petronella 1935-1995
                        James C. 1936-2011

612.   vi. Gustav Basenau b. 1903. d. 29 Nov 1963. m. Elizabeth Marie **Hein**[734] 1901-1999.
            2 children:
                Norman Gustave 1924-1998
                Carol Lois 1931-2019

613.   vii. Edith Bossman b. 7 Mar 1910. d. 14 Apr 1983. m. Peter **Segenvcik** 1906-????. m. Daniel **Gross** 1908-1977.
            1 child:
                Daniel Randolph 1936-2000

607. Adeline **BASENAU** (*BOSSMAN*) (**JURGELEIT**) born 6 Jan 1888 in Javaravas. Daughter of Karl Basenau[606] (1866-1925) and Pauline **Jurkschat**[645] (1866-1924). Baptized at Mariampol Evangelical Lutheran Church. Married Christ **Jurgeleit**[597] (1881-1949) 12 Aug 1906 at Zion Evangelical Lutheran Church. Died 1 Jul 1936. Interment at Lutheran Cemetery. For list of children, see husband Christ Jurgeleit.

608. Johann **BASENAU** (*BOSSMAN*) born 11 Dec 1889 in Javaravas. Son of Karl Basenau[606] (1866-1925) and Pauline **Jurkschat**[645] (1866-1924). Baptized at Mariampol Evangelical Lutheran Church. Married Elizabeth Emma **Günther**[626] (1892-1970) 18 May 1911 in Cleveland by a Justice of the Peace. Died 22 Mar 1947. Interment at Lutheran Cemetery.

631.   i. Arthur Adolph Bossman b. 6 Dec 1912. d. 15 Jul 1988. m. Anna **Sliwinski** 1912-1964. m. Margie Corene **Smylie** 1922-1996.
            1 child:
                Paul 1947-

632.   ii. John Bossman b. 2 Aug 1914. d. 15 Jan 1972.

633.   iii. Charles Bossman b. 10 Dec 1915. d. 29 May 1990. m. Loretta J. **Quirk** 1918-2007.

1 child:
>> Carole J. 1943-

634.   iv. Emma Martha Bossman b. 2 Mar 1920. d. 26 Dec 1993. m. Russell Roberts **Talbot** 1919-1978.
> 2 children:
>> Kathleen L. 1947-
>> David John 1949-1991

609. Amelia "Mollie" **BASENAU** (*BOSSMAN*) (**WORM**) born 7 Mar 1891 in Degučiai. Daughter of Karl Basenau[606] (1866-1925) and Pauline **Jurkschat**[645] (1866-1924). Baptized at Mariampol Evangelical Lutheran Church. Immigrated September 1906 via Baltimore aboard the S.S. *Wittekind*. Married Martin **Worm**[614] (1881-1949) 29 Sep 1907 at Zion Evangelical Lutheran Church. Divorced. Married Walter F. **Love** (1881-????) 26 May 1934 Died 15 May 1937. Interment unknown. For list of children, see husband Martin Worm.

610. Adam "Edward" **BASENAU** (*BOSSMAN*) born 1894 in Marijampolė. Son of Karl Basenau[606] (1866-1925) and Pauline **Jurkschat**[645] (1866-1924). Baptized at Mariampol Evangelical Lutheran Church. Immigrated October 1908 via New York aboard the S.S. *Pennsylvania*. Married Elizabeth **Heitebach** (1901-1984). Died 27 Mar 1952 in Los Angeles, California. Interment unknown.

611. Eva "Evelyn" **BASENAU** (*BOSSMAN*) (**ORTMAN**) (**HORACEK**) born 1900 in Marijampolė. Daughter of Karl Basenau[606] (1866-1925) and Pauline **Jurkschat**[645] (1866-1924). Baptized at Mariampol Evangelical Lutheran Church. Immigrated October 1908 via New York aboard the S.S. *Pennsylvania*. Married Walter J. **Ortman** (1898-1932) 29 Apr 1921 at Zion Evangelical Lutheran Church. Married James Edward **Horacek** (1888-1960) in West Virginia. Died 28 Jan 1976 in Willoughby, Ohio. Interment at Lutheran Cemetery.

635.   i. Russell August Ortman b. 4 Jan 1922. d. 21 Oct 1983. m. Mildred Katherine **Todorovich** 1925-2011.
> 13 children:
>> Patricia A. 1947-
>> Russell A. 1948-
>> Robert D. 1949-
>> Alexander R. 1953-1988
>> Daniel J. 1966-1966
>> Susan
>> Dennis
>> Sonia
>> Jacqueline
>> Ginger
>> Nancy

        Johan
        Ida

636. ii. Walter John Ortman b. 20 Jul 1923. d. 17 Sep 2008. m. Eileen **Gongos** 1935-2008.

637. iii. Robert R. Ortman b. 27 Aug 1924. d. 17 Jul 2004. m. Josephine Ann **Novitski** 1932-2016.
    8 children:
        Thomas
        Cheryl
        Anne
        Christine
        Robert
        Diana
        Agnes
        John

638. iv. William Roy Ortman b. 26 Mar 1926. d. 16 Feb 1991. m. Joan **Susin** 1930-2011.
    3 children:
        Samantha
        Christopher
        Kimberley

639. v. Grace Jeanette Ortman b. 1 Mar 1927. d. Aug 2005. m. Jeffrey **Hayes** 1957-2012.

640. vi. Arlene P. Ortman b. 17 Aug 1928. d. 1 Jul 2014. m. George Fritz **Todorovich** 1919-1999.
    5 children:
        George
        Donald Edward 1949-1999
        Donna
        Gerald
        Cynthia

641. vii. Dorothy Lillian Ortman b. 10 Sep 1929. d. 28 Mar 2002. m. Merrill Morgan **Clair** 1931-2008.
    5 children:
        Merrill
        Daniel
        Colleen
        Shane Walter 1956-2021

642. viii. Richard Elroy Ortman b. 28 Oct 1930. d. 27 Aug 2005. m. Therese Mary **Yestonsky** 1933-2016.
>   2 children:
>   Michael
>   Terri

643. ix. Charlotte Ortman b. 1932. m. Ralph J. **Hayes** 1932-.

612. Gustav "Gust" **BASENAU** (*BOSSMAN*) born 1903 in Marijampolė. Son of Karl Basenau[606] (1866-1925) and Pauline **Jurkschat**[645] (1866-1924). Baptized at Mariampol Evangelical Lutheran Church. Immigrated October 1908 via New York aboard the S.S. *Pennsylvania*. Married Elizabeth **Hein**[734] (1901-1999) 13 Oct 1923 at St. Peter's Evangelical Lutheran Church. Died 29 Nov 1963. Interment at Lutheran Cemetery.

644. i. Norman Gustave Bossman b. 15 Jul 1924. d. 1 Jan 1998. m. Norma L. **Czzar** 1928-????.

645. ii. Carol Lois Bossman b. 3 Jul 1931. d. 5 Mar 2019. m. William Domonic **Amato** 1929-2011.
>   3 children:
>   Linda
>   William
>   Michael

BASCHAR

223. Auguste **BASCHAR (AUKSCHUN)** born 29 Jan 1877 in Degučiai. Daughter of August Baschar and Wilhelmine **Lehmann**. Baptized at Mariampol Evangelical Lutheran Church. Married Leopold **Aukschun**[211] (1871-1919) at Mariampol Lutheran Church in 1897. Immigrated October 1900 via New York aboard the S.S. *Bonn*. Died 4 Jul 1931. Interment at Lutheran Cemetery. For list of children, see husband Leopold Aukschun[211].

1339. Gustav **BASCHAR** born 19 Apr 1882 in Ungurinė.. Son of August Baschar and Wilhelmine **Lehmann**. Baptized and confirmed at Mariampol Evangelical Lutheran Church. Immigrated June 1906 via Baltimore aboard the S.S. *Brandenburg*. Died 16 Dec 1929. Interment at Lutheran Cemetery.

BATKE

722. Emilie **BATKE (HEIN)** born 1871 in Senoji Radiškė. Daughter of Friedrich Batke and Karoline **Hartwig**. Baptized at Kalwaria Evangelical Lutheran Church. Married Adolf **Hein**[713] (1867-1935) 1893 at Kalwaria Evangelical Lutheran Church. Immigrated July 1902 via Baltimore aboard the S.S. *Hannover*. Died 30 Nov 1907. Interment at Lutheran Cemetery. For list of children, see husband Adolf Hein[713].

BAUMANN

909. Emilie **BAUMANN (SCHWED)** born 1892 in Puszogród (no longer exists; was located between Panemunė and Pakuonis). Daughter of Karl Baumann and Karoline **Nibergala**. Baptized at the Goddlau Evangelical Lutheran Church. Immigrated November 1911 via Baltimore aboard the S.S. *Rhein*. Married Adolf **Schwed** (1878-1958) 4 May 1912 at Zion Evangelical Lutheran Church. Died 22 Sep 1967. Interment at Lutheran Cemetery.

    910.   i. Oswald Schwed b. 8 May 1913. d. 27 Oct 1999. m. Olga **Buknat**[905] 1912-1997.
                1 child:
                      Lawrence 1939-2014

    911.   ii. Edith Ida Schwed b. 9 Apr 1916. d. Aug 1978. m. David James **Stewart** 1907-1997.
                2 children:
                      Dorothy 1936-
                      William 1937-

    912.   iii. William Henry Schwed b. 5 Mar 1918. d. 26 Aug 1985. m. Thelma M. **Shearer** 1912-1996. m. Helen **Roll** 1918-1995.
                2 children:
                      William Ronald 1938-2001
                      Dennis James 1942-2000

    913.   iv. Adolf Schwed b. 1919. d. 21 May 1919.

    914.   v. Erna Emilie Schwed b. 12 May 1921. d. 2 Nov 2008. m. Albert Leo **Hess** Jr.[728] 1919-1997.

    915.   vi. Eleanor S. Schwed b. 14 Jul 1924. d. 7 Sep 2012. m. Richard E. **McDonald** 1922-????. m. Albert Charles **Nozik** ????-????.

    916.   vii. Harold Carl Schwed b. 6 Oct 1925. d. 15 Jun 1996. m. Arlene R. **Schollmeyer** 1921-1982.
                2 children:
                      Daniel 1952-1967
                      Susan 1955-1967

917. Olga **BAUMANN (WILK)** born 1895 in Puszogród (no longer exists; was located between Panemunė and Pakuonis). Daughter of Karl Baumann and Karoline **Nibergala**. Baptized at the Goddlau Evangelical Lutheran Church. Married Gustav **Wilk** (1891-1953) 7 Oct 1916 at Zion Evangelical Lutheran Church. Died 17 Jul 1978. Interment at Lutheran Cemetery. For list of children, see husband Gustav Wilk.

BENDER

174. Henriette **BENDER (REINKE)** born 1883 in Paserninkai. Daughter of Karl Felix Bender and Pauline Karoline **Hausrath**. Baptized at Serey Reformed Lutheran Church. Immigrated April 1903 via New York aboard S.S. *Kaiser Wilhelm der Große*. Married Adolf Julius **Reinke**[170] (1876-1951) 26 Apr 1903 at Zion Evangelical Lutheran Church. Died 16 Jun 1961 in Homersville Township, Ohio. Interment at Lutheran Cemetery. For list of children, see husband Adolf Julius Reinke.

175. Auguste **BENDER (SNYDER)** born 1878 in Paserninkai. Daughter of Karl Felix Bender and Pauline Karoline **Hausrath**. Baptized at Serey Reformed Lutheran Church. Married Wilhelm **Snyder [Schneider]** (1880-1963) 3 October 1914 at Zion Evangelical Lutheran Church. Died 27 Nov 1961 in Cleveland Heights. Interment at Lutheran Cemetery.

    176.   i. Helen Snyder b. 6 Jan 1916. d. 16 Jul 1989. m. Joseph P. **Aquilia** 1916-1985.
        4 children:
          Margaret 1937-
          Angela F. 1938-1995
          Joseph 1940-
          Viola C. 1943-2002
    177.   ii. Emma Snyder b. 12 Oct 1918. d. 25 Sep 2017.
    178.   iii. Ruth Snyder b. 7 Sep 1920. d. 2 Apr 2000. m. Paul r. **Babyak** 1917-????.
        1 child:
          Paul R. Jr. 1947-

955. Bertha **BENDER (HIRSCH)** born 1898 in Vilkaviškis. Daughter of Gustav Bender and Natalie **Weinschröder**[575] (1874-1968). Baptized at Wilkowischken Evangelical Lutheran Church. Immigrated February 1914 via Baltimore aboard the S.S. *Cassel*. Married Wilhelm **Hirsch**[952] (1884-1960) 13 Jul 1918 at Zion Evangelical Lutheran Church. Died 17 Apr 1996. Interment at Lutheran Cemetery. For list of children, see husband Wilhelm Hirsch.

BERWING

248. Karl Gustav **BERWING** born about 1864 in Degučiai. Son of Julius Berwing and Pauline Helene **Dikheiser** (1838-1916). Baptized at Mariampol Lutheran Evangelical Church. Married Pauline **Reder** (1860-1922) 1883 at Mariampol Lutheran Evangelical Church. Died 29 Jan 1924. Interment at Lutheran Cemetery.

    249.   i. Adolf Johann Berwing b. 18 Sep 1884. d. 15 Feb 1954. m. Rose Mae **Rost** 1890-1972.
            1 child:
                Rose Elizabeth 1927-2008

    250.   ii. Otto Berwing b. 1886. d. ????.

    251   iii. Auguste Berwing b. 1889. d. 9 May 1979. m. George A **Fife** 1887-1958. m. William D. **Clark** 1896-1963. m. Albert W. **Laws** 1895-1969.
            2 children:
                George Clark 1911-1977
                Mildred Clark 1913-2010

    252.   iv. Oskar Adolf Berwing b. 1891. d. 11 Oct 1946. m. Ida M. **Lang** 1896-1976.
            3 children:
                Dorothy 1915-1992
                Robert A. 1917-1970
                Pauline J. 1933-2017

    253.   v. Bertha Berwing b. 31 Dec 1894. d. 8 Dec 1954. m. Joseph A. **Brown** 1888-1967.
            3 children:
                Harold R.
                Walter Joseph 1914-1978
                Norman Daniel 1920-1985

    254.   vi. Karl Berwing b. 10 Jun 1896. d. 8 Feb 1977. m. Emma J. **Mills** 1901-1933. m. Etna Marie **Gershon** 1896-1967. m. Margaret Louise **Johnston** 1913-1968.

    255.   vii. Mildred Berwing b. 20 Sep 1897. d. 13 Aug 1967. m. William C. **Menzies** 1896-1972.
            2 children:
                Ruth Elizabeth 1918-1994
                Alice Mildred 1918-1991

256. viii. Walter Berwing b. 28 Mar 1900. d. 31 Jul 1999. m. Mildred **Frederick** 1902-1983. m. Lillian C. **Hofmeister** 1901-1987.
2 children:
Carol Jean 1933-2001
Vera Mae 1921-2018

249. Adolf Johann **BERWING** born 18 Sep 1884 in Marijampolė. Son of Karl Gustav Berwing[248] (1864-1924) and Pauline **Reder** (1860-1922). Baptized at Mariampol Evangelical Lutheran Church. Immigrated August 1892 via Baltimore aboard the S.S. *Gera*. Married Rose Mae **Rost** (1890-1972) 30 Jun 1923 at Immanuel Evangelical Lutheran Church. Died 15 Feb 1954. Interment at Lake View Cemetery.

257. i. Rose Elizabeth Berwin b. 18 Jun 1927. d. 11 Apr 2008. m. Kenneth Richards **Lovell** 1927-2011.
4 children:
John
Mark
Linda
Mary

251. Auguste **BERWING (FIFE) (CLARK) (LAWS)** born 1889 in Degučiai. Daughter of Karl Gustav Berwing[248] (1864-1924) and Pauline **Reder** (1860-1922). Baptized at Mariampol Evangelical Lutheran Church. Immigrated August 1892 via Baltimore aboard the S.S. *Gera*. Married George Austin **Fief** (1887-1958) 19 Jul 1911 at St. John's Evangelical Lutheran Church. Divorced 22 Apr 1921. Married William D. **Clark** (1896-????) 4 August 1921 by Justice of the Peace. Divorced. Married Albert W. **Laws** Jr. (1895-1969) 22 May 1937 at Trinity United Brethren in Christ Church, Bowling Green, Ohio. Died 9 May 1978 in Willoughby, Ohio. Interment at Lutheran Cemetery.

258. i. George K. Clark b. 28 Nov 1911. d. 13 Jan 1977. m. Edna F. 1913-1993.
3 children:
Ronald G. 1941-
Pamela D. 1944-2005
James Karl 1949-1996

259. ii. Mildred Clark b. 19 Oct 1913. d. 23 Jan 2010. m. Hugh Hammond **Graham** 1914-2007.
3 children:
Hugh Hamond Jr. 1938-2011

252. Oskar Adolf **BERWING** born 1891 in Degučiai. Son of Karl Gustav Berwing[248] (1864-1924) and Pauline **Reder** (1860-1922). Baptized at Mariampol Evangelical Lutheran Church. Immigrated August 1892 via Baltimore aboard the S.S. *Gera*. Married Ida M. **Lang**[1391] (1896-1976) 11 December 1914 in Cleveland by a Justice of the Peace. Died 11 Oct 1894 in Sharon, Pennsylvania. Interment at Hillcrest Memorial Park, Hermitage, Pennsylvania.

    260.   i. Dorothy Berwing b. 23 Sep 1915. d. 14 Sep 1992. m. William **Rupp** 1914-????.
        4 children:
        Fay E.
        William R.
        Eileen R.

Alan261.   ii. Robert Arthur Berwing b. 4 Dec 1917. d. 18 Oct 1970. m. Alice Laverne **Elliott** 1920-1922.
        4 children:
            Marilyn Ann 1941-1999
            Elizabeth E. 1943-
            Shirley J. 1944-

    262.   iii. Pauline Jeanne Berwing b. 12 Jul 1933. d. 12 Feb 2017. m. Robert Stephen **Mott** 1926-2014.
        6 children:
            Robert Milo 1953-2014
            Lara Jayne 1971-2004

263. Emilie **BERWING** (*ANDEXLER/ANDECHSER*) born 1869 in Degučiai. Daughter of Julius Berwing and Pauline Helene **Dikheiser** (1838-1916). Baptized at Mariampol Evangelical Lutheran Church. Married Karl **Andexler**[264] (1863-1911) 1886 at Mariampol Evangelical Lutheran Church. Died October 1937. Interment at Lutheran Cemetery. For list of children, see husband Karl Andexler.

270. Johann Julius **BERWING** born 28 Apr 1882 in Degučiai. Son of Julius Berwing and Pauline Helene **Dikheiser** (1838-1916). Baptized and confirmed 8 June 1896 at Mariampol Evangelical Lutheran Church. Immigrated June 1899 via New York aboard the S.S. *Augusta Victoria*. Died 4 Dec 1926. Interment at Lutheran Cemetery.

BIRKOBEN / BERKOBEIN / BERKENBEIN

240. Hugo Gustav **BIRKOBEN** born 15 Dec 1882 in Bolcie (Poland). Son of Andreas Birkoben (1857-????) and Helene **Gerulat** (1861-????). Baptized at Wischainy Evangelical Lutheran Church. Immigrated April 1901 via New York aboard S.S. *Königin Luise*. Married Emilie **Budnik** (1882-1915) 14 Nov 1909 at Zion Evangelical Lutheran Church. Died June 1948. Interment at Lutheran Cemetery.

    241.   i. Lillian Birkobein b. 21 Aug 1910. d. bef. 1948. m. ? **Siess**.

    242.   ii. Ruth Amelia Birkoben b. 29 Jan 1912. d. 11 Apr 1998. m. Friedrich Thure **Westberg** 1912-1981.
        1 child:
            Frederick Wallace 1938-2012

244. Karl **BIRKOBEN** born 1884 in Bolcie (Poland). Son of Andreas Birkoben (1857-????) and Helene **Gerulat** (1861-????). Baptized at Wischainy Evangelical Lutheran Church. Married Auguste **Kausch**[246] (1886-1979) 22 April 1906 at Zion Evangelical Lutheran Church. Died 6 Dec 1958. Interment at Lutheran Cemetery.

    245.   i. Oskar Karl Berkoben b. 9 Oct 1907. d. 27 May 1967. m. Freida Marie **Schafer** 1907-1997.
        3 children:
            Kenneth Oscar 1933-
            Orland Carl 1940-
            John Richard 1945-2013

247. Albert **BIRKOBEN** born 1890 in Bolcie (Poland). Son of Andreas Birkoben (1857-????) and Helene **Gerulat** (1861-????). Baptized at Wischainy Evangelical Lutheran Church. Immigrated November 1911 via Philadelphia aboard the S.S. *Chemnitz*. Died August 1955. Interment at Lutheran Cemetery.

BLUM / BLUHM / BLOOM

1270. Gustav **BLUM** born 19 Dec 1890 in Užsieniai. Son of Gustav Blum and Johanna **Leidig**. Baptized and confirmed at Neustadt Evangelical Lutheran Church. Immigrated August 1913 via New York aboard the S.S. *Königin Luise*. Married Martha **Albrecht**[1269] 10 Jul 1923 at St. Paul's Evangelical Lutheran Church. Died April or Feb 1967. Interment unknown.

    1271.   i. Richard Harvey Blum b. 3 Jun 1924. d. 2 Jan 2006. m. Mildred Mary **Lopes** 1924-1988.
        1 child:
            Richard L. b. 1948-

    1272.   ii. Emma D. Blum b. 9 Jun 1926. d. 23 Dec 1978. m. Richard David **Osolin** 1924-1992.
        1 child:
            Richard Louis 1949-1994

BOMBLIS / BUMBLIS

1196. Adolf **BUMBLIS** born 1872 in Ungurinė. Son of Johann Bumblis[1205] (1835-1920) and Anna **Schwed**[1206] (1837-1921). Married Anna **Niederstrass** 1899 at Kalwaria Evangelical Lutheran Church. Married Mathilde **Friedrich**[1181] (1881-1971) 7 Sep 1902 at Zion Evangelical Lutheran Church. Died 1926. Interment at Brooklyn Heights Cemetery, Brooklyn, Ohio.

    1197. i. Olga Bumblis b. 25 Apr 1904. d. 13 Dec 1992. m. John **Komko** 1900-1968.
        1 child:
          John Joseph 1931-2006

    1198. ii. August Bumblis b. 23 Feb 1906. d. 3 Feb 1969. m. Margaret **?** 1908-1979. 2 children:
          Margaret 1927-
          Frances 1937-

    1199. iii. Mary Bumblis b. 28 Dec 1908. d. Jan 1968. m. William **Moyer** ????-1969. m. Roland **Rogers**.
        3 children:
          Joseph Marion 1926-1980
          June 1927-2017
          Evelyn Mae 1928-2014

1201. August Gustav **BUMBLIS** born 1883 likely near Kalvarija. Son of Johann Bumblis[1205] (1835-1920) and Anna **Schwed**[1206] (1837-1921). Immigrated August 1901 via New York aboard the S.S. *Southwark*. Married Anna **Friedrich**[1200] (1886-1938) 26 Apr 1903 at Zion Evangelical Lutheran Church. Died 10 Apr 1952. Interment at Lutheran Cemetery.

    1202. i. John Bumblis b. 1 May 1906. d. 27 Sep 1979.

    1203. ii. August Bumblis b. 3 Aug 1910. d. 23 Oct 1957.

    1204. iii. Mary Bumblis b. 29 Mar 1917. d. 17 Nov 1982.

1205. Johann **BUMBLIS** born 1835 likely somewhere near Krosna. Son of Heinrich Bumblis and Maria **Albrecht**. Married Anna **Schwed**[1206] (1837-1921) 1861 at Mariampol Evangelical Lutheran Church. Immigrated August 1902 via Baltimore aboard the S.S. *Brandeburg*. Died 30 Nov 1920. Interment at Lutheran Cemetery.

    1207. i. Marianna Bumblis b. 1862. d. 22 Aug 1942. m. August **Schmidt**[1212] 1862-1917.

7 children:
> Anna[1213] 1886-1916
> August[1214] 1888-1921
> Albert Ferdinand[1215] 1890-1939
> Eduard C.[1216] 1892-1973
> Friedrich[1217] 1894-1942
> Lillian[1218] 1896-1966
> Elmer[1219] 1901-1970

1208. ii. Anna Bumblis b. Sep 1866. d. 18 Oct 1936. m. Jakob **Klein** 1867-1953.
> 4 children:
> Susan 1890-1966
> Julius James 1894-1974
> Jennie 1897-1982
> Frances 1898-1954

1209. iii. Auguste Bumblis b. 17 Apr 1870. d. 31 Dec 1954. m. Gottfried **Strick** 1873-????.
> 2 children:
> Bertha[1222] 1898-1984
> John[1223] 1907-1992

1196. iv. Adolf Bumblis b. 1872. d. 1926. m. Anna **Niederstrass**. m. Mathilde **Friedrich**[1181] 1881-1971.
> 3 children:
> Olga 1904-1992
> August 1906-1969
> Mary 1908-1968

1210. v. Mathilde Bumblis b. 22 May 1874. d. ????.

1211. vi. Johann Bumblis b. 10 Apr 1876. d. ????. m. Sophia Anna **Pischulia** 1875-1941.
> 5 children:
> August Richard[1224] 1903-1967
> Anna[1225] 1905-1971
> Lilly[1226] 1905-????
> Margaret[1227] 1906-1910
> Elsie[1228] 1909-1910

1201. vii. August Gustav Bumblis b. 1883. d. 10 Apr 1952. m. Anna **Friedrich**[1200] 1886-1938.
> 3 children:
> John 1906-1979
> August 1910-1957

Mary 1917-1982

1208. Marianna **BUMBLIS** (**SCHMIDT**) born 1862 likely near Bukta. Daughter of Johann Bumblis[1205] (1835-1920) and Anna **Schwed**[1206] (1837-1921). Baptized and confirmed at Mariampol Evangelical Lutheran Church. Married August **Schmidt**[1212] (1962-1942) 16 Nov 1884 at Mariampol Evangelical Lutheran Church. Died 22 Aug 1942. Interment at Lutheran Cemetery. For list of children, see husband August Schmidt.

1209. Auguste **BUMBLIS** (**STRICK**) born 17 Apr 1870 in Ungurinė. Daughter of Johann Bumblis[1205] (1835-1920) and Anna **Schwed**[1206] (1837-1921). Baptized and confirmed at Mariampol Evangelical Lutheran Church. Immigrated Sep 1903 via Philadelphia aboard the S.S. *Willehad*. Married Gottfried **Strick** (1873-????) 19 Aug 1904 at Schifflein Christi Evangelical Lutheran Church. Died 1954 in Huntsburg, Ohio. Interment at Chardon Municipal Cemetery, Chardon, Ohio.

- 1222. i. Bertha Strick b. 3 Feb 1898. d. 6 Apr 1984. m. John **Buschner** 1889-1944.
    5 children:
    George 1914-2003
    Elizabeth 1914-1997
    Eleanor 1919-2010
    Margaret 1921-1975
    Dorothy 1923-2006

- 1223. ii. John Strick b. 26 Apr 1907. d. 17 Jun 1992. m. Evelyn **Lang** 1913-1991. m. Margaret **Mulvey** 1927-2016.

1211. Johann **BUMBLIS** born 10 Apr 1876 in Liudvinavas. Son of Johann Bumblis[1205] (1835-1920) and Anna **Schwed**[1206] (1837-1921). Baptized and confirmed at Mariampol Evangelical Lutheran Church. Married Sophia Anna **Pischulia** (1875-1941) [Roman Catholic] 2 Jan 1900 by a Justice of the Peace in Cleveland. Death unknown. Likely interred at Calvary Cemetery.

- 1224. i. August Richard Bumblis b. 26 Feb 1903. d. 6 Aug 1967. m. Grace **Truppo** 1903-1985.

- 1225. ii. Anna Bumblis b. 1905. d. 8 Jul 1971. m. James R. **Parker** 1908-1984.
    6 children:
    Richard James 1930-1992
    Katherine 1931-2016
    Robert W. 1933-
    Betty J. 1935-
    Lenora 1937-2009

Lucille G. 1944-

1226.   iii. Lilly Bumblis b. 1906. d. ????.

1227.   iv. Margaret Bumblis b. 10 Oct 1906. d. 15 Dec 1910.

1228.   v. Elsie Bumblis b. 19 Aug 1909. d. 12 Sep 1910.

BORCHERT

1168. Eva **BORCHERT** (**KALCHERT**) born 1850 in Sejny (Poland). Daughter of Johann Borchert and Marianna **Wisocki**. Married Adolf **Kalchert** (1842-????) 1881 at Kalwaria Evangelical Lutheran Church. Immigrated July 1905 via Baltimore aboard the S.S. *Frankfurt*. Died 29 Sep 1926 in Warrensville, Ohio. Interment at Lutheran Cemetery.

    1169.   i. Gustav August Kalchert b. 1863. d. 28 Oct 1926.

    1170.   ii. Rudolf Kalchert b. 1872. d. Sep 1956. m. Sophia **Wysocki** 1873-1949.
> 6 children:
>> Stephanie 1899-1927
>> John 1901-1980
>> Elizabeth 1902-1995
>> Agnes 1909-????
>> Helen 1910-2000
>> James 1915-1983

    1171.   iii. Ludwig Kalchert b. 15 Dec 1885. d. 19 Nov 1933. m. Bertha **Dikheiser**[966] 1887-1936.
> 5 children:
>> Walter Ludwig[971] 1913-1914
>> Evelyn B.[972] 1916-2007
>> Elmer Leonard[973] 1921-2001
>> Richard Herbert[974] 1925-1995
>> Infant Kalchert[975] 1914-1914

    1172.   iv. Adolf Kalchert b. 15 Sep 1887. d. 31 Jul 1949. m. Lydia **Dikheiser**[1174] 1898-1945.
> 3 children:
>> Allen 1921-1999
>> Norman R. 1923-1994
>> Raymond L. 1923-1987

    1174.   v. Marie Kalchert b. 2 Jun 1890. d. 25 Apr 1955. m. Theodor P. **Sikorski** 1889-1956.
> 2 children:
>> Helen 1915-1976
>> Elsie E. 1927-2018

BRAUER

899. Gustav **BRAUER** born 1892 in Raželiai. Son of Ferdinand Brauer and Maire **Nibergala**. Baptized at Goddlau Evangelical Lutheran Church. Immigrated May 1913 via Philadelphia aboard the S.S. *Chemnitz*. Married Auguste **Buknat** (1896-1985) 20 May 1916 at Zion Evangelical Lutheran Church. Died 13 Feb 1978 in Elyria, Ohio. Interment at Lutheran Cemetery.

    900.   i. Oswald Brauer b. 16 Jul 1917. d. 22 Apr 1981. m. Eleanor **Peters**[885] 1917-2018.
            1 child:
                Cheryl L. 1949-

    901.   ii. Alma Brauer b. 24 Jan 1919. d. 25 Nov 2018. m. Walter Henry **Wolf** 1918-1998.

    902.   iii. Elmer Brauer b. 1920. d. ????.

    903.   iv. Arthur Karl Brauer b. 18 Jun 1925. d. 9 May 2003. m. Geraldine Audrey **Neitzel** 1931-.
            2 children:
                Audrey
                Diane

BUDNIK

243. Emilie **BUDNIK (BIRKOBEN)** born 1882 in Bakšiškiai. Daughter of Friedrich Budnik and Marie **Abramat**. Married Hugo Gustav **Birkoben**[240] (1882-1948) 14 Nov 1909 at Zion Evangelical Lutheran Church. Died 14 Mar 1915. Interment at Lutheran Cemetery. For list of children, see husband Hugo Gustav Birkoben[240].

BUKNAT / BUKNAITIS / BOKNAT

904. Ludwig "Louis" **BUKNAT** born 18 Aug 1888 in Liudvinavas. Son of Georg Buknat and Pauline **Adomat**. Baptized at Mariampol Evangelical Lutheran Church. Married Anna **Kozlowski** (1892-1939) 1911 at Mariampol Evangelical Lutheran Church. Immigrated January 1913 via Baltimore aboard the S.S. *Neckar*. Died 3 Mar 1961. Interment at Lake View Cemetery.

    905.   i. Olga Buknat b. 17 Nov 1912. d. 23 May 1997. m. Oswald **Schwed**[910] 1913-1999.
        1 child:
            Lawrence 1939-2014

    906.   ii. Henry Buknat b. 2 Sep 1914. d. 25 Feb 1997. m. Helene Georgetti **Campbell** 1917-2001.
        2 children:
            Bonnie Lee 1946-1975

    907.   iii. Andrew Biknat b. about. 1915. d. ????.

    908.   iv. Ludwig "Louis" Buknat Jr. b. 29 Dec 1917. d. 10 Mar 2000. m. Lucille E. **Wadsworth** 1919-2006.
        1 child:
            Laura E. 1950-

BURKE

375. Karl Adolf **BURKE** born 1888 in Penkiniai. Son of Karl Alexander Burke and Johanna **Kaufmann**. Baptized and confirmed at Mariampol Evangelical Lutheran Church. Immigrated September 1907 via New York aboard the S.S. *Amerika*. Married Anna **Kinat**[371] (1892-1978) 25 December 1911 at Zion Evangelical Lutheran Church. Died 27 Oct 1918. Interment at Lutheran Cemetery.

    376.   i. Harold Burke b. 1 Jul 1912. d. 5 Nov 1915.

    377.   ii. Clarence Edward Burke b. 24 Jul 1914. d. 26 Nov 1993. m. Louise Emma **Molzan** 1914-2000.

    378.   iii. Leonard Burke b. 22 Dec 1916. d. 10 Oct 1979. m. Hilda **Rinas** 1918-2010.
        2 children:
            Linda 1942-
            Laraine 1948-

    379.   iv. Leroy Burke b. 24 Jul 1918. d. 16 Oct 2000.

1072. Johanna **BURKE** (**MAURUSCHAT**) born 1886 in Bulotiškė. Daughter of Karl Alexander Burke and Johanna **Kaufmann**. Baptized at Mariampol Evangelical Lutheran Church. Immigrated August 1908 via New York aboard the S.S. *Blucher*. Married Eduard **Mauruschat**[1073] (1887-1941) 16 Jul 1911 at Zion Evangelical Lutheran Church. Died 9 Aug 1969. Interment at Lutheran Cemetery. For list of children, see husband Eduard Mauruschat.

1077. Karl Gustav **BURKE** born 1883 in Bulotiškė. Son of Karl Alexander Burke and Johanna **Kaufmann**. Baptized at Mariampol Evangelical Lutheran Church. Immigrated February 1904 via New York. Married Amelia "Millie" **Kinat**[1076] (1893-1940) 25 Dec 1912 at Zion Evangelical Lutheran Church. Died 2 May 1967 in Brooklyn, Ohio. Interment at Lutheran Cemetery.

    1078.   i. Lillian Burke b. 1916. d. 27 Mar 2012. m. Harold W. **Slough** 1912-1977.
        1 child:
            Loyal H. 1926-

    1079.   ii. Evelyn Burke b. 28 Dec 1917. d. 7 Sep 2004. m. Carl **Nehring** 1914-1960. m. Julius Bonyhay.
        3 children:
            Susan A. 1944-
            Gayle I. 1947-

Leanne

1080. iii. Walter Gustave Burke b. 13 Oct 1919. d. 24 Dec 2017. m. Eleanor **Bauer**[1089] 1925-2014.

1081. iv. Vera Burke b. 15 Aug 1922. d. 2005. m. Hermann **Peters**[1054] 1915-2016.
        2 children:
            Sandra 1942-
            Kathleen 1947-

BUSCHAR / BUSCHER

1142. Georg **BUSCHAR** born 23 Apr 1856 in Putriškiai. Son of Heinrich Buschar and Henriette **Hermann**. Likely baptized at Mariampol Evangelical Lutheran Church. Married Julianna Auguste **Putnat**[1143] (1858-1952) 1884 at Kalwaria Evangelical Lutheran Church. Died 1 Jan 1916. Interment at Lutheran Cemetery.

    1144. i. Adeline Buschar b. 8 May 1885. d. 17 Jul 1972. m. Johann **Busdiecker** 1887-1941.
        3 children:
           Elmer Henry 1910-1977
           Eleanor 1911-????
           Luella Martha 1914-1989

    1145. ii. Karl "Charles" Buschar b. 12 May 1887. d. 30 Aug 1958. m. Theresa **Lenk** 1890-1969.
        1 child:
           Harold Richard 1914-1983

    1146. iii. George Buschar b. 26 Jan 1891. d. 6 Oct 1953. m. Emma **Schiemann** 1894-1950.
        2 children:
           Alice Emma 1917-1994
           George John 1920-1966

DANGELAT / DANGELEIT

1022. Anna **DANGELAT (NEIMAN)** born 2 Jul 1902 in Miklausė. Daughter of Ludwig Dangelat (1873-1904) and Albine **Schultz**[1021] (1882-1970). Baptized at Mariampol Evangelical Lutheran Church. Immigrated Nov 1921 via New York aboard the S.S. *Carmania*. Married Gustav **Neumann (NEIMAN)**[1016] (1887-1975) 15 Jul 1922 at Zion Evangelical Lutheran Church. Died 19 Jul 1994. Interment unknown. For list of children, see husband Gustav Neumann.

1023. Ludwig "Louis" **DANGELAT** born 1904 in Miklausė. Son of Ludwig Dangelat (1873-1904) and Albine **Schultz**[1021] (1882-1970). Baptized at Mariampol Evangelical Lutheran Church. Immigrated Nov 1921 via New York aboard the S.S. *Carmania*. Married Pauline **Dill**[1027] (1906-1975) 18 Sep 1926 at Zion Evangelical Lutheran Church. Died 26 Nov 1987. Interment at Lutheran Cemetery.

    1024. Ruth Dengelat b. 1928. d. 1934.

DIKHEISER / DYKHEYSER

264. Pauline Helene **DIKHEISER (BERWING)** born 1838 likely in Degučiai. Daughter of Wilhelm Dikheiser and Karoline Dorothea **Regg**. Likely baptized at Mariampol Evangelical Lutheran Church. Married Julius **Berwing** at Mariampol Evangelical Lutheran Church in 1860. Died 5 April 1916. Interment at Lutheran Cemetery.

    248.   i. Karl Gustav Berwing[248] b. 1864. d. 29 Jan 1924. m. Pauline **Reder** 1860-1922.
        8 children:
            Adolf Johann[249] 1884-1954
            Otto[250] 1886-????
            Auguste[251] 1889-1978
            Oskar Adolf[252] 1891-1946
            Bertha[253] 1894-1954
            Karl[254] 1896-1977
            Mildred[255] 1897-1967
            Walter[256] 1900-1999

    263.   ii. Emilie Berwing[263] b. 1869. d. Oct 1937. m. Karl **Andexler**[264] 1863-1911.
        5 children:
            Edward Adolph[265] 1894-1929
            Karl[266] 1898-1956
            Emma[267] 1902-1994
            Lillian[268] 1907-1964
            Herman[269] 1910-1977

    270.   iii. Johann Julius[270] b. 1882. d. 4 Dec 1926.

964. Adolf Luis **DIKHEISER** born 1863 in Degučiai. Son of Johann Dikheizer and Amelia **Reder**. Baptized at Mariampol Evangelical Lutheran Church. Married Anna **Reinke**[965] (1861-1942) 1885 at Mariampol Evangelical Lutheran Church. Immigrated September 1910 aboard S.S. *Breslau*. Died 11 May 1946. Interment at Lutheran Cemetery.

    966.   i. Bertha Dikheiser b. 1886. d. 11 May 1936. m. Ludwig **Kalchert** 1885-1933.
        5 children:
            Walter Lewis 1913-1914
            Evelyn B. 1916-2007
            Elmer Leonard 1921-2001
            Richard Herbert 1925-1995
            Infant 1914-1914

967. ii. Wanda Dikheiser b. 1891. d. 29 Oct 1918. m. Richard **Nowjak**[118] 1888-1980.
    2 children:
        Alert Walter 1916-2012
        Ella 1918-2008

968. iii. Gustav Ferdinand Dikheiser b. 13 Apr 1895. d. 21 Aug 1963. m. Marie **Muschinski**[1441] 1897-1995.
    2 children:
        Lillian[1448] 1918-1963
        Alfred Gustave[1449] 1920-1997

969. iv. Richard Dikheiser b. 1897. d. 3 Dec 1928.

970. v. Lydia Dikheiser b. 1898. d. 11 Jan 1945. m. Adolf **Kalchert** 1887-1949.
    3 children:
        Allen 1921-1999
        Norman Richard 1923-1994
        Raymond L. 1923-1987

966. Bertha **DIKHEISER (KALCHERT)** born 30 Oct 1886 in Marijampolė. Daughter of Adolf Luis Dikheiser[964] (1863-1946) and Anna **Reinke**[965] (1861-1941). Baptized at Mariampol Evangelical Lutheran Church. Married Ludwig **Kalchert**[1171] (1887-1949) 18 Jun 1911 at Zion Evangelical Lutheran Church. Died 11 May 1936. Interment at Lutheran Cemetery.

971. i. Walter Lewis Kalchert b. 17 Mar 1913. d. 25 Oct 1914.

972. ii. Evelyn B. Kalchert b. 24 Apr 1916. d. 16 Oct 2007. m. Henry Vernon **Roohk** 1907-1992.
    2 children:
        Henry Jr. 1944-
        David L. 1946-

973. iii. Elmer Leonard Kalchert b. 23 Dec 1921. d. 26 Oct 2001.

974. iv. Richard Herbert Kalchert b. 8 Aug 1925. d. 8 Mar 1995. m. Mary Patricia **O'Donnell** 1929-1966.
    6 children:
        Katherine Ann 1949-
        Karen P. 1950-2018

975. v. Infant Kalchert b. 1914. d. 25 Oct 1914

967. Wanda **DIKHEISER** (**NOWJAK**) born 13 Aug 1891 in Degučiai. Daughter of Adolf Luis Dikheiser[964] (1863-1946) and Anna **Reinke**[965] (1861-1942). Baptized and confirmed at Mariampol Evangelical Lutheran Church. Married Richard **Nowjak**[118] (1888-1980) 25 Aug 1915 at Zion Evangelical Lutheran Church. Died 29 Oct 1918. Interment at Lutheran Cemetery. For list of children, see husband Richard Nowjak.

968. Gustav Ferdinand **DIKHEISER** born 13 Apr 1895 in Marijampolė. Son of Adolf Luis Dikheiser[964] (1863-1946) and Anna **Reinke**[965] (1861-1942). Baptized and confirmed at Mariampol Evangelical Lutheran Church. Married Marie **Muschinski** (1897-1995) 19 Sep 1917 in Cleveland by a Justice of the Peace. Died 21 Aug 1963 in Long Beach, California. Interment at Forest Lawn Memorial Park, Cypress, California.

> 976. i. Lillian Dorothy Dikheiser b. 22 Jun 1918. d. 18 Oct 1963. m. Melvin Walter **Gee** 1916-1985.
> 2 children:
> Shirley M.
>
> 977. ii. Alfred Gustave Dikheiser b. 1 Jan 1920. d. 21 Apr 1997. m. Erna A. **Davies** 1914-????. m. Dorothy Mae **Miles** 1923-1972.
> 1 child:
> Wayne William 1947-1995

1173. Lydia **DIKHEISER** (**KALCHERT**) born 1898 in Degučiai. Daughter of Adolf Louis Dikheiser[964] (1863-1946) and Anna **Reinke**[965] (1861-1942). Baptized at Mariampol Evangelical Lutheran Church. Married Adolf **Kalchert**[1172] 31 Dec 1918 at Zion Evangelical Lutheran Church. Died 11 Jan 1945. Interment at Lutheran Cemetery. For list of children, see husband Adolf Kalchert.

DIKSCHAT / DUKSCHAT / DICK

1351. Richard Emil **DIKSCHAT** („**DICK**") born 20 Dec 1886 in Marijampolė. Son of Georg Dikschat and Luise **Arndt**. Baptized and confirmed at Mariampol Evangelical Lutheran Church. Immigrated September 1907 via Baltimore aboard the S.S. *Frankfurt*. Died 10 Oct 1924. Interment at Highland Park Cemetery, Highland Hills, Ohio.

DILL / DILEWSKI / DYLEWSKI

1025. Karl **DILL** born 1870 in Poluńce (Poland). Son of Ludwig Gottlieb Dill and Henriette **Krüger**. Baptized at Seine Evangelical Lutheran Church. Immigrated July 1904 via New York aboard the S.S. *Polacia*. Married Angeline **Reinke**[1031] (1880-1969) 5 Oct 1900 at Zion Evangelical Lutheran Church. Died 15 Apr 1943. Interment at Lutheran Cemetery.

    1026. i. Henry Dill b. 12 Jul 1901. d. 19 Dec 1985. m. Margaret **Wonderly** 1902-1989.
        1 child:
           Evelyn 1936-1999

    1027. ii. Pauline Dill b. 29 Dec 1906. d. 5 Apr 1975. m. Ludwig "Louis" **Denglat**[1023] 1904-1987.
        1 child:
           Ruth 1928-1934

    1028. iii. Gustave Dill b. 28 Jul 1909. d. 14 Feb 1995.

    1029. iv. Regina Wanda Dill b. 9 Dec 1911. d. 24 Jan 1983. m. Edward **Prokes** 1907-1978.
        1 child:
           Jean 1936-

    1030. v. Lydia Dill b. 23 Aug 1916. d. 15 Aug 2002.

1500. Johann **DILL (DILEWSKI)** born 31 Dec 1898 in Mockai. Son of August Dilewski and Emilie Blaar. Baptized at Seine Evangelical Lutheran Church. Married Karoline **Keller**[1501] (1899-1993) 15 Jun 1924 at Kalwaria Evangelical Lutheran Church. Immigrated March 1952 via New York aboard the U.S.S. *General Harry Taylor*. Died 27 Jul 1977 in Euclid, Ohio. Interment at Hope Memorial Gardens, Hinckley, Ohio.

    1502. i. Ewald Dill b. 24 May 1924. d. 1945.

    1503. ii. Johann Dill (Jr). b. 19 Sep 1928. d. 30 Sep 2016. m. Wanda **Fechner** 1935-.
        4 children:
           Helen[1509] 1960-
           Herbert[1510] 1961-
           Monica[1511] 1971-
           Michael[1512] 1973-

    1504. iii. Erwin Dill b. 4 Jul 1930. d. 18 Jul 2007. m. Bertha G. **Kuck** 1937-.

3 children:
> Heike[1513] 1958-
> Gerhard[1514] 1961-
> Reinhard[1515] 1966-

1505. iv. Alma Dill b. 2 Nov 1931. d. 2 Oct 2014. m. Oswald **Hempel** 1923-2010.
> 4 children:
>> Edith[1516] 1952-
>> Ingrid[1517] 1953-
>> Irene[1518] 1954-
>> Walter[1519] 1959-

1506. v. Walter Dill b. 22 May 1934. d. 11 Jun 2023. m. Magdalena **Krieger** 1940-2019.
> 3 children:
>> Walter Jr.[1521] 1964-
>> Manfred[1522] 1967-
>> Linda[1523] 1972-

1507. vi. Erna Dill b. 12 Apr 1935. d. 4 Dec 1993. m. Ferdinand Heinrich **Rein** 1934-2013.
> 8 children:
>> Helga[1524] 1959-2021
>> Karin[1525] 1960-
>> Monika[1526] 1962-
>> Karl Helmut[1527] 1968-
>> Erika[1528] 1970-
>> David[1529] 1972-
>> Lydia[1530] 1975-
>> Sylvia[1531] 1977-

1508. vii. Julius Dill b. 7 May 1937. m. Almut **Gerdes** 1945-.
> 5 children:
>> Margaret[1532] 1966-
>> Elisabeth[1533] 1967-
>> Marianna[1534] 1969-
>> Norman[1535] 1974-
>> Heidi Martha[1536] 1982-

1503. Johann **DILL** Jr. born 19 Sep 1928 in Vaiponiškė. Son of Johann Dill[1500] (1898-1977) and Karoline **Keller**[1501] (1899-1977). Baptized at Kalwaria Evangelical Lutheran Church. Immigrated October 1951 via New York aboard the U.S.S. *General W. G. Haan*. Married Wanda **Fechner** (1935-) 30 Nov 1957 at Zion Evangelical Lutheran Church. Died 30 Sep 2016 in Willoughby, Ohio. Interment at Hope Memorial Gardens, Hinckley, Ohio.

1509. i. Helen Dill b. 9 Feb 1960. m. Scott W. **Ullman** 1962-.
3 children:
Michelle
Joseph
Nathaniel

1510. ii. Herbert Dill b. 23 Dec 1961. m. Cheryl G. **Smitley** 1965-.
2 children:
Hannah
Joshua

1511. iii. Monica Dill b. 30 Mar 1971. m. Stephen W. **Jones** 1968-.
2 children:
Caleb
Elisabeth

1512. iv. Michael Dill b. 10 Sep 1973. m. Shelley L. **Hagerman** 1980-.

1504. Erwin **DILL** born 4 Jul 1930 in Vaiponiškė. Son of Johann Dill[1500] (1898-1977) and Karoline **Keller**[1501] (1899-1977). Baptized at Kalwaria Evangelical Lutheran Church. Immigrated March 1952 via New York aboard the U.S.S. *General Harry Taylor*. Married Bertha G. **Kuck** (1937-). Died 18 Jul 2007 in Eastlake, Ohio. Interment at Lutheran Memorial Park, Hinckley, Ohio.

1513. i. Heike Dill b. 16 Jun 1958. m. Ernest R. **Kleine** 1953-.
4 children:
Dan
Linda
Elise
Ben

1514. ii. Gerhard Dill b. 11 Jun 1961. m. Cathy M. **Swartz** 1960-.

1515. iii. Reinhard Dill b. 14 Jul 1966. m. Jeanette **LaRiccia.**

1505. Alma **DILL (HEMPEL)** born 2 Nov 1931 in Vaiponiškė. Daughter of Johann Dill[1500] (1898-1977) and Karoline **Keller**[1501] (1899-1977). Baptized at Kalwaria Evangelical Lutheran Church. Married Oswald **Hempel**[1516] (1923-2010) June 1951 in Germany. Immigrated May 1952 via New York aboard Flying Tiger Line Flight 229. Died 2 Oct 2014 in Las Vegas, Nevada. Interment at Hope Memorial Gardens, Hinckley, Ohio. For list of children, see husband Oswald Hempel.

1506. Walter **DILL** born 22 May 1934 in Vaiponiškė. Son of Johann Dill[1500] (1898-1977) and Karoline **Keller**[1501] (1899-1977). Baptized at Kalwaria Evangelical Lutheran Church. Immigrated March 1952 via New York aboard U.S.S. *General Harry Taylor*. Married Magdalena **Krieger** (1940-2019). Died 11 Jun 2023 in Brunswick, Ohio. Interment at Hope Memorial Gardens, Hinckley, Ohio.

    1521.   i. Walter Dill Jr. b. 27 Feb 1964.

    1522.   ii. Manfred Dill b. 26 Jul 1967. m. Susan E. **Marcis** 1966-.
            3 children:
                Jessica
                Steven
                Eric

    1523.   iii. Linda Dill b. 3 Jun 1972. m. Dennis P **Goodhart** II 1977-.
            2 children:
                Alania
                Dennis III

1507. Erna **DILL (REIN)** born 12 Apr 1935 in Vaiponiškė. Daughter of Johann Dill[1500] (1898-1977) and Karoline **Keller**[1501] (1899-1977). Baptized at Kalwaria Evangelical Lutheran Church. Immigrated March 1952 via New York aboard the U.S,S *General Harry Taylor*. Married Ferdinand Heinrich **Rein** (1934-2013) 13 Oct 1956 at Zion Evangelical Lutheran Church. Died 4 Dec 1993 in Seven Hills, Ohio. Interment at Hope Memorial Gardens, Hinckley, Ohio.

    1524.   i. Helga Rein b. 26 Apr 1959. d. 4 Dec 2021.

    1525.   ii. Karin Rein b. 22 Dec 1960. m. David **Resor** 1954-2016.
            2 children:
                Stephanie Joy
                Emily Michele

    1526.   iii. Monika Rein b. 20 Apr 1962. m. Rev. Christopher **Richardson** 1956-.

    1527.   iv. Rev. Karl Helmut Rein b. 18 Nov 1968. m. Linda **Schramke**. m. Pamela **Lewis**.
            3 children:
                Daniel Karl
                Alison Jean
                Katherine Joy

    1528.   v. Erika Rein b. 15 Mar 1979. m. Gregory J. **Petrus** 1967-.

1529. vi. David Rein b. 9 Oct 1972.

1530. vii. Lydia Rein b. 22 Jan 1975. m. Rev. James David **Lathrop** 1968-.
3 children:
Luke James
Sean
Anna Sophia

1531. viii. Sylvia Rein b. 24 Nov 1977. m. ? **Glosson**.
1 child:
Rylie Ruth

1508. Julius **DILL** born 7 May 1937 in Vaiponiškė. Son of Johann Dill[1500] (1898-1977) and Karoline **Keller**[1501] (1899-1977). Baptized at Kalwaria Evangelical Lutheran Church. Immigrated March 1952 via New York aboard the U.S.S. *General Harry Taylor*. Married Almut **Gerdes** (1945-) at Immanuel Lutheran Church.

1532. i. Margaret Dill b. 29 Jan 1966. m. David Dale **Schreffler** 1970-.

1533. ii. Elizabeth Dill b. 14 Mar 1967. m. Yuriy A. **Dzambasow** 1969-.
3 children:
Elissa
Michael
David

1534. iii. Marianna Dill b. 13 Jan 1969. m. Rev. Gerhard P. **Grabenhofer** 1968-.
3 children:
Sigrid
Dieter
Claudia

1535. iv. Norman Dill b. 23 Apr 1974. m. Brittany N. **Kistler**.
2 children:
Aiden
Lucas

1536. v. Heidi? Martha Dill b. 11 Sep 1982. m. Walter **Klump**.
3 children:
Nolan
Hannah
Nora

DINGFELD / DINGFELDT

627. Anna Helene **DINGFELD (KINSKI)** born 1878 in Čižiškiai. Illegitimate daughter of Marianna **Dingfeldt (Günther)**. Stepdaughter of Andreas **Günther**. Baptized at Wischtiten Evangelical Lutheran Church. Married August Julius **Kinski** (1875-1956) 24 Nov 1900 at Zion Evangelical Lutheran Church. Died 24 Mar 1932. Interment at Lutheran Cemetery.

> 628. i. Walter Kinski b. 27 Jan 1903. d. 27 Sep 1987. m. Opal Irene **Cox** 1904-1982. m. Margaret **Hajovsky** 1903-1986.
>
> 629. ii. Martha M. Kinski b. 12 Mar 1904. d. 11 Mar 2002. m. Victor Kenneth **Nickel** 1901-1975.
> > 3 children:
> > > Gail 1932-
> > > Annette 1936-
> > > Lowell 1944-
>
> 630. iii. Oscar Kinski b. 13 Jul 1905. d. 9 Mar 1980. m. Martha Betty **Nichols** 1905-2004.

1409. Wilhelmine **DINGFELD (KALWEIT)** born 20 Nov 1867 in Čižiškiai. Daughter of Christian Dingfeld and Anna **Alexander**. Baptized and confirmed at Wischtiten Evangelical Lutheran Church. Married Christian **Kalweit**[1408] (1861-1932) 1890 at Wischtiten Evangelical Lutheran Church. Died 14 Jan 1950. Interment at Lutheran Cemetery. For list of children, see husband Christian Kalweit.

1461. Elizabeth **DINGFELD (DÖRSCH)** born 3 Nov 1879 in Čižiškiai. Daughter of Christian Dingfeld and Anna **Alexander**. Baptized and confirmed at Wischtiten Evangelical Lutheran Church. Married August **Dörsch** (1873-1934). Died 28 Oct 1950. Interment at Lutheran Cemetery.

> 1462. i. Florence A. Dörsch b. 31 Aug 1899. d. 9 Sep 1943. m. Geroge D. **Smith** 1898-1976.
> > 3 children:
> > > Georgette Florence 1918-1981
> > > Virginia Mae 1919-1999
> > > George Dewey Jr. 1922-2010
>
> 1463. ii. Arthur Richard Dörsch b. 15 Nov 1904. d. 27 Jul 1972. m. Anne **Lucak** 1912-2003.
> > 1 child:
> > > Janice 1936-2021

DOCZKIS / DOCZKAT / DUTCHCOT

96. Johann **DOCZKIS** („**DOCZKAT**") born 14 Dec 1883 in Kregždžiai. Son of Johann Doczkis and Wilhelmine Anna **Klotzober**. Baptized and confirmed at Wischtiten Evangelical Lutheran Church. Immigrated Jan 1903 via New York. Married Bertha **Klotzhober**[1365] 30 Sep 1903 at First St. Paul's Evangelical Lutheran Church in Pittsburg, Pennsylvania. Died 24 Apr 1953. Interment at Knollwood Cemetery, Mayfield Heights, Ohio.

   97. i. Edward Doczkat b. 13 Dec 1904. d. 15 Jan 1994. m. Celia **Cendrowski** 1907-1984.
       1 child:
           Barbara 1931-

   98. ii. Herman J. Doczkat b. 12 Feb 1907. d. 4 Nov 1972. m. Bertha **Reusch** 1906-1996.
       2 children:
           Dolores D. 1930-2020
           Nancy 1936-2021

   99. iii. Lawrence Albert Dutchcott b. 25 Jan 1910. d. 8 Sep 2005. m. Jennie **Vidmar** 1911-2003.

   100. iv. Laura Louise Dutchcot b. 24 Sep 1911. d. 14 Apr 2003. m. Harold Ray **Bell** 1909-1990.
        2 children:
            Bonnie R. 1943-
            Cheryl L. 1945-

   101. v. John Walter Dutchcot b. 18 Oct 1913. d. 8 Dec 2006. m. Alma L. **Schwed**[94] 1918-2007.
        1 child:
            Judy A. 1947-

   102. vi. Ruth Helen Doczkat b. 13 Oct 1915. d. 15 Aug 1998. m. John **Petsche** 1899-1975.

143. Emilie **DOCZKIS** (*DOCZKAT*) (**FISCHER**) born 5 Aug 1894 in Kregždžiai. Daughter of Johann Doczkis and Wilhelmine Anna **Klotzober**. Baptized and confirmed at Wischtiten Evangelical Lutheran Church. Married Heinrich **Fischer**[137] (1888-1972). Died 20 Sep 1932. Interment at Lutheran Cemetery. For list of children, see husband Heinrich Fischer.

1360. Georg **DOCZKIS** (*DUTCHCOT*) born 28 Feb 1886 in Kregždžiai. Son of Johann Doczkat and Wilhelmine Anna **Klotzhober**. Baptized and confirmed at Wischtiten Evangelical Lutheran Church. Married Helene **Klotzhober**[1361] (1887-1934) likely in Pennsylvania. Died June 1954. Interment at Lutheran Cemetery.

    1362. i. Martha Emilie Dutchcot b. 2 Jul 1908. d. 8 Jun 1983. m. Raymond Frank **Breskvar** 1907-1984.
        4 children:
            Ray 1931-
            Ronald 1935-
            Marilyn 1937-
            Michele 1946-

    1363. ii. Albert George Dutchcott b. 23 May 1911. d. 23 Nov 1989. m. Emma **Turk** 1915-1992.
        1 child:
            Carol Ada 1934-1998

    1364. iii. Ruth Dutchcott b. 13 Oct 1915. d. 15 Aug 1998.

DORN

650. Eduard Martin **DORN** born 1851 in Widugiery (Poland). Son of Ferdinand Dorn and Anna **Grazulis**. Baptized at Seine Evangelical Lutheran Church. Married Karoline **Borchert** (1853-1911) 1874 at Kalwaria Evangelical Lutheran Church. Died 30 Sep 1908. Interment at Woodland Cemetery.

    651.   i. Ludwig Dorn b. 1875. d. ????.

    652.   ii. Adele Emilie Dorn b. 1878. d. 20 Oct 1957. m. Karl **Roloff** 1876-1942.
            4 children:
                Natalie 1905-1931
                Benjamin 1909-1978
                Carl 1911-1983
                Margaret 1913-1990

    653.   iii. Marianna "Marie" Dorn b. 1881. d. 11 May 1956. m. Josef **Hausrath** 1882-1956.
            5 children:
                Florence 1908-1995
                Elise 1912-????
                Elenore Freida 1913-1989
                Harold J. 1916-1971
                Eugene 1920-1992

    654.   iv. Eduard Wilhelm Dorn b. 1885. d. ????.

    655.   v. Robert Dorn b. 30 Oct 1896. d. 23 Nov 1969. m. Claire **Miller** 1895-1978.

    656.   vi. Lillian "Tillie" Dorn b. 1897. d. ????. m. Edgar Allen **Warren** 1893-1966.
            1 child:
                Robert 1928-

652. Adele Emilie **DORN** (**ROLOFF**) born 1878 in Miklausė. Daughter of Eduard Martin Dorn[650] (1851-1908) and Karoline **Borchert** (1853-1911). Baptized at Kalwaria Evangelical Lutheran Church. Married Karl **Roloff** (1876-1942) 19 Jul 1903 at Zion Evangelical Lutheran Church. Died 20 Oct 1957. Interment at Lutheran Cemetery.

    653.   i. Natalie Roloff b. 23 May 1904. d. 20 Oct 1931.

654. ii. Benjamin Roloff b. 1 Dec 1905. d. 8 Mar 1978. m. Edna **Johnson** 1907-1981.

655. iii. Carl Roloff b. 22 Jan 1911. d. 28 Jan 1983. m. Virginia **Weise** 1922-1979.

656. iv. Margaret Roloff b. 2 Apr 1913. d. 18 Sep 1990. m. James L. **Reycraft** 1891-1983.

653. Maria **DORN (HAUSRATH)** born 1881 in Miklausė. Daughter of Eduard Martin Dorn[650] (1851-1908) and Karoline **Borchert** (1853-1911). Baptized at Kalwaria Evangelical Lutheran Church. Married Josef **Hausrath**[657] (1882-1956) 28 Nov 1907 at Zion Evangelical Lutheran Church. Died 11 May 1956. Interment at Lutheran Cemetery. For list of children, see husband Josef Hausrath.

ECKERT

1159. Ludwig "Louis" Rudolf **ECKERT** born 10 Aug 1861 in Patašinė. Son of Ludwig Eckert and Marianna **Jung**. Baptized and confirmed at Mariampol Evangelical Lutheran Church. Married Eva **Putnat** (1864-1958). Died 22 Feb 1935. Interment at Knollwood Cemetery, Mayfield Heights, Ohio.

    1160. i. Karl "Charles" Adam Eckert b. 20 Nov 1885. d. 11 Sep 1975. m. Berta Luise **Grigat**[316] 1887-1925.
> 3 children:
>> Florence C.[317] 1910-1970
>> Raymond Charles[318] 1917-1994
>> Harold Richard[319] 1925-1963

    1161. ii. Anna Eckert b. 11 Mar 1891. d. 2 Apr 1891.

    1162. iii. Marie Eckert b. 21 Oct 1892. d. 9 Aug 1931. m. Robert Boleslaw **Hein** 1886-1932.
> 2 children:
>> Helmer 1913-1999
>> Kenneth Robert 1921-1986

    1163. iv. Ludwig "Lewis" Eckert Jr. b. 9 Feb 1895. d. 26 Mar 1993. m. Beatrice M. **Aldrich** 1897-1976.
> 3 children:
>> Irene Rose 1917-2003
>> Hazel L. 1919-2007
>> Ludwig "Lewis" Martin III 1921-2005

    1164. v. Martha Lusie Eckert b. 28 Oct 1897. d. 13 Jun 1987. m. George William **Raquet** 1898-1987.
> 5 children:
>> Marianna Ruth 1917-2004
>> Marie Anne 1918-????
>> Laverne 1921-????
>> Beverly 1931-????
>> Ronald 1936-

    1165. vi. Paul A. Eckert b. 19 Jul 1901. d. 18 Sep 1923. m. Gladys E. **Smith** 1902-1998.

    1166. vii. George Adalbert Eckert b. 6 Jul 1904. d. 10 Feb 1992. m. Katherine Dolores **Schuster** 1908-1989.
> 2 children:
>> Marjorie L. 1929-2017

George Jr. 1931-2014

1167. viii. Albert John Eckert b. 12 Aug 1907. d. 10 Mar 1957. m. Dorothea **Schwartz** 1906-1996.
1 child:
Jeannette 1930-2002

1418. Johanna Karoline **ECKERT (FRANULEWICZ)** born 24 Sep 1858 in Krikštonys. Daughter of Friedrich Eckert and Karoline **Maier**. Baptized at Serey Reformed Lutheran Church. Married Julius **Franulewicz**[1417] (1860-1925) 1882 at Serey Reformed Lutheran Church. Died 27 Dec 1922. Interment at Lutheran Cemetery. For list of children, see husband Julius Franulewicz.

EICHELBERGER

1301. Rudolf Oskar **EICHELBERGER** born 1 Aug 1871 somewhere near Sudargas. Son of Julius Eichelberger and Pauline **Dikheiser**. Baptized at Sudgaren Evangelical Lutheran Church. Immigrated September 1891 via Baltimore aboard the S.S. *Hanover*. Married Mary "May" **Jühlich** 27 Jun 1925 by a Justice of the Peace in North Olmsted, Ohio. Died 22 Dec 1940. Interment unknown.

ELMENTHALER

773. Johann Adolf **ELMENTAHLER** born 1854 in Krikštonys. Son of Johann Elmenthaler and Karoline **Wichmann**. Married Emilie **Hartig** (1862-1949) 1880 at Serey Reformed Lutheran Church. Died 18 Jan 1927. Interment at Lutheran Cemetery.

    774.   i. William Elmenthaler b. 9 Jul 1892. d. 22 Nov 1969. m. Lillian **Horn** 1893-????.
                  3 children:
                        Lillian Ida 1916-2001
                        Ralph William 1920-1969
                        Ruth 1926-1998

    775.   ii. Ruth Elmenthaler b. 30 Jun 1903. d. 9 Jul 1984. m. Walter Elmer **Conrad** 1903-1982.
                  2 children:
                        Marjorie Ruth 1923-2015
                        Violet 1926-1996

ERNST

935. Albert **ERNST** born 1896 in Seirijai. Son of Karl Ernst and Pauline **Tiedemann**[961] (1861-1942). Baptized at Serey Reformed Lutheran Church. Immigrated April 1910 via Baltimore aboard the S.S. *Rhein*. Married Olga **Hirsch**[934] (1898-1954) 25 Mar 1916 at Zion Evangelical Lutheran Church. Died 31 May 1981. Interment at Lutheran Cemetery.

    936. i. Raymond Ernst b. 23 Jan 1917. d. 12 Jun 2000. m. Selma Hedwig **Wenger** 1917-2015.
        2 children:
            Ronald R. 1944-1985
            Ruth Ann 1948-2006

    937. ii. Irene Olga Ernst b. 10 Apr 1919. d. 2 Jun 1994. m. Alvin C. **Haas** 1920-1986.
        1 child:
            Alene 1944-2016

960. Emilie **ERNST (WEINSCHRÖDER)** born 1889 in Seirijai. Daughter of Karl Ernst and Pauline **Tiedemann**[961] (1861-1942.) Baptized at Serey Reformed Lutheran Church. Married Julius **Weinschröder**[569] (1886-1964) 15 Jun 1907 at Zion Evangelical Lutheran Church. Died 3 Aug 1957. Interment at Lutheran Cemetery. For list of children, see husband Julius Weinschröder.

ERZTHALER / STAYLER

1259. Marie Emma **ERZTHALER** (**STOSSUN**) born 16 Nov 1873 in Kregždžiai. Daughter of August Erzthaler (1847-1934) and Marie **Maczulat**. Baptized and confirmed at Wischtiten Evangelical Lutheran Church. Married Gustav **Stossun**[1258] (1866-1926) 31 Dec 1896 at Zion Evangelical Lutheran Church. Died 18 Feb 1966. Interment at Lutheran Cemetery. For list of children, see husband Gustav Stossun.

1261. Henriette **ERZTHALER** (**WAGNER**) (**SPURGAT**) born 16 Apr 1886 in Kregždžiai. Daughter of August Erzthaler (1847-1934) and Helene **Klotzober**. Baptized and confirmed at Wischtiten Evangelical Lutheran Church. Married Johann **Wagner**[1262] (1883-1921) 3 Sep 1905 at Zion Evangelical Lutheran Church. Married Jakob **Spurgat**[1303] (1890-1967) 7 Aug 1926 at St. John's Lutheran Church. Died 21 Oct 1969. Interment at Lutheran Cemetery. For list of children, see husband Johann Wagner.

1266. Karl Friedrich **ERZTHALER** born 24 Mar 1898 in Kregždžiai. Son of August Erzthaler (1847-1934) and Helene **Klotzober**. Likely baptized at Wischtiten Evangelical Lutheran Church. Immigrated July 1914 via New York aboard the S.S. *Vaterland*. Died 2 Oct 1971. Interment at Lutheran Cemetery.

ESSEL

279. Eduard **ESSEL** born 1877 in Romanowce (Poland). Son of Leopold Essel and Pauline **Herr**. Baptized at Seine Evangelical Lutheran Church. Immigrated November 1898 via Baltimore aboard the S.S. *Willehad*. Married Mathilde **Klein** (1878-1979) 9 Sep 1901 at St. Paul's Evangelical Lutheran Church. Died 24 Sep 1919. Interment at Lutheran Cemetery.

    280.   i. Lydia Essel b. 25 Sep 1902. d. 30 May 1915.

    281.   ii. Mathilde "Tillie" Essel b. 8 Dec 1905. d. 5 Oct 1969. m. Harry W. **Pierson** 1902-1970.
        1 child:
            Harry Pierson 1926-2017

    282.   iii. Ernest Essel b. 27 May 1911. d. 15 Apr 1997.

283. Wilhelmine Henriette **ESSEL** (*FILLER*) (*FIELER*) (**KIRSCHNICK**) born 1878 in Romanowce (Poland). Daughter of Leopold Essel and Pauline **Herr**. Baptized at Seine Evangelical Lutheran Church. Immigrated June 1898 via Baltimore aboard S.S. *Crefeld*. Married Johann **Filler** (*FIELER*) (1875-1904) 19 Nov 1899 at St. Paul's Evangelical Church. Married Ferdinand **Kirschnick** (1863-1924) 3 Sep 1905 at St. Paul's Evangelical Lutheran Church. Died 20 Nov 1965. Interment at Lutheran Cemetery.

    284.   i. Ottilie "Tillie" Fieler b. 12 May 1901. d. 14 Sep 1951. m. Eduard **Gerlat** 1895-1977.
        2 children:
            Leonard Edward 1923-2010
            Norman George 1927-1996

    285.   ii. Wilhelmine "Wilma" Fieler "Kirschnick" b. 9 Nov 1904. d. 17 Oct 1941.

    286.   iii. Arthur John Kirschnick b. 6 Mar 1907. d. 5 Jan 1987. m. Helen **Konopa** 1917-2012.
        1 child:
            Melvin 1941-

    287.   iv. Lillian J. Kirschnick b. 9 Oct 1909. d. 24 Jan 1985.

    288.   v. Harold George Kirschnick b. 23 Apr 1914. d. 27 Oct 1996. m. Katherine Ann **Guist** 1919-2003.
        1 child:
            Robert Harold 1941-2013

289. vi. Eleanor Marie Kirschnick b. 2 Dec 1918. d. 27 Dec 1989. m. Rudolph Joseph **Cherne** 1916-1984.
    2 children:
        Roy 1942-
        Dolores 1944-

290. Eduard Adolf **ESSEL** born 30 Oct 1860 in Romanowce (Poland). Son of Leopold Essel and Pauline **Herr**. Baptized at Seine Evangelical Lutheran Church. Married Julia **Hintz** (1872-1949). Died 12 Jan 1945. Interment at Knollwood Cemetery, Mayfield Heights, Ohio.

291. i. Henry Louis Essel b. 3 Feb 1889. d. 20 Dec 1939. m. Anna Maria Louise **Lüdtke** 1892-1976.
    3 children:
        Ruth 1917-1949
        Grace Marie 1919-2005
        Ralph Henry 1923-1988

292. ii. Emma P Essel b. Jul 1891. d. 7 Oct 1962. m. Ernst F. **Lüdtke** 1891-1940.

293. iii. Rudolf Ludwig Essel b. 15 Mar 1892. d. 8 Jan 1960. m. Mary Anna **Lösch** 1894-1983.
    4 children:
        Leroy Howard 1920-1983
        Donald John 1924-1997
        Marian 1930-2019
        Robert Rudolph 1932-1933

294. iv. Theodore Edward Essel b. 21 Feb 1894. d. 16 Feb 1966. m. Emma A **Neumann**[1381] 1896-1980.
    3 children:
        Betty A. 1924-1926
        Albert Edward 1925-1976
        Edith E. 1927-

295. v. Wilhelmine "Minnie" Essel b. 15 Nov 1895. d. 10 Sep 1963. m. Peter Thomas **Howard** 1891-1920. m. Johann **Jurkschat (Yurkschatt)**[1056] 1893-1975.
    6 children:
        Hattie 1917-1993
        Leonard G. 1919-1945
        Evelyn 1921-1970
        Wilma „Minnie" 1926-2014
        John Adolph 1932-2019

Ruth F. 1936-2017

296.   vi. Walter Abel Essel b. 2 Jan 1898. d. 8 Apr 1974. m. Emeline „Emma" ? 1905-1987.

297.   vii. Olga Theodora Essel b. 16 May 1900. d. 29 Dec 1978. m. August William **Stobbe** 1885-1962.
       2 children:
          Clifford
          Warren

298.   viii. Evelyn Wanda Marie Essel b. 25 Mar 1907. d. 21 Jan 1995. m. William Frederick **Haase**[704] 1903-1972.
       2 children:
          Barbara 1933-
          Bruce

299.   ix. Dorothy Ethel Essel b. 1 Aug 1909. d. 20 Feb 1999. m. George A **Poe** 1909-????. m. John Canvas **White** 1913-1974.

300.   x. Raymond Paul Essel b. 11 Sep 1914. d. 8 Apr 1974.

301.   xi. Florence Essel b. 25 Mar 1917. d. 25 Sep 1918.

302. Eduard Karl **ESSEL** born 1871 in Romanowce (Poland). Son of Leopold Essel and Pauline **Herr**. Baptized at Seine Evangelical Lutheran Church. Married Emilie **Bucholtz** (1871-1961) 17 Feb 1902 at St. Paul's Evangelical Lutheran Church. Died 12 May 1961. Interment at Lutheran Cemetery.

   303.   i. Emma A Essel b. 1 Apr 1903. d. 3 Jul 1959. m. John Ernst **Huerster** 1900-1977.
          2 children:
             Eleanore June 1934-2012
             Grace

   304.   ii. Bertha Pauline Essel 18 Jun 1905. d. 19 Dec 1981. m. Arthur Felix **Huelsmann** 1905-1979.
          1 child:
             Betty Jane 1933-2012

   305.   iii. Harry Carl Essel b. 1 Feb 1901. d. 1 Jan 1997.

   306.   iv. Lillian Pauline Essel b. 9 Jun 1911. d. 2 Aug 1990. m. Louis **Villepique** 1913-????. m. John Benjamin **Kling** 1952-2012.
          1 child:
             Linda K. 1952-2012

307. Marie **ESSEL (GOLON) (SPRINGMAN)** born 1874 in Romanowce (Poland). Daughter of Leopold Essel and Pauline **Herr**. Baptized at Seine Evangelical Lutheran Church. Married Franz Wilhelm Julius **Springman** (1866-1908). Married Gustav Edward **Gollon (Golon)** 27 March 1910 at St. Paul's Evangelical Lutheran Church. Died 29 May 1960. Interment at Lutheran Cemetery.

> 308.   i. Ottilie "Tillie" Springman. 12 Dec 1894. d. 1941. m. Karl **Schink** 1892-1973.
>
> > 1 child:
> > Howard Charles 1918-1919
>
> 309.   ii. Leona Lydia Golon b. 26 Oct 1910. d. 25 May 1951. Twin of Lillian Golon.[310]
>
> 310.   iii. Lillian Golon b. 26 Oct 1910. d. 7 Jul 1998. Twin of Leona Lydia Golon.[309]

315. Anna **ESSEL (WIEMERT)** born 1881 in Romanowce (Poland). Daughter of Leopold Essel and Pauline **Herr**. Baptized at Seine Evangelical Lutheran Church. Married August Martin **Wiemert**[311] (1874-1957) 20 Jan 1901 at St. Paul's Evangelical Lutheran Church. Died 5 Dec 1963. Interment at Northfield Macedonia Cemetery, Northfield, Ohio. For list of children, see husband August Martin Wiemert.

FILIER / FILLER / FIEHLER

1543. Wilhelmine **FILIER (TIESLAUK)** (*TISCHLER*)) likely born 1878 in Pogorzałek (Poland) with the name „Helene." Daughter of Johann Filier and Anna **Jugutszki** (1838-1917). Baptized at Wischainy Evangelical Lutheran Church. Immigrated Sep 1897 via Boston aboard the S.S. *Bohemia*. Married Jakob **Tieslauk**[1572] 6 Oct 1898 at Zion Evangelical Lutheran Church. Died 29 Jan 1944. Interment at Lutheran Cemetery . For list of children, see husband Jakob Tieslauk.

FISCHER

136. Helene **FISCHER (SCHWAND)** born 28 Sep 1895 in Klėtkininkai. Daughter of Karl Fischer and Anna **Schütz**. Baptized and confirmed at Wischtiten. Immigrated June 1921 via New York aboard the S.S. *Hudson*. Married Gustav **Schwandt**[134] (1890-1956) 27 Dec 1921 at St. Johannes Independent Evangelical Church. Died 7 Aug 1947. Interment at Knollwood Cemetery, Mayfield Heights, Ohio. For list of children, see husband Gustav Schwandt.

137. Heinrich **FISCHER** born 1888 in Klėtkininkai. Son of Karl Fischer and Anna **Schütz**. Baptized and confirmed at Wischtiten Evangelical Lutheran Church. Immigrated September 1906 via Baltimore aboard the S.S. *Breslau*. Married Emilie **Doczkat (Doczkis)**[143] (1894-1932) 15 October 1913 at Bethlehem Church. Married Catherine **Bernhardt** 14 August 1937 at St. John's Lutheran Church. Died 15 Oct 1972. Interment at Lutheran Cemetery.

    138. i. Harold Gustave Fischer b. 11 Jan 1914. d. 21 Dec 1968. m. Betty Jane **Völker Gillick** 1915-????. m. Rosalie Ann **Fortuna** 1916-1998.
        3 children:
            Nancy 1933-
            Barbara 1935-
            Richard H. 1944-

    139. ii. Alma L. Fischer b. 11 Dec 1915. d. 16 Nov 1995. m. Robert L. **Batchlet** 1913-1970.
        1 child:
            Robert Louis Jr. 1939-1979

    140 iii. Howard Henry Fischer b. 4 Jan 1919. d. 8 Jul 1993. m. Anna **Dannenberg** 1923-1989.

    141. iv. Edward Walter Fischer b. 3 Jan 1921. d. 3 Jan 2013. m. Olga **Hray**.
        1 child:
            Lawrence

    142. v. Richard Arnold Fischer b. 22 Feb 1925. d. 21 Apr 2000. m. Margie **Feldbush** 1927-????.

FRANULEWITZ / FRANULEWICZ / FRANLEY

481. Mathilde Pauline **FRANULEWICZ (TIEDMANN)** born 1857 in Pilokalnis (near Liškiava). Daughter of Karl Franulewicz and Eva **Lechner**. Baptized at Serey Reformed Lutheran Church. Married Julius **Tiedmann**[420] (1859-1918) 1882 at Serey Reformed Lutheran Church. Immigrated June 1903 via New York aboard the S.S. *Batavia*. Died 13 May 1905. Interment in Woodland Cemetery. For list of children, see husband Julius Tiedmann.

1416. Pauline Bertha **FRANULEWICZ (PUDIMAT)** born 1887 in Liškiava. Daughter of Julius Franulewicz[1417] (1860-1925) and Johanna Karoline **Eckert**[1418] (1858-1922). Baptized at Serey Reformed Lutheran Church. Married Heinrich **Pudimat**[1415] (1879-1942) 20 Aug 1904 at Zion Evangelical Lutheran Church. Died 2 Mar 1921. Interment at Lutheran Cemetery. For list of children, see husband Heinrich Pudimat.

1417. Julius **FRANULEWICZ (FRANULEWICH)** born 9 Mar 1860 in Liškiava. Son of Karl Franulewicz and Eva **Lechner**. Baptized at Serey Reformed Lutheran Church. Married Johanna Karoline **Eckert**[1418] (1858-1922) 1882 at Serey Reformed Lutheran Church. Immigrated Feb 1900 via New York aboard the S.S. *Phoenicia*. Died 26 Apr 1925 in Chardon, Ohio. Interment at Lutheran Cemetery.

    1419.   i. Adolf Franulewicz b. 1883. d. 1885.

    1420.   ii. Amalie Franulewicz b. 1885. d. ????.

    1416.   iii. Pauline Bertha Franulewicz b. 1887. d. 2 Mar 1921. m. Heinrich **Pudimat**[1415] 1879-1942.
                7 children:
                      Elizabeth 1906-1914
                      Alma 1907-1984
                      Lillian Pauline 1907-2003
                      Olga Marie 1909-2011
                      Albert Arnold 1917-1996
                      Edward Julius 1919-2001
                      Wilber Eric 1921-1999

    1421.   iv. Gustav Franulewicz b. ????. d. 1894.

    1422.   v. Angelika Franulewicz b. ????. d. 1894.

1423.   vi. Olga Franulewicz b. 4 Mar 1898. d. 2 Jun 1988. m. William Edward **Hinz** 1898-1986.
        4 children:
            Ruth E. 1920-2010
            Dorothy E. 1926-2018
            Grace 1930-
            Barbara 1940-

1424.   vii. Eduard Franulewicz b. 1899. d. 24 Jul 1918.

1425.   vii. Karl Franulewicz b. 17 Sep 1897. d. 27 May 1982. m. Clara A. **Metzdorf** 1900-1982.
        1 child:
            Harold C. 1919-2002

1423. Olga **FRANULEWICZ (HINZ)** born 4 Mar 1898 in Liškiava. Daughter of Julius Franulewicz[1417] (1860-1925) and Johanna Karoline **Eckert**[1418] (1858-1922). Baptized at Serey Reformed Lutheran Church. Married William Edward **Hinz** (1898-1986). Died 2 Jun 1988 in Collier County, Florida. Interment at Naples Memorial Gardens Cemetery, North Naples, Florida.

1435.   i. Ruth Eva Hinz b. 7 Oct 1920. d. 18 Nov 1920. m. Robert H. **Boyle** 1920-1987.
        2 children:
            Sandra L. 1947-
            Bonnie J. 1949-

1436.   ii. Dorothy E. Hinz b. 24 Sep 1926. d. 9 May 2018. m. Richard **Bliss** 1924-1957.
        2 children:
            Richard S. 1947-2018

1437.   iii. Grace Hinz b. 1930. m. Richard E. **Zielske**.

1438.   iv. Barbara Hinz b. 11 Mar 1942.

1424. Eduard **FRANULEWICZ** born 17 Sep 1899 in Seirijai. Son of Julius Franulewicz[1417] (1860-1925) and Johanna Karoline **Eckert**[1418] (1858-1922). Baptized at Serey Reformed Lutheran Church. Struck by lightning and died 24 Jul 1918 in Hamden Township, Ohio. Interment at Lutheran Cemetery.

FRENKEL

1407. Malwine **FRENKEL (PUSKAT)** born 3 Jul 1882 in Kybartai. Daughter of Anton Frenkel and Rosalie **Walinski**. Baptized and confirmed at Neustadt Evangelical Lutheran Church. Married August **Puskat**[1404] (1880-1950) 17 May 1902 at Third Reformed [Lutheran] Church. Died 19 Nov 1951. Interment at Hillcrest Cemetery, Bedford Heights, Ohio. For list of children, see husband August Puskat.

FRIEDKE / FRETKE

1536. August **FRIEDKE** (*FRETKE*) born 1 Apr 1892 in Prapuntai. Son of Johann Friedke (1866-1908) and Anna Marianna **Meier** (1863-1938.) Baptized and confirmed at Serey Reformed Lutheran Church. Immigrated Oct 1913 via New York aboard the S.S. *Frankfurt*. Married Marianna **Reinke**[1042] (1886-1956). Died 28 May 1966 in Mantua, Ohio. Interment at Lutheran Cemetery.

FRIEDRICH

1175. Gottlieb Ludwig **FRIEDRICH** born about 1825 near Marijampolė. Son of Gottlieb Friedrich and Dorothea **Spiess**. Married Marie **Gleid**[1176] (1840-1922) 1861 at Mariampol Evangelical Lutheran Church. Died 10 Mar 1920. Interment at Lutheran Cemetery.

    1177. i. Henriette Friedrich b. 1866. d. ????.

    1178. ii. Eduard Friedrich b. 1869. d. ????.

    1179. iii. Ernestine Friedrich b. 1871. d. 19 Jan 1942. m. Gottlieb **Schröder**[1180] 1876-1961.
> 5 children:
>> Otto[1181] 1901-1988
>> Marie 1903-1994
>> Walter[1182] 1907-1990
>> Albert[1183] 1910-1911
>> Arthur[1184] 1912-1979

    1180. iv. Karl Friedrich b. 1 Jan 1873. d. 12 Mar 1950. m. Amelia **Schröder** 1865-1900. m. Helene „Lena" **Schröder** 1878-1933.
> 7 children:
>> Ottilie 1893-1962
>> Emma Ernestine 1895-1969
>> Olga A. 1902-1910
>> Charles 1908-1908
>> Elmer O. 1909-1990
>> Milton W. 1911-1962
>> Clarence W. 1915-1978

    1181. v. Mathilde Friedrich b. 1 May 1881. d. 17 May 1971. m. Adolf **Bumblis** 1872-1926.
> 3 children:
>> Olga 1905-1992
>> August 1906-1969
>> Marie 1908-1968

    1182. vi. Anna Friedrich b. 1886. d. 16 Feb 1938. m. August Gustav **Bumblis** 1882-1951.
> 3 children:
>> John 1907-1979
>> August 1910-1957
>> Marie 1917-1982

1179. Ernestine **FRIEDRICH (SCHRÖDER)** born 1871 in Seimeniškiai. Daughter of Gottlieb Ludwig Friedrich[1175] (1825-1920) and Marie **Gleid**[1176] (1840-1922). Confirmed at Mariampol Evangelical Lutheran Church. Married Gottlieb **Schröder**[1180] (1876-1961) 12 Jan 1901 at Zion Evangelical Lutheran Church. Died 1961. Interment at Lutheran Cemetery. For list of children, see husband Gottlieb Schröder.

1186. Karl **FRIEDRICH** born 1 Jan 1873 in Seimeniškiai. Son of Gottlieb Ludwig Friedrich[1175] (1825-1920) and Marie **Gleid**[1176] (1840-1922). Confirmed at Mariampol Evangelical Lutheran Church. Married Amelia **Schröder**[1187] (1865-1900) 24 Sep 1892 at Bethlehem Evangelical Lutheran Church in Detroit, Michigan. Married Helene "Lena" **Schröder**[1188] 1878-1933 27 Oct 1900 at Zion Evangelical Lutheran Church. Died 12 Mar 1950. Interment Lutheran Cemetery.

> 1189. i. Ottilie Friedrich b. 22 Jul 1893. d. 25 Aug 1962. m. Michael G. **Scheipner** 1889-1952.
> 2 children:
> Elenore 1915-2012
> Ruth 1917-1986

> 1190. ii. Emma Ernestine Friedrich b. 8 Nov 1895. d. 18 May 1969. m. Joseph **Cihak** 1893-1968.

> 1191. iii. Olga A. Friedrich b. 14 Jun 1902. d. 5 Apr 1910.

> 1192. iv. Charles Friedrich b. 2 Feb 1908. d. 2 Feb 1908.

> 1193. v. Elmer O. Friedrich b. 19 Apr 1909. d. 20 Jun 1990.

> 1194. vi. Milton W. Friedrich b. 30 Nov 1911. d. 1 Apr 1962. m. Helen V. **Urban** 1908-1997.

> 1195. vii. Clarence W. Friedrich b. 27 Oct 1915. d. 28 Feb 1978. m. Dorothy M. **Morsefield** 1914-1988.
> 2 children:
> Roger Alan 1944-
> Linda 1949-

1181. Mathilde **FRIEDRICH (BUMBLIS)** born 1881 near Krosna. Daughter of Gottlieb Ludwig Friedrich[1175] (1825-1920) and Marie **Gleid**[1176] (1840-1922). Married Adolf **Bumblis**[1196] (1872-1926) 7 Sep 1902 at Zion Evangelical Lutheran Church. Died 17 May 1971. Interment at Brooklyn Heights Cemetery, Brooklyn, Ohio. For list of children, see husband Adolf Bumblis.

1200. Anna **FRIEDRICH (BUMBLIS)** born 1886 in Krosna. Daughter of Gottlieb Ludwig Friedrich[1175] (1825-1920) and Marie **Gleid**[1176] (1840-1922). Baptized at Kalwaria Evangelical Lutheran Church. Married August Gustav **Bumblis**[1201] (1882-1951) 26 Apr 1903 at Zion Evangelical Lutheran Church. Died 16 Feb 1938. Interment at Lutheran Cemetery. For list of children, see husband August Gustav Bumblis.

GERULAT / GERULAITIS / GERLAT

930. Bertha **GERULAT (LANG)** born 17 Mar 1894 in Vazniškiai. Daughter of Johann Gerulat and Auguste **Getz**. Baptized and confirmed at Mariampol Evangelical Lutheran Church. Immigrated October 1913 via New York aboard the S.S. *Rhein*. Married Karl **Lang**[926] (1895-1971) 26 Jan 1920 at Zion Evangelical Lutheran Church. Died 24 Oct 1989 in Westlake, Ohio. Interment at Lutheran Cemetery. For list of children, see husband Karl Lang.

931. Eduard **GERULAT (GERLAT)** born 1895 in Vazniškiai. Son of Johann Gerulat and Auguste **Getz**. Baptized and confirmed at Mariampol Evangelical Lutheran Church. Immigrated October 1913 via New York aboard the S.S. *Rhein*. U.S. WWI veteran. Married Ottilie "Tillie" **Kirschnick** (1901-1951) 10 Jun 1922 at Zion Evangelical Lutheran Church. Died 16 Nov 1977, Lake County, Ohio. Interment at Knollwood Cemetery, Mayfield Heights, Ohio.

    932.   i. Leonard Edward Gerlat b. 27 Apr 1923. d. 10 Mar 2010. m. Dories E. **Bedford** ????-????.
    2 children:
        Alan
        Barbara

    933.   ii. Norman Gerlat b. 13 Feb 1927. d. 7 Oct 1996. m. Shirley A. **Kvarda**. ????-2016.

GESCHWANDTNER

320. Olga **GESCHWANDTNER (MÜLLER)** (*MILLER*) born 14 Mar 1907 in Lauckaimis. Daughter of Josef Geschwandtner and Anna **Jekewitz** (1870-1953). Married Hermann **Müller** (1901-????) 6 Sep 1925, likely at Neustadt Evangelical Lutheran Church. Immigrated April 1927 via New York aboard the S.S. *Washington*. Died 27 Nov 1985. Interment at Sunset Memorial Park, North Olmsted, Ohio.

    321.   i. Gertrude Miller b. 26 Sep 1928. m. David H. **Clements** (1926-).

    322.   ii. Marlene Ruth Miller b. 6 May 1933. m. Donald Raymond **Krieger** (1932-).
            1 child:
                Raymond William 1953-

323. Anna **GESCHWANDTNER (DRESCHER)** born 29 Aug 1901 in Lauckaimis. Daughter of Josef Geschwandtner and Anna **Jekewitz** (1870-1953). Baptized and confirmed at Neustadt Evangelical Lutheran Church. Married August Wilhelm **Drescher** (1896-1945) May 1929 at Pillkallen, East Prussia. Immigrated April 1950 via New York aboard the S.S. *Washington*. Died 16 Aug 1990. Interment at Sunset Memorial Park, North Olmsted, Ohio.

    324.   i. Elisabeth Anna Drescher b. 13 Dec 1930. d. 8 July 2014. m. ? **Becker**.

    324   ii. Siegfried Drescher.

GLEICHFORSCH

1090. Adolf **GLEICHFORSCH** born 1896 in Olendrai. Son of Karl Gleichforsch (1860-1927) and Henriette **Weier** (1865-1941). Baptized and confirmed at Kalwaria Evangelical Lutheran Church. Married Marie **Lauks**[1091] (1904-1972) 26 Dec 1924 at Mariampol Evangelical Lutheran Church. Immigrated April 1955 via Pan American Airways. Died 5 Apr 1968. Interment at Lake View Cemetery.

    1092. i. Adolf Gleichforsch b. 31 Aug 1925. d. 31 Jul 1944.

    1093. ii. Olga Gleichforsch b. 26 Nov 1930. d. 31 Jul 1978. m. Adolf Günther **Neubauer** 1924-1962.
        2 children:
            Edmund Adolf 1948-2009
            Edith Gertrude 1956-

1093. Olga **GLEICHFORSCH (NEUBAUER)** born 26 Nov 1930 in Ramanavas. Daughter of Adolf Gleichforsch[1090] (1896-1968) and Marie **Lauks**[1091] (1904-1972). Baptized at Mariampol Evangelical Lutheran Church. Married Adolf Günther **Neubauer** (1924-1962) in Germany. Immigrated August 1955 via New York aboard the U.S.S. *General W. C. Langfitt*. Died 31 Jul 1978 in Geneva, Ohio. Interment at Lake View Cemetery.

    1094. i. Edmund Adolf Neubauer b. 7 Jan 1948. d. 16 Jun 2009. m. Rosemary **Vassil** 1937-2013. Engaged to Donna **Zohos**.

    1095. ii. Edith Gertrude Neubauer b. 29 Aug 1956. m. Karl Richard **Landsmann** 1953-.
        1 child:
            Richard Jeremy 1979-

GLEID / GLEIDT

1176. Marie **GLEID (FRIEDRICH)** born around 1840 near Marijampolė. Daughter of Martin Gleid and Eva **Pakeraitis**. Married Gottlieb Ludwig **Friedrich**[1175] (1825-1920) 1861 at Mariampol Evangelical Lutheran Church. Died 1922. Interment at Lutheran Cemetery. For list of children, see husband Gottlieb Ludwig Friedrich.

GÜNTHER / GINTER

386. Bertha **GINTER** (**KLOTZOBER**) born 1887 in Wiżajny (Poland). Daughter of Andreas Ginter and Maria **Dingfeld**. Married Matthias Martin **Klotzober**[380] (1887-1958) 17 Oct 1908 at Zion Evangelical Lutheran Church. Died 23 Sep 1916. Interment at Lutheran Cemetery. For list of children, see husband Matthias Martin Klotzober.

457. Julius **GÜNTHER** (**GINTER**) born November 1867 in Wiżajny (Poland). Son of Gottlieb Günther and Anna **Jodauk**. Baptized and confirmed at Wischainy Evangelical Lutheran Church. Married Wilhelmine **Lettke** (1869-1915) 28 Jan 1893 at Zion Evangelical Lutheran Church. Married Henriette **Schröder**[455] 5 Jan 1925 at Zion Evangelical Lutheran Church. Died 5 Feb 1956. Interment at Lutheran Cemetery.

    458.   i. Edward Albert Guenther b. 26 Nov 1893. d. 12 Nov 1977. m. Anna **Benzin** 1892-1958. m. Marie **Smith** 1900-1981.
              2 children:
                  Leroy 1917-1999
                  Jeanne C. 1928-2016

    459.   ii. Harry Guenther b. 28 Oct 1895. d. 15 Apr 1986. m. May B. **Schiemann** 1896-1984.
              1 child:
                  Joyce 1919-

    460.   iii. Alice Elsie Guenther b. 30 Nov 1897. d. 12 Jan 1980. m. Michael **Rachul** 1892-1966.
              2 children:
                  Norma 1919-2018
                  Roy Walter 1921-2010

    461.   iv. Emma Guenther b. 2 Oct 1900. d. 17 Jul 1952. m. George C. **Plescott** 1900-1978.

    462.   v. Walter Guenther b. 17 Sep 1905. d. 9 Feb 1998. m. Bernice **Edgerton** 1911-2010.

    463.   vi. Otto Guenther b. 15 Aug 1908. d. 4 Jun 1958. m. Anne **?**.

622. August **GÜNTHER** (*GUENTER*) born 24 Jan 1890 in Wiżajny (Poland). Son of Andreas Ginter and Maria **Dingfeld**. Baptized at Wischainy Evangelical Lutheran Church. Married Helene **Lang** (1893-1977) 22 Nov 1913 at Zion Evangelical Lutheran Church. Died 26 Aug 1926. Interment at Lutheran Cemetery.

623. i. Howard W. Guenther b. 21 Jul 1915. d. 19 Feb 1918.

624 ii. Leonard Earl Guenther b. 17 Dec 1917. d. 9 Jun 2010. m. Ruth Ottilie **Scheipner** 1917-1986. Betty June **?** 1918-2012.
> 1 child:
>> Howard Earl Jr. 1942-2006

625. iii. Ray Arthur Guenther b. 22 Sep 1920. d. 7 Dec 1988. m. Lillian Marie **Hellgren** 1921-1981.
> 3 children:
>> Karen Lee 1946-2017

626. Elizabeth Emma **GÜNTHER** (*GINTER*) (**BASENAU**) (***BOSSMAN***) born 5 Apr 1892 in Wiżajny (Poland). Daughter of Andreas Ginter and Maria **Dingfeld**. Baptized at Wischainy Evangelical Lutheran Church. Married Johann **Basenau**[628] (**Bossman**) (1889-1947) 18 May 1911 in Cleveland by a Justice of the Peace. Died 7 Jun 1970. Interment at Lutheran Cemetery. For list of children, see husband Johann Basenau.

GRIGAT / GRIGAITIS

105. Emilie **GRIGAT** (**PASEKEL**) born 1873 near Marijampolė. Daughter of Johann Grigat and Elisabeth „Luise" **Keslau**. Married Ludwig „Louis" **Pasekel**[103] 1894 at Kalwaria Evangelical Lutheran Church. Immigrated via Baltimore June 1905 aboard S.S. *Chemnitz*. Died 7 Dec 1953. Interment at Knollwood Cemetery, Mayfield Heights, Ohio. For list of children, see husband Ludwig „Louis" Pasekel.

106. Marie **GRIGAT** (**NEUBACHER**) born 1884 in Bukta. Daughter of Johann Grigat and Elisabeth „Luise" **Keslau**. Baptized and confirmed at Mariampol Evangelical Lutheran Church. Married Albert Egan **Neubacher** (1879-1948) in or near Essen, Germany. Emigrated in September 1905 via Baltimore aboard S.S. *Darmstadt*. Died in Broward County, Florida, July 1967. Interment unknown.

   107. i. Erna "Emma" Neubacher b. 22 Dec 1904. d. 31 Dec 1972.

   108. iii. Arthur Neubacher b. 20 Oct 1906. d. 11 Nov 1956. m. Ivy Miriam **Emerson** 1912-1995.

   109. iv. Alfred Neubacher b. 15 Sep 1908. d. 17 Oct 1976. m. Elsie **Klempan** 1913-1997.
   2 children:
   Donald Alan 1939-2022
   Noreen G. 1945-

   110. v. Ida Neubacher b. 23 Aug 1910. d. 27 Nov 1997. m. Otto Adolf **Rauth** 1912-1992.
   1 child:
   Marilyn 1936-2021

316. Berta Louise **GRIGAT** (**ECKERT**) born 1887 in Bukta. Daughter of Johann Grigat and Elisabeth „Luise" **Keslau**. Baptized at Mariampol Evangelical Lutheran Church. Married Karl "Charles" A. **Eckert**[1160] (1885-1975) 26 Feb 1908 at St. Paul's Evangelical Lutheran Church. Died 13 Aug 1925. Interment at Knollwood Cemetery, Mayfield Heights, Ohio.

   317. i. Florence Eckert b. 24 Dec 1910. d. 13 Mar 1970. m. Joseph **Prissinger** 1909-2003.
   1 child.
   Carole V. 1939-

   318. ii. Raymond Charles Eckert b. 9 Apr 1917. d. 20 Mar 1994. m. Doris M. 1920-2003.

        2 children:
            Dale R 1946-
            Dennis P. 1949-

319.   iii. Harold Richard Eckert b. 7 May 1925. d. 5 Dec 1963. m. Edith Mae **Albert** 1926-2007.
        2 children:
            Alan R. 1948-
            Karen J.

GRÜBNER / GRIBNER

987. August **GRÜBNER** (*GRIBNER*) born 16 Jun 1877 in Būriškės. Son of Karl Grübner and Anna **Jonakat**. Baptized and confirmed at Mariampol Evangelical Lutheran Church. Immigrated August 1903 via New York aboard the S.S. *Kaiser Wilhelm II*. Married Emilie **Wisgin**[986] (1877-1926) 13 Aug 1904 at Schifflein Christi Evangelical Lutheran Church. Died 9 Feb 1937. Interment at Lutheran Cemetery.

    988.   i. Oscar Gribner b. 31 Oct 1902. d. 10 Mar 1976.

    989.   ii. Arthur Robert Gribner b. 15 Dec 1905. d. 20 Nov 1972. m. Marie **Naymik** 1912-2009.
            2 children:
                Bernard 1939-2016
                Marlene 1948-

    990.   iii. Auguste Gribner b. 17 Jul 1907. d. 30 Jan 1978.

    991.   iv. James Reinhold Gribner b. 14 Jul 1911. d. 1 Jan 1989. m. Rose **Pasco** 1919-2011. m. Josie **Buckner** 1928-2007.

    992.   v. Edna Gribner b. 4 Dec 1916. d. 1 Jul 2005.

GUDAT / GUDAITIS

1231. Emilie **GUDAT** (**NEUMANN**) born 3 May 1895 in Romanowo (current location unknown but near Marijampolė). Daughter of August Gudat and Anna **Tolgas**. Baptized and confirmed at Mariampol Evangelical Lutheran Church. Married Karl **Neumann**[1230] 16 Oct 1915 at Zion Evangelical Lutheran Church. Died 19 Mar 1995. Interment at Lutheran Cemetery. For list of children, see husband Karl Neumann.

1311. Leopold **GUDAT** born 18 Sep 1886 in Kalvarija. Son of Josef Gudat and Eva **Baltrunat**. Baptized and confirmed at Kalwaria Evangelical Lutheran Church. Married Marie **Schütz**[1318] (1885-1975) in 1905 at Kalwaria Evangelical Lutheran Church. Immigrated December 1906 via New York aboard the S.S. *Albano*. Died 13 Jun 1948 in Beech Grove, Indiana. Interment at Concordia Cemetery, Beech Grove, Indiana.

    1312. i. Karl "Charles" Gudat b. 8 Feb 1909. d. 6 Sep 1978. m. Marie **Pesanti** 1914-????.
        2 children:
           Richard Karl 1932-2011
           Lawrence 1938-

    1313. ii. Anna Gudat b. 31 Oct 1911. d. 26 May 1984. m. Joseph **Duganitz** 1910-1995.
        2 children:
           Joseph G. 1932-
           Joanne Elizabeth 1935-2021

    1314. iii. Edward Gudat b. 11 Dec 1918. d. 10 Feb 1997. m. Mary **McDonald** 1924-2005. Twin of Otto Gudat.[1315]
        1 child:
           Shawn 1956-

    1315. iv. Otto Gudat b. 11 Dec 1918. d. 4 Apr 2004. m. Freda Lucille **Brown** 1918-2013. m. Sophrona Myrtle **Pulp** 1927-2017.
        8 children:
           Michael
           Connie
           Carter Wayne
           Linda L.
           Sonny Tex
           Sandra
           Debra
           Thomas Joe 1958-1960

1324. Matthias Leopold **GUDAT** born 1882 in Trakėnai. Son of Josef Gudat and Eva **Baltrunat** (1857-1926). Baptized at Mariampol Evangelical Lutheran Church. Immigrated April 1906 via New York aboard the S.S. *Rugia*. Married Emilie "Millie" **Schütz**[1319] 9 May 1909 at Zion Evangelical Lutheran Church. Divorced 20 Mar 1922. Death and interment details unknown.

    1325.   i. Richard Lewis Gudat b. 25 Aug 1911. d. 23 Jul 1977. m. Stella **Laskowski** 1913-1984.
              3 children:
                    Dolores 1934-
                    Richard L. 1936-
                    William E. 1941-

GUTMANN

1049. Karl Johann **GUTMANN** born 1894 in Bukta. Son of Johann Gutmann and Dorothea **Wellert**. Baptized and confirmed at Mariampol Evangelical Lutheran Church. Immigrated April 1913 via New York aboard the S.S. *President Grant*. Married Pauline **Reinke**[1040] (1895-1987) 27 Apr 1921 in Cleveland by a Justice of the Peace. Died 9 Mar 1966. Interment unknown.

    1050.   i. Howard William Gutman b. 10 Aug 1922. d. 4 Nov 1998. m. Eleanor Amelia **Peters**[1063] 1921-2011.
         1 child:
            Richard Howard 1947-1944

    1064.   ii. Edna Ruth Gutman b. 9 Dec 1923. d. 29 Mar 2003. m. Adam **Schmidt** 1921-????.
         1 child:
            Karen Ruth 1966-

HAASE / HASE / HAZE

697. August **HAASE** born 1869 in Derviniai. Son of Johann Haase and Helene **Blaar**. Baptized and confirmed at Kalwaria Evangelical Lutheran Church. Married Amalie **Konrad**[707] (1868-1943) 1888 at Mariampol Evangelical Lutheran Church. Immigrated June 1895 via New York aboard the S.S. *Normannia*. Died 7 Mar 1946. Interment at Lutheran Cemetery.

    698.   i. Anna Haase b. 1889. d. 16 Jul 1974. m. Charles **Gall** 1875-1961.
        4 children:
            Elmer Andrew 1914-1931
            Anna Louise 1916-2011
            Arthur 1920-2019
            Walter 1921-2015

    699.   ii. Karl "Charles" August Haase b. 1890. d. 27 May 1968. m. Bessie A. **Korbler** 1890-????.

    700.   iii. Emma Haase b. 31 Jul 1895. d. 20 Aug 1982. m. Albert **Heinrich**[68] 1892-1959.
        4 children:
            Alma Louise[72] 1918-1918
            Robert August[73] 1919-1919
            Albert Carl[74] 1921-1921
            Mildred[75] 1922-1938

    701.   iv. Ottilie Haase b. 31 Mar 1897. d. 21 Nov 1982. m. Carl K. **Grunwald** 1894-1967.
        2 children:
            Norma 1928-
            Robert Carl 1932-2018

    702.   v. Bertha Haase b. 14 Apr 1899. d. 23 Nov 1988. m. Elmer **Just** 1898-1946.
        1 child:
            Allan D 1931-

    703.   vi. Wilhelmine Haase b. 27 Mar 1901. d. 3 Apr 1984. m. George C. **Plescott** 1900-1978.

    704.   vii. William Frederick Haase b. 15 Jan 1903. d. 22 Apr 1972. m. Evelyn Wanda Marie **Essel**[298] 1907-1995.
        2 children:
            Barbara 1933-
            Bruce C. 1944-

705. viii. Louise Haase b. 6 Jan 1908. d. 7 Apr 1992. m. Frank Doral **Conkle** 1907-1988.
    1 child:
        Raymond Roland 1928-2008

706. ix. Arthur Haase b. 15 Jan 1913. d. 24 Feb 1997. m. Margaret Dorothy **Wittine** 1915-1993.
    1 child:
        Jeffery A. 1947-1986

698. Anna **HAASE (GALL)** born 1888 in Degučiai. Daughter of August Haase[698] (1869-1946) and Amalie **Konrad**[707] (1868-1943). Baptized at Kalwaria Evangelical Lutheran Church. Immigrated June 1895 via New York aboard the S.S. *Normannia*. Married Karl "Charles" **Gall** (1875-1961) 13 Jul 1918 at St. Paul Lutheran Church in Valley City, Ohio. Died 16 Jul 1974. Interment at St. Paul Lutheran Cemetery, Valley City, Ohio.

708. i. Elmer Andrew Gall b. 6 Jun 1914. d. 30 May 1931.

709. ii. Anna Louise Gall b. 24 May 1916. d. 24 Jan 2011. m. Walter **Sluberski** 1917-????. m. Ted Albert **Cznadel** 1918-1995. m. Dwight Edward **Wood** 1906-1977.
    2 children:
        Thomas 1940-
        Nancy Lee 1944-2009

710. iii. Arthur Carl Gall b. 15 Jun 1919. d. 10 Dec 2019. m. Alice **Petropoulos** 1925-????.
    2 children:

711. iv. Walter Gall b. 3 Feb 1921. d. 13 Dec 2015. m. Suzanne Marie **Schelosky** 1925-1967.
    2 children:
        Sue Carol 1944-
        Elaine 1948-

699. Karl „Carl" August **HAASE** born 1890 in Degučiai. Son of August Haase[698] (1869-1946) and Amalie **Konrad**[707] (1868-1943). Baptized at Kalwaria Evangelical Lutheran Church. Immigrated June 1895 via New York aboard the S.S. *Normannia*. Married Bessie Ann **Korbler** (1894-1935) 28 Jun 1916 at St. Paul's Evangelical Lutheran Church. Married Ila M. **Herran** (1891-1970) 15 Apr 1939 at Ninth Reformed Lutheran Church. Died 27 May 1968 in West Palm Beach, Florida. Interment at East Cleveland Township Cemetery.

712. Carl Richard Haase b. 19 Aug 1917. d. 16 Oct 1918.

HABERSAT

806. Karl **HABERSAT** born 29 Sep 1884 in Beržiniai. Son of Gottlieb Habersat and Catherine **Grün**. Baptized and confirmed at Mariampol Evangelical Lutheran Church. Immigrated May 1904 via New York aboard the S.S. *Patricia*. Married Julianna **Heller** (1884-1967) 3 Apr 1907 at Zion Evangelical Lutheran Church. Died 29 Jul 1909. Interment at Lutheran Cemetery.

HARTIG

325. Julius Karl **HARTIG** born 1883 in Balbieriškis. Son of Johann Friedrich „Franz" Hartig and Auguste **Ackermann**. Baptized at Prenen Lutheran Church. Immigrated July 1909 via New York aboard the S.S. *Amerika*. Married Anna **Reichel**[328] (1888-1973) 15 Oct 1913 by a Justice of the Peace. Died 6 Jan 1956. Interment at Lake View Cemetery.

    326.   i. Bertha Hartig b. 30 Dec 1914. d. 29 Jul 2012. m. Edward Jerome **Bowers** 1906-1942. m. George H. **Bonko** 1906-????. m. **Hunter**.
           3 children:
                Anne M. 1938-
                Dixie Lee
                Edward Jr.

    327.   ii. Frederick Julius Hartig b. 6 Jul 1917. d. 17 May 2002. m. Betty Jane **Agan** 1921-1991.
           4 children:
                Frederick K 1946-
                Richard A 1947-
                Eric S 1949-
                Phillip Thomas 1952-1998

944. Auguste Bertha **HARTIG** (**KIESLING**) (**HIRSCH**) born 1868 Pošnia. Daughter of Ferdinand Hartig and Julia **Ackermann**. Baptized at Serey Reformed Lutheran Church. Married Adolf **Kiesling** (????-1895) 1890 at Serey Reformed Lutheran Church. Married Gottlieb **Hirsch**[938] (1872-1961) 1898 at Serey Reformed Lutheran Church. Died 10 May 1944. Interment at Lutheran Cemetery. For list of additional children, see husband Gottlieb Hirsch.

    945.   i. August Kiesling b. 1891. d. ????.

    946.   ii. Hedwig "Hattie" Kiesling b. 1893. d. 12 Aug 1937. m. William C. **Perry**[1115] 1891-1973.
           4 children:
                William 1913-2005
                Robert Carl 1919-1995
                Thomas Donald 1921-2006
                Dorothy Ruth 1925-2016

    947.   iii. Emilie Anna Kiesling b. 26 Jul 1895. d. 26 Sep 1979. m. Eberly George **Clayton** 1896-1967.
           1 child:
                Howard Alvin 1918-2006

HASENHEIT

1338. Ottilie "Tillie" **HASENHEIT (MÜLLERSZKOWSKI)** born 1859 in Antakalnis. Daughter of Efrom Hasenheit and Julianna **Walter**. Baptized at Goddlau Evangelical Lutheran Church. Married Friedrich **Müllerszkowski (Millerskofski)** 1883 at Goddlau Evangelical Lutheran Church. Died 22 Jul 1935 in Garfield Heights, Ohio. Interment at St. John Lutheran Cemetery, Garfield Heights, Ohio.

HAUSRATH

129. August **HAUSRATH** born 18 Oct 1880 in Butrimiškės. Son of Karl Hausrath and Amalie Jung. immigrated June 1900 via New York aboard the S.S. *Bremen*. Married Emma **Dei** (1882-1977) 1903 at Zion Evangelical Lutheran Church. A well-known entrepreneur and business owner in the Collinwood neighborhood. Grandfather of the artist Joan Hausrath. Helped save the lives of children during the 1908 Collinwood school fire. Died 12 Dec 1971 in Mayfield Heights. Interment at Knollwood Cemetery, Mayfield Heights, Ohio.

    130.   i. Lillian Hausrath b. 4 May 1904. d. 31 Mar 2007.

    131.   ii. Hearld Hausrath b. 14 Nov 1906. d. 4 Jul 1999. m. Josephine **Walker** (1913-2004).
        2 children:
            James A. 1945-1978
            Joan b. 1942-

    132.   iii. Violet "Hazel" Hausrath b. 24 Oct 1908. d. 10 Jun 1977. m. Jack Clarkson **Evans** (1907-1977).
        2 children:

    133.   iv. Myrtle Cora Hausrath b. 30 Jul 1911. d. 20 Nov 2006. m. Alexander Voros **Wrought** (1900-1971).
        2 children:
            Susan Kate 1947-2022

482. Eva **HAUSRATH (TIEDMANN)** born 1883 in Pryga. Daughter of Gustave "Just" Hausrath and Emilie **Herbst**. Baptized at Serey Reformed Lutheran Church. Married Adolf Eduard **Tiedmann**[422] (1885-1963) 3 Oct 1907 in Cleveland by a Justice of the Peace. Died 11 May 1942. Interment at Lutheran Cemetery. For list of children, see husband Adolf Eduard Tiedmann.

657. Josef **HAUSRATH** born 1885 in Puńsk (Poland). Son of Gottlieb Hausrath and Pauline **Wildauer**. Baptized at Seine Evangelical Lutheran Church. Married Marie **Dorn**[653] (1881-1956) 28 Nov 1907 at Zion Evangelical Lutheran Church. Died 28 May 1956. Interment at Lutheran Cemetery.

    658.   i. Florence Hausrath b. 4 Nov 1908. d. 29 Aug 1995. m. Lloyd G. **Speth** 1903-1972.
        1 child:
            Joan 1935-

    659.   ii. Elsie Hausrath b. 1912. d. ????.

660. iii. Eleanor Frieda Hausrath b. 1 Sep 1913. d. 24 Apr 1989. m. Albert E. **Scharfetter** 1914-1969.
   2 children:
   Sandra W. 1939-
   Gregory P. 1949-

661. iv. Harold Josef Hausrath b. 6 Mar 1916. d. 4 Nov 1971. m. Evelyn R. **Woidtke** 1918-1990.
   2 children:
   Michael D. 1945-
   Karen E. 1951-

662. v. Eugene Robert Hausrath b. 27 Mar 1920. d. 31 Jan 1992. m. Murial **Walsh** 1924-2010.
   3 children:
   Gary
   Bruce
   Diane

672. Dorothea "Dora" HAUSRATH (HERR) born 1879 in Puńsk (Poland). Daughter of Gottlieb Hausrath and Pauline **Wildauer**. Baptized at Seine Evangelical Lutheran Church 1877. Married Ferdinand **Herr**[668] (1867-1955) 15 Feb 1890 at Zion Evangelical Lutheran Church. Divorced. Death and interment information unknown. For list of children, see husband Ferdinand Herr.

673. Ferdinand HAUSRATH born 1865 in Puńsk (Poland). Son of Gottlieb Hausrath and Pauline **Wildauer**. Baptized at Seine Evangelical Lutheran Church in 1877. Married Karoline **Kinat**[683] (1870-1931) 4 Aug 1888 at Zion Evangelical Lutheran Church. Died 3 Jul 1939. Interment at St. John Lutheran Cemetery.

684. i. Caroline Hausrath b. 2 Jun 1889. d. 5 Sep 1889.

685. ii. Bertha Emilie Hausrath b. 14 Aug 1890. d. 6 Aug 1976. m. John Beter Hartman **Ehlers** 1890-1981.
   4 children:
   Marie 1922-
   Johan Frederick 1923-2005
   Lois Elizabeth 1925-2018

686. iii. Pauline Augusta Hausrath b. 29 Oct 1891. d. 30 Nov 1971. m. Edwin Frederick **Niemeier** 1891-1965.
   3 children:
   Harriet E. 1916-2012
   Robert R. 1917-1917
   Virginia 1923-2016

687.   iv. William Hausrath b. 29 Mar 1893. d. 14 Oct 1957. m. Lucy Ernestine **Bandelow** 1894-1961.
        4 children:
            Ruth Lucille 1917-1998
            Ellen 1921-
            Richard William 1922-2010
            James Earl 1928-2013

688.   v. Harry Arthur Hausrath b. 13 Sep 1894. d. 29 Dec 1980. m. Rosalie **Buchholz** 1895-1946. m. Erna **Bargmann Hysner** 1904-1962.
        1 child:
            Dorothy 1920-2010

689.   vi. Edna Marie Hausrath b. 23 Mar 1896. d. 15 Mar 1989. m. Robert G. **Brockman** 1889-1967.
        2 children:
            Robert Walter 1918-2005
            Eugene William 1923-1991

690.   vii. George Hausrath b. 10 Jun 1897. d. 12 Jun 1897.

691.   viii. Walter Michael Hausrath b. 29 Sep 1898. d. 18 Feb 1970. m. Alma Clara Elizabeth **Guelker** 1901-1959.
        2 children:
            Walter Paul 1923-1972
            Norma Florence 1924-2013

692.   ix. Arthur Henry Hausrath b. 20 Jul 1900. d. 25 Aug 1978. m. Alma Anna **Boehmert** 1899-1984.
        2 children:
            Donald Arthur 1923-2005
            Marjorie Ruth 1927-2020

693.   x. Florence Harriet Hausrath b. 7 Jan 1902. d. 27 Nov 1988. m. John N. **Jacobs** ????-????.

694.   xi. Clara H. Hausrath b. 19 Feb 1903. d. 15 Mar 1991. m. Paul Elsworth **Giebner** 1907-1991.
        2 children:
            Donna Jean 1930-1990
            Thomas P. 1939-

695.   xii. Louise Eleanor Hausrath b. 18 Oct 1904. d. 6 Feb 1991. m. Arthur Rudolph Hermann **Schmidt** 1900-1955.
        2 children:
            Arthur Rudolf Hermann 1927-1981

                Jane L. 1935-2017

696.   xiii. Lenoard Ferdinand Hausrath b. 21 Apr 1909. d. 26 Dec 1994. m. Lydia Emily **Heinrich** 1910-1999.
        2 children:
            Dwayne F. 1929-1929
            Carol Marie 1931-2009

1285. August Johann **HAUSRATH** born 15 Jan 1905 in Butrimiškės. Place of baptism unknown. Son of Friedrich Hausrath and Pauline **Peters**. Married Marie **Schmanski** (Russian Orthodox; 1913-1955) in Lithuania. Immigrated October 1949 via New York aboard the U.S.S. *General Muir*. Married Herta Auguste **Petz** (1911-1994) 18 Aug 1956 at Shore Haven Lutheran Church in Euclid, Ohio. Died 20 Aug 1985 in Florida. Interment unknown.

HEIMERT

544. Anna Dorothea **HEIMERT (UNTERBERGER)** born 1864 in Krasenka. Daughter of Johann Heimert and Dorothea **Unterberger**. Baptized and confirmed at Mariampol Evangelical Lutheran Church. Married Friedrich **Unterberger**[537] (1864-1950) 1887 at Mariampol Evangelical Lutheran Church. Immigrated June 1892 via Baltimore aboard the S.S. *Braunschweig*. Died 19 Mar 1925. Interment at Lutheran Cemetery. For list of children, see husband Friedrich Unterberger.

HEIN

713. Adolf **HEIN** born 1867 in Przystawańce (Poland). Son of Karl Hein and Julianna **Juletzki**. Baptized at Seine Evangelical Lutheran Church. Married Emilie **Batke**[722] (1871-1907) 1893 at Kalwaria Evangelical Lutheran Church. Immigrated July 1902 via Baltimore aboard the S.S. *Hannover*. Married Marianna **Kinat**[723] (1881-1954) 28 Dec 1907 at Zion Evangelical Lutheran Church. Died 3 Sep 1935. Interment at Lutheran Cemetery.

　　714.　　i. Friedrich Wilhelm Hein b. 1901. d. 22 Feb 1912.

　　715.　　ii. Anna Luise Hein b. 8 Oct 1902. d. 1903.

　　716.　　iii. Emily A. Hein b. 21 May 1904. d. 22 Aug 1989. m. George Gustave **Wohlfeil** 1902-1965.
　　　　　　　3 children:
　　　　　　　　　Arlene Martha 1926-2004
　　　　　　　　　Thomas G. 1930-2016
　　　　　　　　　Sharon H. 1938-

　　717.　　iv. Oscar Hein b. 1 Oct 1908. d. 18 Jul 1980. m. Helen Rose **Gruss** 1910-1998. m. Lydia M. **Cussack** 1915-2002.
　　　　　　　3 children:
　　　　　　　　　Jacqueline 1937-
　　　　　　　　　David 1939-
　　　　　　　　　Robert G. 1948-

　　718.　　v. Olga Marianna Hein b. 30 Dec 1909. d. 2 Mar 1987. m. George Arthur **Rindfleisch** 1910-1995. m. Peter C. **Perusek** 1917-1995.
　　　　　　　1 child:
　　　　　　　　　Beverly 1932-2009

　　719.　　vi. Bertha Hein b. 23 Aug 1911. d. 1 Apr 1999. m. Emil R. **Makahusz** 1909-1983.
　　　　　　　1 child:
　　　　　　　　　Richard Alan: 1932-2017

　　720.　　vii. Walter Hein b. 26 Jul 1914. d. 7 Jan 1984. m. Margaret A. **Makahusz** 1914-1986.
　　　　　　　3 children:
　　　　　　　　　Walter 1936-
　　　　　　　　　Ronald 1939-
　　　　　　　　　Audrey J. 1940-

721.   viii. Martha Hein b. 19 Mar 1915. d. 14 Jan 1997. m. Wilber A. **Boehm** 1915-2000.

730. Andreas „Heinrich" **HEIN** born Przystawańce (Poland). Son of Karl Hein and Julianna **Juletzki**. Baptized at Seine Evangelical Lutheran Church. Married Adeline **Pudimat**[740] (1876-1956) 1896 at Seine Evangelical Lutheran Church. Died 8 Jan 1949. Interment at Lutheran Cemetery.

   731.   i. Emma Hein b. 9 Jul 1897. d. 2 Jul 1984. m. Karl **Schneider**[477] (1892-1961).
        1 child:
           Leonard Carl[476] 1916-1990

   732.   ii. Adolph William Hein b. 18 Feb 1898. d. 11 Nov 1984. m. Gladys L. **Kerslake** 1896-1989.
        3 children:
           Virginia 1922-
           Alice Jean 1924-
           Richard 1935-

   733.   iii. Henry Hein Jr. b. 4 Jan 1901. d. 28 Dec 1992. m. Helen **Mckransky** 1903-????. m. Florentine Catherine **Groff** 1906-1979.
        1 child:
           Gloria H. 1923-1986

   734.   iv. Elisabeth Hein b. 14 Nov 1901. d. 6 Jul 1999. m. Gustav **Basenau** (**Bossman**)[612] 1902-1963.
        2 children:
           Norman G.[644] 1924-1998
           Carol Lois[645] 1931-2019

   735.   v. Albertine Hein b. 26 Mar 1907. d. 24 Dec 2000. m. Joseph L. **Thresher** 1904-1976.
        2 children:
           Doris J. 1924-1969
           Roger Leonard 1934-

   736.   vi. Emil Hein b. 22 Mar 1909. d. 8 Dec 1974. m. Valerie **Ference** 1910-1992.

   737.   vii. Edwin Hein b. 8 Mar 1912. d. 29 Dec 2001. m. Mary **Lawrence** 1914-2021.
        1 child:
           James Robert 1946-1989

738.   viii. Alma Hein b. 9 May 1916. d. 10 Mar 2014. m. Thomas **Macintosh** 1912-1979. m. John Edward **Griffin** 1914-1951.

739.   ix. Gloria Hein b. 10 Dec 1923. d. 28 Apr 1986. m. Herman **Thompson.**

741. Amelia **HEIN (LIER)** (***LEAR***) born 1877 in Przystawańce (Poland). Daughter of Karl Hein and Julianna **Juletzki**. Baptized at Seine Evangelical Lutheran Church. Married August **Lier**[742] (1869-1939) 18 Aug 1898 at German Reformed Church, Plymouth, Pennsylvania. Died 13 Feb 1948. Interment at Hillcrest Cemetery, Bedford Heights, Ohio. For list of children, see husband August Lier.

755. Leopold **HEIN** born 1885 in Kybartai (Lazdijai district). Son of Karl Hein and Julia **Juletzki**. Baptized at Kalwaria Evangelical Lutheran Church. Immigrated July 1906 via Baltimore aboard the S.S. *Main*. Married Marie **Pudimat**[760] (1887-1995) 10 May 1913 at St. Peter's Evangelical Lutheran Church. Died 30 May 1936. Interment at Lutheran Cemetery.

756.   i. Arthur Carl Hein b. 15 Feb 1914. d. 11 Mar 1915.

757.   ii. Gertrude Ruth Hein b. 11 Apr 1917. d. 11 Jul 2011. m. Albert James **Slater** 1911-1980.
       3 children:
           Michael R. 1946-
           Susan L. 1947-
           Merrilea Ruth 1948-1948

758.   iii. Robert William Hein b. 6 Feb 1921. d. 17 Mar 1999. m. Ruth Velma **Erricson** 1922-1989. m. Margaret Anne **Watts** 1921-2010.
       1 child:
           Lindsay Jane 1946-2003

759.   ix. Roy Carl Hein b. 12 Jul 1924. d. 16 Oct 2015. m. Jeanne **Honschopp** 1923-2013.
       4 children:

761. Julius **HEIN** born 1890 in Kybartai (Lazdijai district). Son of Karl Hein and Julia **Juletzki**. Baptized at Kalwaria Evangelical Lutheran Church. Immigrated October 1906 via Baltimore aboard the S.S. *Köln*. Married Adeline **Podzis**[765] (1891-1963) 24 May 1913 at St. Peter's Evangelical Lutheran Church. Died 5 Jan 1970 in Mayfield Heights, Ohio. Interment at Lutheran Cemetery.

762.   i. Howard Arthur Hein b. 12 Feb 1914. d. 22 May 1998. m. Felice **Armstrong** 1914-1978.
       1 child:
           Patricia Doris 1941-2009

763. ii. Wilber Erick Hein b. 10 Feb 1921. d. 15 Aug 1999.

764. iii. Doris Adeline Hein b. 23 Jul 1926. d. 19 Mar 2007. m. Leonard Paul **Obert** 1922-1967.
   1 child:

1307. Rudolf **HEIN** born 30 Jan 1902 in Poluńce (Poland). Son of Johann Hein and Emilie **Neumann**. Baptized at Seine Evangelical Lutheran Church. Married Meta **Grau** (1919-2009). Immigrated December 1951 via New York aboard the U.S.S. *General R. M. Blatchford.* Died 12 May 1979. Interment at Lutheran Cemetery.

   1308. i. Karl Emil Hein b. 13 Aug 1938. m. Dorothy **Malek**.
      2 children:
         Christa
         Laura

   1309. ii. Wilhelm Hein b. 2 Dec 1946.

   1310. iii. Irene Marta Hein b. 4 Mar 1949. m. James **Hall**.

1477. Ludwig „Louis" **HEIN** born 1866 in Puńsk (Poland). Son of Andreas "Heinrich" Hein and Karoline **Ziermann**. Baptized and confirmed at Seine Evangelical Lutheran Church. Married Johanna **Schröder** (1869-1959) 8 Nov 1890 at Zion Evangelical Lutheran Church. Died 4 May 1952 in Euclid, Ohio. Interment at Lutheran Cemetery.

   1478. i. Olga B. Hein b. 7 Jul 1896. d. 11 Apr 1978. m. Walter F. **Meyer** (1894-1963).

   1479. ii. Frederick A. Hein b. 7 Jun 1909. d. 10 Sep 1993. m. Mary **Jones** 1912-2004. m. Dorothea **Schneider** 1909-????.
      2 children:
         Bernard P. 1931-2000
         Frederick Jr. 1945-2011

1480. Amelia **HEIN** (**STOSSUN**) (*STASUN*) born 1871 in Puńsk (Poland). Daughter of Andreas "Heinrich" Hein and Karoline **Ziermann**. Baptized and confirmed at Seine Evangelical Lutheran Church. Married Karl **Stasun** (1867-1936). Died 17 Feb 1932. Interment at Lake View Cemetery.

   1481. i. Emilie Stasun b. 5 Jul 1891. d. 3 Apr 1972. m. Lawrence William **de Beauclair** 1892-1975.
      1 child:
         Jeanne Irene 1918-2003

1482. ii. Amalie Stasun b. 19 Dec 1892. d. 19 Sep 1897.

1483. iii. Helene Stasun b. 19 Dec 1894. d. 11 Sep 1895.

1484. iv. Ernestine Stasun b. 30 Jul 1896. d. ????.

1485. v. Irene Stasun b. 31 Jul 1897. d. 20 Nov 1962. m. Leslie George **Raquett** 1890-1964.

1538. Josef **HEIN** born 29 Feb 1876 in Wiłkopedzie (Poland). Son of Justine **Hein**. Baptized at Seine Lutheran Church. Immigrated May 1901 via New York aboard the S.S. *Pennsylvania*. Married Pauline **Herr**[1537] 11 Jan 1905 at Zion Evangelical Lutheran Church. Died 11 May 1947. Interment at Knollwood Cemetery, Mayfield Heights, Ohio.

1539. i. Edward E. Hein b. 3 Feb 1906. d. 14 Nov 1989. m. Elvera **Schultz** 1907-1999.

1540. ii. Clara Pauline Hein b. 20 Aug 1910. d. 2 Feb 1979.

1541. iii. Elsie Marie Hein b. 13 Jan 1913. d. 22 Aug 2001. m. Clarence Frederick **Boester** 1914-1998.
    2 children:
        Sue E. 1943-
        Lynn M. 1944-

HEINRICH / HENRY

67. August **HEINRICH** (*HENRY*) born about 1855 in Ungurinė. Son of Karl Heinrich and Helene **Pfeifer**. Married Emilie **Nowiak**[82] (1863-1945) at Wirballen Evangelical Lutheran Church 31 Aug 1879. Died 5 Jul 1916. Interment at Knollwood Cemetery, Mayfield Heights, Ohio.

    68.   i. Albert Heinrich b. 24 Apr 1892. d. 12 Sep 1959. m. Emma **Haase**.
            1 child:
                Mildred Heinrich

    69.   ii. Edmund Heinrich b. 1894. d. 15 Sep 1975. m. Emma P **Plescott** 1896-1975.
            2 children:
                Edmund August 1922-1977
                Joseph John 1915-2012

    70.   iii. Adolf Eduard b. 4 Mar 1896. d. 1978. m. Loretta **Boers** 1901-1975.
            2 children:
                Marjorie 1930-1987
                Loretta 1933-

    71.   iv. August Hermann b. 1899. d. 3 Feb 1959. m. Adeline **Plescott** 1904-2000.
            2 children:
                Adel
                Esther

68. Albert **HEINRICH** born 24 Apr 1892 in Degučiai. Son of August Heinrich[67] (1855-1916) and Emilie **Nowiak**[82] (1863-1945). Baptized at Mariampol Evangelical Lutheran Church. Married Emma **Haase**[700] (1895-1982) 25 Jan 1918 at Zion Evangelical Lutheran Church. Died 12 Sep 1959 in West Palm Beach, Florida. Interment at Lutheran Cemetery.

    72.   i. Alma Louise Heinrich b. 11 Oct 1918. d. 12 Dec 1918.

    73   ii. Robert August Heinrich b. 2 Oct 1919. d. 13 Nov 1919.

    74.   iii. Albert Carl Heinrich b. 31 Mar 1921. d. 19 Apr 1921.

    75.   iv. Mildred Heinrich b. 28 Sep 1922. d. 28 Aug 1938.

69. Edmund **HEINRICH** born 1894 in Degučiai. Son of August Heinrich[67] 1855-1916 and Emilie **Nowiak**[82] 1863-1945. Baptized at Mariampol Evangelical Lutheran Church. Married Emma **Plescott** 20 Oct 1921 at Zion Evangelical Lutheran Church. Died 15 Sep 1975. Interment at Whitehaven Memorial Park, Mayfield, Ohio.

    76.   i. Edmund August Heinrich b. 2 Aug 1922. d. 22 May 1977. m. Jean Victoria **Dear** 1922-2006.

    77.   ii. Florence Emma Heinrich b. 12 Feb 1924. d. 18 Feb 1999. m. Joseph John **Gregor** Jr 1915-2012.

70. Adolf Eduard **HEINRICH** born 4 Mar 1896 in Degučiai. Son of August Heinrich[67] (1855-1916) and Emilie **Nowiak**[82] (1863-1945.) Baptized at Mariampol Evangelical Lutheran Church. Married Loretta **Boers** 1901-1975 18 Sep 1926 at Zion Evangelical Lutheran Church. Died 17 Mar 1978. Interment at Sunset Memorial Park, North Olmsted, Ohio.

    78.   i. Majorie Heinrich b. ca. 1930. d. 1987. m. John R. **Wolfs** 1917-1986.

    79.   ii. Loretta Heinrich b. ca. 1933.

71. August Hermann **HEINRICH** born 1899 in Degučiai. Son of August Heinrich[67] (1855-1916) and Emilie **Nowiak**[82] (1863-1945.) Baptized at Mariampol Evangelical Lutheran Church. Immigrated via Baltimore in September 1907 aboard the S.S. *Frankfurt*. Married Adeline **Plescott** (1904-2000) 17 Dec 1925 at Zion Evangelical Lutheran Church. Died 3 Feb 1959. Interment at Lutheran Cemetery.

    80.   i. Adel Heinrich b. 20 Jul 1926.

    81.   ii. Esther Florence Heinrich b. 18 Jan 1935. d. 28 Sep 2023. m. Andrew **Broccone** 1933-1986.
            2 children:
                Marc
                Mandy

982. Marie **HEINRICH (REDER)** born 17 Feb 1891 in Urbantai. Daughter of Matthias Heinrich and Julianna **Plitzuweit**. Baptized and confirmed at Neustadt Evangelical Lutheran Church. Immigrated May 1910 via New York aboard the S.S. *Rotterdam*. Married Gustav **Reder**[978] (1893-1972) 4 Jul 1914 at Zion Evangelical Lutheran Church. Died 16 Mar 1960 in Conneaut, Pennsylvania. Interment at Albion Cemetery, Albion, Pennsylvania. For list of children, see husband Gustav Reder.

994. Bertha **HEINRICH** (**WISGIN**) born 25 Dec 1894 in Urbantai. Daughter of Matthias Heinrich and Julianna **Plitzuweit**. Baptized and confirmed at Neustadt Evangelical Lutheran Church. Married Richard **Wisgin**[983] (1884-1976) 1 Dec 1917 at Zion Evangelical Lutheran Church. Died May 1991. Interment at Knollwood Cemetery, Mayfield Heights, Ohio. For list of children, see husband Richad Wisgin.

995. August **HEINRICH** born 15 Jan 1893 in Urbantai. Son of Matthias Heinrich and Julianna **Plitzuweit**. Baptized and confirmed at Neustadt Evangelical Lutheran Church. Immigrated February 1923 via New York aboard the S.S. *Manchuria*. Died 18 May 1977. Interment unknown.

1397. Karl **HEINRICH** (*HENRY*) born 1866 in Ungurinė. Son of Karl Heinrich and Helene **Pfeifer**. Baptized and confirmed at Mariampol Evangelical Lutheran Church. Married Anna **Palenschat** 8 Jul 1893 at St. Peter's Evangelical Lutheran Church. Died 28 Nov 1935. Interment at Highland Park Cemetery, Highland Hills, Ohio.

    1398. i. Mildred Emilie Henry b. 2 Aug 1894. d. 3 Sep 1980. m. Erwin P. **Milde** 1895-1987.
        4 children:
            Leonard M. 1916-1985
            Myrtle E. 1923-2004
            Erwin C. 1927-1999
            Anne L. 1929-2020

    1399. ii. Walter Heinrich b. 2 Apr 1898. d. 6 Jan 1900.

    1400. iii. Ewald Henry b. 29 Jul 1901. d. Mar 1957. m. Hannah Elizabeth **Lang**[1386] 1903-1996.
        4 children:
            Lois Ann 1923-2004
            Elaine Doris 1927-1931
            Charles Edwin 1932-2022
            Judith 1939-

    1401. iv. Albert Henry b. 13 Apr 1905. d. 1 Jul 1975. m. Emma **Jesset**[882] 1903-1994.
        2 children:
            Mildred 1932-
            Richard W. 1943-

    1402. v. Arthur Heinrich b. 24 Nov 1908. d. 25 Jan 1910.

1499. Johann **HEINRICH** born 13 May 1978 in Urbantai. Son of Matthias Heinrich and Julianna **Plitzuweit**. Baptized and confirmed at Neustadt Evangelical Lutheran Church. Died 4 Apr 1908. Interment at Lutheran Cemetery.

HEMPEL

1516. Oswald **HEMPEL** born 17 Mar 1923 in Cigoniškiai. Son of Ferdinand Hempel (1893-1953) and Marianna **Friedke** (1894-1969). Baptized at Serey Reformed Lutheran Church. Married Alma **Dill**[1505] (1931-2010) June 1951 in Germany. Immigrated May 1952 via New York aboard *Flying Tiger Line,* Flight 229. Died 2 Aug 2010 in Parma, Ohio. Interment at Hope Memorial Gardens, Hinckley, Ohio.

    1517.   i. Edith Hempel b. 29 Jan 1952. m. Jeffrey L. **Johnson** 1947-????.
               1 child:
                    Rebecca Karoline 1980-

    1518.   ii. Ingrid Hempel b. 4 Feb 1953. m. John E. **Hamilton** 1942-2023.

    1519.   iii. Irene Hempel b. 5 Sep 1954. m. Robert S. **Jakubcin** 1951-????.

    1520.   iv. Walter Hempel b. 17 Apr 1959.

HERR

668. Ferdinand **HERR** born 1867 in Zwirgzda (Poland). Son of Ferdinand Herr and Karoline **Essel**. Baptized at Seine Evangelical Lutheran Church. Immigrated May 1888. Married Dorothea **Hausrath**[672] (1877-????) 15 Feb 1890 at Zion Evangelical Lutheran Church. Divorced. Married Caroline **Hein** (1865-1941) 19 Jul 1915 in Cleveland by a Justice of the Peace. Died 4 Jun 1955. Interment at East Cleveland Township Cemetery.

    669.   i. Anna Auguste Herr b. 31 Jul 1891. d. Apr 1972. m. David Craig **Adie** 1888-1943.
        1 child:
           Jean Cooper 1919-2015

    670.   ii. Harold Ferdinand Herr b. 16 Jan 1898. d. 9 Feb 1970. m. Gladys Jane **Bauchmire** 1902-1997.
        1 child:
           Martha 1939-

    671.   iii. Arthur Gottlieb Herr b. 19 Feb 1901. d. Apr 1972. m. Ruth M. **Hanlon** 1899-2002.
        2 children:
           Marta Jeanne 1930-2017
           William Frederick 1932-2015

1537. Pauline **HERR (HEIN)** born 28 Aug 1887 in Mostowo (no longer exists; was located near Klejwy, Poland). Daughter of Ferdinand Herr and Marianna **Dill** (1861-1933.) Baptized at Seine Evangelical Lutheran Church. Immigrated May 1903 via New York aboard the S.S. *Frankfurt*. Married Josef **Hein**[1538] (1876-1947) 11 Jan 1905 at Zion Evangelical Lutheran Church. Died 30 Sep 1968 in Santa Ana, California. Interment at Knollwood Cemetery, Mayfield Heights, Ohio. For list of children, see husband Josef Hein.

HESS

725. Johann **HESS** born 1888 in Kasteletiškė. Son of Johann Hess and Helene **Hein**. Baptized at Kalwaria Evangelical Lutheran Church. Married Emilie **Kinat**[724] (1887-1939) 1913 at Mariampol Evangelical Lutheran Church. Immigrated May 1913 via Baltimore aboard the S.S. *Cassel*. Died 5 Feb 1976 in Warren, Ohio. Interment unknown.

    726.   i. Adolf August Hess b. 1913. d. 30 Sep 1939. m. Muriel Mabel **Hesse** 1909-2001.
            1 child:
                Loralie Anne 1936-2010

    727.   ii. Emma Emilie Hess b. 11 Jan 1915. d. 30 Nov 1989. m. Steve **Pinko** 1904-1982.
            1 child:
                Steven 1949-

    728.   iii. Albert Leopold Hess. B. 25 Jan 1916. d. 18 Sep 1997. m. Erna Emily **Schwed**[914] 1921-2008.

    729.   iv. Freida Elizabeth Hess b. 5 Mar 1917. d. 26 Sep 2008. m. Edwin Allison **Farley** 1909-1980.
            2 children:
                Georgene 1941-
                Lester 1947-

HIRSCH

403. Albertine "Bertha" **HIRSCH** (**MAI**) (*MAY*) born 1888 in Laukinčiai. Daughter of Georg Leopold Hirsch (1836-1904) and Michaeline **Heidebruch**. Baptized at Serey Reformed Lutheran Church. Married Alexander **Mai**[397] (1883-1942) in Pittsburgh, Pennsylvania. Died 12 Dec 1963. Interment at Lutheran Cemetery. For list of children, see husband Alexander Mai.

934. Olga **HIRSCH** (**ERNST**) born 1898 in Gervėnai. Daughter of August Adam Hirsch and Emilie **Meier**. Baptized at Serey Reformed Lutheran Church. Immigrated August 1913 via Baltimore aboard the S.S. *Main*. Married Albert **Ernst**[935] (1896-1981) 25 Mar 1916 at Zion Evangelical Lutheran Church. Died August 1954. Interment at Lutheran Cemetery. For list of children, see husband Albert Ernst.

938. Gottlieb **HIRSCH** born 1872 in Gervėnai. Son of Leopold Hirsch (1836-1906) and Pauline **Schütz** (1842-1880). Baptized at Serey Reformed Lutheran Church. Married Berta **Hartig**[944] (1868-1944) 1898 at Serey Reformed Lutheran Church. Died 15 Feb 1961. Interment at Lutheran Cemetery.

    939.   i. Olga Hirsch b. 20 Aug 1899. d. 18 Apr 1983. m. Johann Gustav **Hirsch** 1888-1948. m. Malcome D. **Tyler** 1892-1969. m. Andrew C. **Baran** 1888-1959.
        2 children:
            Harold J. 1919-1963
            June 1924-1966

    940.   ii. Oswald E. Hirsch b. 11 Mar 1902. d. 19 Dec 1996. m. Elizabeth **Leopold** 1904-1982.
        1 child:
            Kathryn 1929-1992

    941.   iii. Edmund Arthur Hirsch b. 3 Jun 1905. d. 27 Jun 1966. m. Isabell **Apanaites** 1912-1989.
        1 child:
            Edmund D. 1941-2014

    942.   iv. Albert Hirsch b. 10 Sep 1907. d. 21 May 1979. m. Joanna **Stepanovich** 1919-2022.
        2 children:
            Anette 1942-
            Thomas A. 1946-

    943.   v. Alvin C. Hirsch b. 11 Jan 1912. d. 19 Apr 2001. m. Margaret Mary **Jira** 1916-2014.

2 children:
>William B. 1941-2007
>Dennis Paul 1947-2010.

952. Wilhelm **HIRSCH** born 1884 in Pošnia. Son of Leopold Hirsch (1836-1904) and Michaline **Heidebruch** (1857-1902). Baptized at Serey Reformed Lutheran Church. Immigrated November 1904 via New York. Married Berta **Bender**[955] (1898-1996) 13 July 1918 at Zion Evangelical Lutheran Church. Died 19 Dec 1960. Interment at Lutheran Cemetery.

>953. i. Arthur Wilhelm Hirsch b. 26 May 1919. d. 10 May 2011. m. Esther Marie **Grieg** 1922-1996.
>>1 child:
>>>Pamela J. 1948-

>954. ii. Gertrude Hirsch b. 7 Feb 1921. d. 4 Jan 2022. m. Steven **Baer** 1916-1989.
>>6 children:
>>>Denise Holly 1964-
>>>Deborah
>>>Cheryle
>>>Douglas
>>>Bruce
>>>Nancy

956. Auguste **HIRSCH (LEHMANN)** born 1891 in Laukinčiai. Daughter of Leopold Hirsch (1836-1904) and Michaline **Heidebruch** (1857-1902). Baptized at Serey Reformed Lutheran Church. Immigrated October 1907 via New York aboard the S.S. *Zeeland*. Married Matthias **Lehmann**[82] (1886-1942) 14 Jan 1922 at Zion Evangelical Lutheran Church. Died January 1978. Interment at Lutheran Cemetery. For list of children, see husband Matthias Lehmann.

958. Albine **HIRSCH (WEINSCHRÖDER)** born 1894 in Laukinčiai. Daughter of Leopold Hirsch (1836-1904) and Michaline **Heidebruch** (1857-1902). Baptized at Serey Reformed Lutheran Church. Married Leon **Weinschröder**[574] (1891-1969) 23 May 1914 at Zion Evangelical Lutheran Church. Died 23 Dec 1986. Interment at Lutheran Cemetery.

959. Julius **HIRSCH** born 1897 in Laukinčiai. Son of Leopold Hirsch (1836-1904) and Michaline **Heidebruch** (1857-1902). Baptized at Serey Reformed Lutheran Church. Married Cassie **Holdaway** (1903-1984) 6 Jan 1925 in Cleveland by a Justice of the Peace. Died 31 Oct 1980. Interment at Lutheran Cemetery.

HUBERT

1102. Anna Helene **HUBERT** (**PERRY**) born 5 Jul 1876 in Karklupėnai. Daughter of Johann Hubert (1835-????) and Magdalene **Muk** (1837-????). Baptized at Wirballen Evangelical Lutheran Church. Married Thomas **Perry**[1096] (1870-1955) likely at Wirballen. Immigrated June 1903 via New York aboard the S.S. *Pretoria*. Died 8 Apr 1942. Interment at Lutheran Cemetery. For list of children, see husband Thomas Perry.

JESSAT / JESSET / JANZAT / JANSZAT

875. Gustav August **JESSAT** (*JESSET*) born 1868 in Degučiai. Son of Adolf Jessat and Amelia **Berwing**. Baptized and confirmed at Mariampol Evangelical Lutheran Church. Married Anna **Andechser**[874] (1865-1957) in 1889 at Mariampol Evangelical Lutheran Church. Died 15 Nov 1936. Interment at Highland Park Cemetery, Highland Hills, Ohio.

876. i. Bertha Jessat b. 1891. d. 26 Nov 1971. m. Christian **Springborn** 1890-1931. m. Arthur C. **Kramer** 1893-1973.
   2 children:
   William L. 1910-1972
   Eleanor 1912-1983

877. ii. Charles Jesset b. 26 Nov 1893. d. 15 May 1959. m. Augusta **Hook** 1896-1982.
   1 child:
   Earl 1915-1990

878. iii. Edward Jesset b. 30 Mar 1895. d. 19 Oct 1972. m. Beta L. A. **Moorman** 1893-1979.
   3 children:
   Leonard E. 1921-1944
   Arthur Elroy 1923-2007
   Bernice 1924-2008

879. iv. William Jesset b. 31 Dec 1897. d. 4 Aug 1955. m. Laura Dagmar **Silverberg** 1903-1999.
   1 child:
   Joan D. 1931-2010

880. v. Otto Jessat b. 1898. d. 11 Jun 1900.

881. vi. Fred Jessat b. 1900. d. 23 Jan 1902.

882. vii. Emma Jesset b. 18 Nov 1903. d. 22 Feb 1994. m. Albert William **Henry**[1401] 1905-1975.
   2 children:
   Mildred Elaine 1933-
   Richard W. 1943-

883. viii. Leonard Gustave Jessat b. 20 Oct 1912. d. 12 Jan 1994. m. Mary Elisabeth **Stokes** 1912-1993.
   1 child:
   Shirley Elaine 1935-2006

JONAT / JONAITIS / JONATH

827. Johann **JONAT** born 24 Jun 1892 in Turgalauks. Son of August Jonat and Anna **Leichert**. Baptized and confirmed at Mariampol Evangelical Lutheran Church. Immigrated June 1910 via New York aboard the S.S. *Barbrossa*. Married Amalie "Molly" **Lukat**[831] (1897-1972) 21 Nov 1915 at Zion Evangelical Lutheran Church. Died 17 May 1960 in Indianapolis, Indiana. Interment at Woodland Cemetery.

    828.   i. Harold John Jonath b. 26 Dec 1916. d. 8 Feb 1984. m. Gladys M. **Spoonamore** 1922-2008.
            4 children:
                Judy L. 1943-
                William H. 1946-
                John David 1947-2000
                Evelyn R. 1949-1993

    829.   ii. Ernst Adolf Jonath b. 28 Aug 1918. d. 1 Apr 1990. m. Lela **Goltz** 1920-????.
            2 children:
                Beverly A. 1942-
                Gayle L. 1947-

    830.   iii. Eleanor Martha Jonath b. 12 Jan 1923. d. 27 Nov 2012. m. William Thomas **Springer** 1921-1984.
            4 children:
                Patricia N. 1943-
                Marvin E. 1946-
                Karen E. 1947-
                James C. 1949-

JURGELEIT / YURGELEIT / URGELEIT

596. Christine **JURGELEIT** (**KONRAD**) born 1875 in Cyrailė. Daughter of Christian Jurgeleit and Julainna **Anderkat**. Baptized and confirmed at Kalwaria Evangelical Lutheran Church. Married Ludwig "Louis" **Konrad**[588] 14 May 1898 at German Evangelical Lutheran Church in McKeesport, Pennsylvania. Died May 1949. Interment at Lutheran Cemetery. For list of children, see husband Ludwig "Louis" Konrad.

597. Christ **JURGELEIT** (***URGELEIT***) born 12 Feb 1881 in Cyrailė. Son of Christian Jurgeleit and Julainna **Anderkat**. Baptized and confirmed at Kalwaria Evangelical Lutheran Church. Immigrated April 1901 via New York. Married Adeline **Basenau** (**Bossmann**) 12 Aug 1906 at Zion Evangelical Lutheran Church. Died 1949. Interment at Lutheran Cemetery.

  598. i. John Herman Urgeleit b. 27 Sep 1907. d. 12 Jul 1965. m. Gertrude **Bartell** 1909-1993.

  599. ii. Edith Urgeleit b. 11 Jan 1910. d. 18 Aug 2005. m. Charles Joseph **Sierputowski (Siers)** 1914-2002.
    1 child:
      Sharon Lynn 1940-1992

  600. iii. Leonard Christian Urgeleit b. 4 Jun 1912. d. 5 Apr 1987. m. Theresa **Fritz** 1915-2000.
    2 children:
      Leonard R. 1940-
      David Nelson 1948-2012

  601. iv. Mildred Urgeleit b. 18 Jan 1920. d. 1 Feb 1978. m. Karoly John **Ferencz** Sr. 1914-1996.
    1 child:
      Charles J. 1950-

  602. v. Charlotte Irene Urgeleit b. 14 Mar 1923. d. 8 May 2003. m. Regis Leo **Morgan** 1919-1980.
    2 children:
      Susan 1946-
      Gwenne 1947-

  603. vi. Lois Pauline Urgeleit b. 8 Dec 1926. d. 24 Jul 1995. m. Robert Edward **Hotes** 1927-2006.
    1 child:
      Cynthia L. 1947-.

604.   vii. Lloyd Carl Urgeleit b. 8 Dec 1926. d. 1 Nov 2014.

JURGELEWICZ / JURGELEWITZ

397. Berta **JURGELEWITZ (LANG)** born 14 Jul 1893 in Vilkaviškis. Daughter of Friedrich Johann Jurgelewitz and Auguste **Henk**. Baptized and confirmed at Wilkowischken Evangelical Lutheran Church. Immigrated July 1911 via New York aboard the S.S. *Geo. Washington*. Married Ludwig **Lang**[395] (1875-1962) 31 May 1913 at St. Paul's Evangelical Lutheran Church. Died 2 Feb 1962. Interment at Crown Hill Cemetery, Twinsburg, Ohio. For list of children, see husband Ludwig Lang.

1279. Emma **JURGELEWITZ (LANG)** born 18 Mar 1887 in Vilkaviškis. Daughter of Friedrich Johann Jurgelewitz and Auguste **Henk**. Baptized and confirmed at Wilkowischken Evangelical Lutheran Church. Married Ferdinand **Lang**[1278] (1878-1960) in 1906 at Mariampol Evangelical Lutheran Church. Died 16 Sep 1959 in Ashtabula, Ohio. Interment at Crown Hill Cemetery and Mausoleum, Twinsburg, Ohio. For list of children, see husband Ferdinand Lang.

JURKSCHAT / YURKSCHAT / JURKSCHAITIS / URKSCHAT

329. Adolf **JURKSCHAT** born 2 Jan 1872 in Javaravas. Son of Ludwig Jurkschat (1824-1904) and Pauline **Zink** (1833-1909.) Baptized and confirmed at Mariampol Evangelical Lutheran Church. Married Emilie **Martinkat** in 1889 at Mariampol Evangelical Lutheran Church. Immigrated June 1913 via Baltimore aboard the S.S. *Eisenach*. Died 6 Aug 1936. Interment at Lutheran Cemetery.

> 330. i. Johann Jurkschat b. 14 Jun 1908. d. 13 Jun 1943. m. Emma Lydia **Baseleben**.

645. Pauline **JURKSCHAT** (**BASENAU**) (**BOSSMAN**) born 1866 in Javaravas. Daughter of Ludwig Jurkschat (1824-1904) and Pauline **Zink** (1833-1909.) Baptized and confirmed at Mariampol Evangelical Lutheran Church. Married Karl **Basenau**[606] (1866-1925) in 1888 at Mariampol Evangelical Lutheran Church. Immigrated October 1908 via New York aboard the S.S. *Pennsylvania*. Died 28 Apr 1924. Interment at Lutheran Cemetery. For list of children, see husband Karl Basenau.

646. Anna **JURKSCHAT** (**PAMPUS**) (**BOSSMAN**) born 28 Apr 1874 in Javaravas. Daughter of Ludwig Jurkschat (1824-1904) and Pauline **Zink** (1833-1909). Baptized and confirmed at Mariampol Evangelical Lutheran Church. Married Gustav **Pampus**[647] (1893-1922) 10 Jan 1914 at Zion Evangelical Lutheran Church. Married Karl **Basenau**[606] (1866-1925) 10 Jan 1925. Died 27 Apr 1944. Interment at Lutheran Cemetery. For list of children, see husband Gustav Pampus.

1056. Johann **JURKSCHAT** (*YURKSCHAT*) born 1893 in Kvietiškis. Son of Johann Jurkschat and Auguste **Blum**. Baptized at Mariampol Evangelical Lutheran Church. Immigrated January 1913 via Baltimore aboard the S.S. *Eisenach*. Married Auguste **Pempus** (1896-1924) 10 Apr 1915 at Zion Evangelical Lutheran Church. Married Wilhelmine **Essel**[295] (1895-1963) 18 Apr 1925 at Bethlehem Evangelical Lutheran Church. Died 21 Feb 1975, Holmes County, Ohio. Interment at Lutheran Cemetery.

> 1057. i. Hattie Anna Yurkschat b. 11 Mar 1917. d. 28 Apr 1993. m. Henry Peter **Dries** 1907-1976.
>> 2 children:
>> Richard E. 1939-2013
>> Ralph Leonard 1946-2005

> 1058. ii. Leonard Gustave Yurkschatt b. 27 Feb 1919. d. 14 Aug 1945.

1059. iii. Evelyn Hannah Yurkschat b. 1921. d. 19 Nov 1970. m. Adolph Howard **Peters**[1055] 1919-2010.

1060. iv. Wilma Minnie Yurkschat b. 23 Jun 1926. d. 15 May 2014. m. Elmer Walter **Witt** 1936-2000.
    2 children:
        Elmer Walter Jr. 1949-2006
        Laura Gayle

1061. v. John Adolph Yurkschat b. 25 Dec 1932. d. 21 Nov 2019. m. Carol Jean **Loew** 1935-.
    2 children:
        Judith Fern 1956-
        Justina 1966-1966

1062. vi. Ruth Yurkschat b. 15 Dec 1935. d. 23 May 2017. m. Lynn **Shephard**.
    2 children:
        Jeff
        Scott

KALCHERT

1169. Gustav August **KALCHERT** born 1863 in Resuras. Son of Adolf Kalchert and Helene Julianna **Müller**. Baptized at Mariampol Evangelical Lutheran Church. Died 28 Oct 1926. Interment at Lutheran Cemetery.

KALWEIT / KALLWEIT / KALWAITIS

1408. Christian **KALWEIT** born 1 Nov 1861 Rėčiūnai. Son of Johann Kalweit and Karoline **Mietzke**. Baptized and confirmed at Wischtiten Evangelical Lutheran Church. Married Wilhelmine **Dingfeld**[1409] (1867-1950) in 1890 at Wischtiten Evangelical Lutheran Church. Died 7 Apr 1932. Interment at Lutheran Cemetery.

    1410.   i. Ottilie Bertha Kalweit b. 23 Oct 1892. d. 21 Jan 1969. m. Guy Carleton **Kendall** 1895-1962.
                2 children:
                        Pauline Martha 1920-1954
                        Evelyn Roselle 1927-2009

    1411.   ii. Emma Martha Kalweit b. 4 Mar 1894. d. 3 Feb 1978.

    1412.   iii. Harold Albert Kalweit b. 29 Apr 1896. d. 21 May 1948. m. Rose G. **Mickovsky** 1893-1986.
                1 child:
                        Alice Marie 1930-2005.

    1413.   iv. Albina Kalweit b. 22 Apr 1900. d. 14 Feb 1987.

    1414.   v. Walter Kalweit b. 7 Sep 1904. d. 4 Oct 1980.

KAPTEIN

331. Eduard "Emmanuel" **KAPTEIN** born 1883 in Mureikai. Son of Julius Kaptein and Auguste **Rebner**. Likely baptized at Schaken Evangelical Lutheran Church. Immigrated August 1912 via Baltimore aboard the S.S. *Brandenburg*. Married Emma **Kaptein**[353] (1890-1967) 10 May 1913 at Third Reformed Lutheran Church. Died 23 Feb 1947. Interment at Lake View Cemetery.

    332.   i. Ruth Kaptein b. 25 Sep 1925. d. 11 Feb 2016. m. Frank John **Cronin** 1924-2001.

    333.   ii. Edna Kaptein b. 27 Feb 1914. d. 18 Dec 2003. m. Christopher **Nelson** 1907-1989.
        2 children:
            Sandra
            Jackie

    334.   iii. Edward Kaptein Jr. b. 11 Mar 1919. d. 22 Mar 1994. m. Anna **Zajac** 1921-2012.

    335.   iv. Walter Frederick Kaptein b. 15 Feb 1921. d. 12 Feb 2002. m. Helen Josephine **Newman** 1923-2011.

336. Gustav **KAPTEIN** born around 1890, likely in Mureikai. Son of Julius Kaptein and Auguste **Rebner**. Likely baptized at Schaken Evangelical Lutheran Church. Immigrated May 1910 via Baltimore aboard the S.S. *Cassel*. Married Marie **Puschkat** (1896-1932) 1 August 1914 at Third Reformed Lutheran Church. Died 27 Sep 1936. Interment at Zion Lutheran Cemetery, Maple Heights, Ohio.

    337.   i. Gustav Richard Kaptein b. 19 Dec 1916. d. 15 Oct 1983. m. Dorothy Ruth **Sloop** 1922-1994. m. Lois Ann **Cummings** 1928-2015.
        3 children:
            Rev. Curtis Clark 1948-2002
            Dale E. 1949-1966
            Frieda 1953-1962

    338.   ii. Arthur George Kaptein b. 1 Jun 1918. d. 27 Oct 1979. m. Mary Mae 1927-1971. m. Ruth Marie **Tipping** 1923-2002.

    339.   iii. Elmer Edmond Kaptein b. 14 Jun 1920. d. 8 Jan 2007. m. Mary Ada **Kinzy** 1927-2021.
        1 child:
            Edmond Forrest

340. iv. Lillian Ruth Kaptein b. 2 Apr 1923. d. 6 Dec 1987. m. Arthur **Puskat**[1405] 1906-1998.
   2 children:
   Beverly A 1936-
   Ralph A 1949-

341. v. Harold William Kaptein b. 5 Aug 1928. d. 23 Feb 2007. m. Agnes M. **Scheimann** 1929-2018.
   4 children:
   Joseph
   Judith
   Linda
   Theresa

342. Ottilie **KAPTEIN (LOGIES)** born 3 Mar 1895 in Mureikai. Daughter of Julius Kaptein and Auguste **Rebner**. Baptized at Schaken Evangelical Lutheran Church. Married Karl **Logies**[343] (1887-1985) 14 Feb 1919 at Zion Evangelical Lutheran Church. Died 29 Jan 1983. Interment at Lutheran Cemetery. For list of children, see husband Karl Logies.

353. Emma **KAPTEIN (KAPTEIN)** born about 1890 likely in Vyžpiniai. Daughter of Eduard Samuel Kaptein and Anna Emma **Wilk**. Likely baptized at Schaken Evangelical Lutheran Church. Immigrated August 1912 via Philadelphia aboard the S.S. *Brandenburg*. Married Eduard **Kaptein**[331] (1883-1947) (relationship undetermined) 10 May 1913 at Third Reformed Lutheran Church. Died 19 Jan 1967 in Los Angeles, California. Interment at Lake View Cemetery. For list of children, see husband Eduard Kaptein.

KAUSCH

246. Auguste **KAUSCH** (**BIRKOBEN**) born 1886 in Maude (Poland). Daughter of Friedrich Kausch and Wilhelmine **Abramat**. Baptized at Wischainy Evangelical Lutheran Church. Married Karl **Birkoben**[244] (1884-1958) 22 Apr 1906 at Zion Evangelical Lutheran Church. Died 26 Sep 1979. Interment at Lutheran Cemetery. For list of children, see husband Karl Birkoben.

998. Helene **KAUSCH** (**TENNEBOR**) born 1863 in Okliny, (Poland). Daughter of Johann Kausch and Karoline **Kremer**. Baptized at Wischainy Evangelical Lutheran Church. Married Georg **Tennebor**[997] (1862-1926) in 1883 at Wischainy Evangelical Lutheran Church. Immigrated February 1902 via New York aboard the S.S. *Southwark*. Died 19 Mar 1925. Interment at Lutheran Cemetery. For list of children, see husband Georg Tennebor.

KELLER

1501. Karoline **KELLER (DILL)** born 24 Dec 1899 in Folwark Sejny, (Poland). Daughter of Adolf Keller and Marianna **Neitzel**. Baptized at Seine Evangelical Lutheran Church. Married Johann **Dill**[1500] (1898-1977) 15 Jun 1924 at Kalwaria Evangelical Lutheran Church. Died 23 Jan 1993 in Eastlake, Ohio. Interment unknown. For list of children, see husband Johann Dill.

KEMERAIT / KEMMERAIT / KEMERAITIS

357. Adolf **KEMERAIT** born 17 Jan 1874 in Bukta. Son of Friedrich Kemerait and Christine **Kalweit**. Baptized and confirmed at Mariampol Evangelical Lutheran Church. Married Emilie **Tieslau**[363] (1880-1943) 25 Nov 1902 at Mariampol Evangelical Lutheran Church. Immigrated April 1903 via Philadelphia aboard the S.S. *Victoria*. Died 15 Mar 1938. Interment at Knollwood Cemetery, Mayfield Heights, Ohio.

    358.   i. Gustave Kemerait b. 8 Jun 1904. d. 27 Jun 1949. m. Philomena Marie **Bruckner** 1907-1993.
            4 children:
                Patricia 1932-
                Robert 1936-
                Edward Gustav 1929-2000
                Donald James 1936-1992

    359.   ii. Emma Kemerait b. 23 Nov 1906. d. 1 Jan 1999. m. James W. **Kaye** 1904-1973.
            2 children:
                Richard 1934-
                Janice 1936-

    360.   iii. Lillian Kemerait b. 28 Jun 1913. d. 17 Dec 1985. m. Theodore E. **Meyers** 1910-1975.
            2 children:
                Kurt T. 1942-
                Susan E. 1945-

    361.   iv. Edna Kemerait b. 20 Aug 1916. Twin of Elinor Kemereit.[362]

    362.   v. Elinor Kemereit b. 20 Aug 1916. Twin of Edna Kemerait.[361]

KIESLING / KIZLING

946. Hedwig „Hattie" **KIESLING** (**PERRY**) born 1893 in Alytus. Daughter of Adolf Kiesling (????-1895) and Bertha **Hartig**[944] (1868-1944). Baptized at Serey Reformed Lutheran Church. Married William C. **Perry**[1115] (1891-1973) 7 May 1913 in Cleveland by a Justice of the Peace. Died 12 Aug 1937. Interment at Lutheran Cemetery.

    948.   i. William Perry b. 24 Sep 1913. d. 13 May 2005. m. Frances Evelyn **O'Grady** 1923-2010.

    949.   ii. Robert Carl Perry Sr. b. 25 Jan 1919. d. 21 May 1995. m. Elizabeth Mary **Reardon** 1922-2004.
            2 children:
                Robert Jr. 1943-
                Thomas J. 1945-

    950.   iii. Thomas Donald Perry b. 22 Dec 1921. d. 17 Jan 2006. m. Dorothy J. **Sedej** 1926-2011.

    951.   iv. Dorothy Ruth Perry b. 27 Jan 1925. d. 12 Nov 2016. m. Jack Linn **Wise** 1924-2010.
            3 children:
                James L. 1949-

KINAT / KINAITIS / KENAT

371. Anna **KINAT** (**BURKE**) (**SCHULTZ**) born 1892 in Kybartai (Lazdijai district). Daughter of Karl Kinat and Anna **Reidel**. Baptized at Kalwaria Evangelical Lutheran Church. Immigrated June 1910 via New York aboard the S.S. *Bremen*. Married Karl Adolf **Burke**[375] (1888-1918) 25 December 1911 at Zion Evangelical Lutheran Church. Married Edward **Schultz** (1886-1959) 11 Oct 1919 at Zion Evangelical Lutheran Church. Died 4 Oct 1978. Interment at Lutheran Cemetery. For additional list of children, see husband Karl Adolf Burke.

    372.   v. Eduard Schultz Jr. b. 24 Aug 1920. d. 21 Jul 2000. m. Norma Berta **Wisgin**[985] 1921-2013.

    373.   vi. Erna Schultz b. 26 Sep 1921. d. 29 Jul 1997. m. Friedrich Gustav **Pretzloff** (*Pretzlav*) 1918-1998.
              5 children:
                    Gary 1945-
                    Deborah 1946-
                    Heather 1948-

    374.   vii. Herbert Schultz b. 25 May 1924. d. 9 Mar 2013. m. Mary D. **Obreza** 1924-2019.
              2 children:
                    Herbert Lynn Jr. 1951-2023
                    Connie

    375.   viii. Raymond O. Schultz b. 9 Dec 1929. d. 30 May 2017. m. Margaret Ann.
              2 children:
                    Eric
                    Charles

483. August „Augustis" **KINAT** (***KINAITIS***) born 23 Apr 1879 in Widugiery (Poland). Son of Franz Kinat (1860-????) and Auguste **Schmidt** (1856-1939). Baptized at Seine Evangelical Lutheran Church. Confirmed at Mariampol Evangelical Lutheran Church. Married Pauline **?** (1900-????). Immigrated November 1949 via New York aboard the U.S.S. *General Harry Taylor*. Died 3 Dec 1962. Interment at Lutheran Cemetery.

484. Ferdinand **KINAT** born 1866 in Widugiery (Poland). Son of Ludwig Kinat and Karoline **Herbst**. Baptized at Seine Evangelical Lutheran Church. Married Mathilde **Richter** (1871-1927) 23 Jul 1890 at Zion Evangelical Lutheran Church. Married Albine **Schultz** (1882-1970) 22 Aug 1914 at Zion Evangelical Lutheran Church. Died 18 Apr 1926. Interment at Woodland Cemetery.

485.   i. Ottilie Kinat b. 7 Jun 1891. d. 22 Apr 1965. m. Adam **Kless**[518] (1884-1968).
> 5 children:
>> Eugene 1913-2006
>> Malvern 1913-1980
>> Adeline 1920-1999
>> Elizabeth 1922-2008
>> Robert Charles 1929-2004

486.   ii. Elmer Kinat b. 1892. d. 29 Sep 1899.

487.   iii. Louis Alex Kinat b. 4 Jul 1894. d. 26 Feb 1924. m. Irene **Aukens** 1898-1957.
> 2 children:
>> Justine Irene 1917-2004
>> Richard Owen 1921-1982

488.   iv. Ruth M. Kinat b. 24 Jan 1896. d. 29 Dec 1947. m. Alfred Riley **Newkirk** 1891-????.
> 1 child:
>> Ruth Alice 1919-1995

489.   v. Esther Kinat b. 25 May 1897. d. 13 Sep 1983. m. Raymond **Garcia** Lopez 1895-1942. m. Nicholas C. **Korver** 1880-1926. m. Friedrich **Kless**[524] 1886-1964.
> 3 children:
>> Evelyon Olivia 1919-1977
>> Ester Gertrude 1922-2012
>> Nancy L. 1934-

490.   vi. Olivia L. Kinat b. 12 May 1899. d. 30 Sep 1975. m. Edward Carl **Wolf** 1892-1986.
> 2 children:
>> Elieen 1924-
>> Lucille 1927-

491.   vii. Kurt Kinat b. 26 Dec 1901. d. 28 May 1918.

492.   viii. Tabitha Kinat b. 15 Sep 1905. d. 2 Nov 1991. m. Paul Carl **Arndt** 1905-1985.
> 2 children:
>> Paul C 1932-
>> Dorothy 1934-2018

493. ix. Edith Lydia Kinat b. 21 Jan 1907. d. 17 Feb 1946. m. Harvey Christian **Weber** 1905-1987.
    1 child:
        Charles Harvey 1933-1976

494. x. Vera L. Kinat b. 16 Feb 1909. d. 30 Jan 1973. m. Ernest Jud **Hooker** 1904-1985.
    1 child:
        Sidney Roger 1929-2003

495. xi. Malvenia Kinat b. 29 Apr 1912. d. 16 Jun 1983. m. William Henry **Jarmush** 1910-????.
    2 children:
        Elaine 1930-2016
        Dolores 1934-

496. xii. Ralph Carl Kinat b. 2 May 1915. d. 10 Dec 1979. M. Martha **Sichau** 1918-????.
    1 child:
        Lindel R. 1945-

497. Adolf **KINAT** born 1864 in Widugiery (Poland). Son of Ludwig Kinat and Karoline **Herbst**. Baptized at Wischainy Evangelical Lutheran Church. Married Anna **Schmidt** (1859-1921) 1884 at Kalwaria Evangelical Lutheran Church. Died 1 Oct 1936. Interment in Woodland Cemetery.

498. i. Natalie "Nattie" "Hattie" Kinat b. 9 Dec 1885. d. 10 Jan 1955. m. Josef **Augustat** (1885-1908). m. Julius **Garchow** 1883-1924. m. Max J. **Bavernitz** 1877-1928. m. Joseph J. **Koubek** 1877-1963. m. ? **Beingesser**. m. Paul Lewis **Fischer** 1900-1972.
    2 children:
        Joseph Adolf Hugh 1908-1980
        Walter Julius 1920-1920

499. ii. Lillian Pauline Kinat b. 22 Dec 1889. d. 9 Jan 1963. m. Gustav A. **Nelson** 1884-1968.
    1 child:
        Howard J. 1909-????

500. iii. Anna Kinat b. 1 Jun 1892. d. 19 Nov 1979. m. Paul **Belling** 1879-1948.
    1 child:
        Kenneth Walther 1912-1997

501. iv. Harold Adelbert Kinat b. 27 Aug 1896. d. 12 Apr 1983. m. Elizbaeth Frances **Decker** 1905-1964.

502.   v. Walter Kinat b. 18 Dec 1898. d. 17 Jun 1966. m. Marie A. **Kos** 1900-1994.
>   1 child:
>> Wilbur Walter 1920-1999

674. Emilie **KINAT** (**KURBAN**) (*CORBAN*) born 1874 in Widugiery (Poland). Daughter of Georg Kinat and Auguste Justine **Paul** (1844-1922). Baptized at Seine Evangelical Lutheran Church. Married Gottlieb **Kurban** (1868-1925) 20 Jan 1892 at Zion Evangelical Lutheran Church. Died 25 Sep 1946. Interment at St. John Lutheran Cemetery.

    675.   i. Emma Emilie Corban b. 31 Jan 1893. d. 10 Aug 1893.

    676.   ii. Adolf Hermann Corban b. 22 Apr 1894. d. 25 Nov 1918.

    677.   iii. Frederick Arthur Corban b. 15 Feb 1897. d. 19 Feb 1950. m. Dorothea J. **Dunkel** 1896-1973.
>   1 child:
>> Roy Arthur 1928-1989

    678.   iv. George Corban b. 29 Jun 1899. d. 6 May 1971. m. Elsie **Reeve** 1906-1984.

    679.   v. John Clarence Corban b. 27 Aug 1904. d. 9 Jun 1961. m. Frances Alfretta **Bryan** 1906-1972.

    680.   vi. Helen Corban b. 30 Aug 1908. d. 17 Aug 2001. m. Frederick **Theuerkauf** 1907-1988.
>   1 child:
>> Wade F. 1946-

    681.   vii. Edwin F. Corban b. 17 Jul 1911. d. 26 May 1977,

    682.   viii. Herbert Raymond Corban b. 1 Oct 1913. d. 18 Aug 1976. m. Alma Virginia **Petshe** 1915-2001.
>   2 children:
>> Dennis J. 1944-
>> Ronald H. 1948-

683. Karoline **KINAT** (**HAUSRATH**) born 1870 in Widugiery (Poland). Daughter of George Kinat and Auguste Justine **Paul** (1844-1922). Baptized at Seine Evangelical Lutheran Church. Married Ferdinand **Hausrath**[673] (1865-1939) 4 Aug 1888 at Zion Evangelical Lutheran Church. Died 5 Apr 1931. Interment at St. John Lutheran Cemetery. For list of children, see husband Ferdinand Hausrath.

723. Marianna **KINAT** (**HEIN**) born 1881 in Widugiery (Poland). Daughter of Johann Kinat and Helene **Steinert**. Baptized at Seine Evangelical Lutheran Church. Married Adolf **Hein**[713] (1867-1935) 28 Dec 1907 at Zion Evangelical Lutheran Church. Died 1 Nov 1954. Interment at Lutheran Cemetery. For list of children, see husband Adolf Hein.

724. Emilie **KINAT** (**HESS**) born 1887 in Widugiery (Poland). Daughter of Johann Kinat and Helene **Steinert**. Baptized at Seine Evangelical Lutheran Church. Married Johann **Hess**[725] (1888-1976) in 1911 at Mariampol Evangelical Lutheran Church. Died 18 Jun 1939. Interment at Knollwood Cemetery, Mayfield Heights, Ohio. For list of children, see husband Johann Hess.

1076. Amelia „Millie" **KINAT** (**BURKE**) born 1893 in Kybartai (Lazdijai district). Daughter of Karl Kinat and Anna **Reidel**. Baptized at Kalwaria Evangelical Lutheran Church. Immigrated May 1912 via Baltimore aboard the S.S. *Rhein*. Married Karl Gustav **Burke**[1077] (1883-1967) 25 Dec 1912 at Zion Evangelical Lutheran Church. Died 2 Feb 1940. Interment at Lutheran Cemetery. For list of children, see husband Karl Gustav Burke.

1352. August **KINAT** born 22 Jun 1895 in Kauniškiai. Son of Karl Kinat and Anna **Reidel**. Baptized and confirmed at Seine Evangelical Lutheran Church. Immigrated July 1913 via Philadelphia on the S.S. *Frankfurt*. Married Justine **Klaus**[1353] (1889-1950) 29 Oct 1921 at Zion Evangelical Lutheran Church. Died 22 Sep 1955. Interment at Lutheran Cemetery.

1354. Eduard Karl **KINAT** (*KENAT*) born 1886 in Widugiery (Poland). Son of Karl Kinat and Anna **Reidel**. Baptized at Seine Evangelical Lutheran Church. Immigrated May1902 via Baltimore aboard the S.S. *Cassel*. Married Emma **Blase** (1888-1977) 24 Jul 1907 at Zion Evangelical Lutheran Church. Died 1957. Interment at Saint Paul Lutheran Cemetery in Westlake, Ohio.

    1355. i. Velma Kenat b. 8 Jun 1910. d. 14 Jun 1986. m. Friedrich **Bender** 1906-1990).
        1 child:
           Betty Jane 1933-

    1356. ii. Eleanor M. Kenat b. 21 Oct 1912. d. 2 Oct 2006. m. Joseph T. **Jurcak** 1904-1998.
        1 child:
           Joyce Norma 1941-2007

    1357. iii. Clarence Louis Kenat b. 9 Jun 1915. d. 3 Sep 1980. m. Mary **?** 1915-1983.
        2 children:
           Gayle M. 1947-

Marlene E. 1950-

1358. iv. Harold Kenat b. 11 Sep 1918. d. 31 Mar 1979.

1359. v. Norma Gertrude Kenat b. 20 Sep 1920. d. 11 Dec 2001. m. Edward J. **Miller** 1919-2010.

KIRSCHNER / KROSCHNEWSKI

32. Auguste **KIRSCHNER (NOVACK)** (*NOWIAK*) born about 1878 likely near Marijampolė. Daughter of August Kirschner (*Kroschnewski*) and Henriette **Mett**. Married Georg **Nowiak**[62] (*Novack*). Died 21 May 1936. Interment at Lutheran Cemetery.

    33.   i. Edward Novack b. 26 May 1903. d. 20 Oct 1964. m. Rose **Engle** 1907-1991.
            2 children:
                Joan 1945-
                Edward Jr. 1947-1947

    34.   ii. William Novack b. 18 Oct 1904. d. 9 Sep 1977. m. Wilma **Phelps** 1909-1983.
            1 child:
                Shirley Mae 1932-1977

    35.   iii. Emma "Emily" Novack b. 1905. d. 20 Dec 1986. m. George **Weymark**. m. Edward **Pachasa**.
            5 children:
                Robert D. 1938-2018
                Doris J. 1940-
                Nancy
                Donald
                Cheryl

    36.   iv. Bertha Anna Novack. b 19 Aug 1909. d. 5 May 1978. m. Herman W. **Schuster**.
            2 children:
                Richard H. 1937-
                Ruth A. 1942-

    37.   v. George Novack Jr. b. 6 Feb 1910. d. 21 Nov 1961.

    38.   vi. Olga Novack b. 6 Feb 1915. d. 29 May 1975. m. Anton **Schmidt** 1908-1987.
            2 children:
                Edward Anthony 1937-1997
                Linda M. 1948-

    39.   vii. Gustav Novack b. 21 Jul 1918. d. 6 Aug 2006. m. Mildred Lucille **Young** 1922-2005.
            2 children:
                Keith D.
                Kenneth B.

40. Pauline **KIRSCHNER** (*LEHMAN*) (**LEHMANN**) born about 1880 likely near Marijampolė. Daughter of August Kirschner (*Kroschnewski*) and Henriette **Mett**. Married Matthias **Lehmann**[82] 4 May 1907 at Zion Evangelical Lutheran Church. Divorced. Married John **Drangel** 25 Nov 1921 by Justice of the Peace. Died 25 Jan 1942. Interment at Lutheran Cemetery.

    41.   i. William Lehman b. 31 Mar 1909. d. 4 Feb 1985. m. Emily **Epler** 1909-1974.

    42.   ii. Edward J. Lehman b. 13 May 1910. d. 26 Nov 1948. m. Frances **Ewerth** 1915-????.
        2 children:
            Edward Jr 1935-2002
            Audrey Jane 1943-1983

43. Anna **KIRSCHNER (LANGMEYER)** born 23 Jun 1883 in Gudinė. Baptized at Mariampol Evangelical Lutheran Church. Daughter of August Kirschner ("**Kroschnewski**") and Henriette **Mett**. Married Johann **Langmeyer** 9 Dec 1906 at Zion Evangelical Lutheran Church. Died 6 Nov 1963. Interment at Lutheran Cemetery.

    44.   i. Emma Langmeyer b. ca. 1908. d. Nov 1969. m. Thomas W. **Schofield**.
        1 child:
            Thomas A. 1924-2004

    45.   ii. Anna Langmeyer b. 10 May 1909. d. 31 Mar 1961, m. William **Larsen** 1911-????.
        1 child:
            Joyce 1935-2006

    46.   iii. Olga "Sally" Pauline Langmeyer b. 3 Apr 1911. d. 1 Jan 2002. m. Harold M. **Dietrich** 1908-2003.
        2 children:
            Richard Melvin 1928-2006
            Sally Marlene 1934-2006

47. Jeanette Johanna **KIRSCHNER (SALEKER)** born 8 Sep 1888 in Gudinė. Baptized at Mariampol Evangelical Lutheran Church. Daughter of August Kirschner (*Kroschnewski*) and Henriette **Mett**. Immigrated Jun 1906 via Baltimore. Married Gustav Adolf **Saleker**[17] 10 Dec 1908 at Schifflein Christi Evangelical Lutheran Church. Died 14 Dec 1941. Interment at Lutheran Cemetery. For list of children, see husband Gustav Adolf Saleker.

48. Emilie **KIRSCHNER (WITLIB)** born 1 May 1891 in Gudinė. Baptized at Mariampol Evangelical Lutheran Church. Daughter of August Kirschner ("**Kroschnewski**") and Henriette **Mett**. Married Julius **Witlib** 1885-1958. Died 27 Nov 1940. Internment at Lutheran Cemetery.

    49.   i. Millie Witlib b. 12 Mar 1909. d. 19 May 1909.

    50   ii. Gustave Witlib b. 8 Apr 1910. d.????.

    51.   iii. Herman Witlib b. 21 Jun 1911. d. 11 Jul 1934.

    53.   iv. Edith Witlib b. 17 Jun 1913. d. 26 Mar 1935.

    54.   v. Jeanette Witlib b. 7 Oct 1914. d. 8 Oct 1931. m. Edward **Clayton.**

KLAUS

1353. Justine **KLAUS (KINAT)** born 20 Oct 1889 in Olginiai (no longer exists; near Vaitkabaliai). Daughter of Karl Klaus (????-1896) and Christine **Wanagas** (1858-1926). Baptized and confirmed at Wischainy Evangelical Lutheran Church. Married August **Kinat**[1352] (1895-1955) 29 Oct 1921 at Zion Evangelical Lutheran Church. Died 16 Jun 1950. Interment at Lutheran Cemetery.

KLESS / KLEES / KLÖS / KLOSS / KLASS

503. Marie **KLESS** (**RICHTER**) born 1873 in Bambiniai. Daughter of Friedrich Kless and Marie **Neubacher** (????-1920). Baptized at Wischainy Evangelical Lutheran Church. Married August **Reiter** (1871-1947) 1890 at Wischainy Evangelical Lutheran Church. Died 17 Aug 1962. Interment at Knollwood Cemetery, Mayfield Heights, Ohio. For list of children, see husband August Reiter.

507. Karoline "Lena" **KLESS** (*KENNATH*) (**KENAT**) born 6 Feb 1880 in Tupikai (near Aštriakalnis). Daughter of Friedrich Kless and Marie **Neubacher**. Baptized at Wischainy Evangelical Lutheran Church. Married Edward Adolf **Kennath** (1877-1958) 23 Nov 1904 at Zion Evangelical Lutheran Church. Died 23 Aug 1953. Interment at Lake View Cemetery.

    508.   i. Alvina Kennath b. 26 Aug 1905. d. 8 Jul 1993. m. Robert F. **Doughty** 1900-????.

    509.   ii. Ralph Edward Kennath b. 24 Mar 1907. d. 5 Jun 1975. m. Margaret Estella **Perkins** 1910-1996. m. Charlotte Mary **Beszpremi** 1908-1996.

    510.   iii. Gertrude Kennath b. 24 Oct 1914. d. 29 Jun 1991. m. William K. **Numan** 1905-1980.

    511.   iv. Harvey Edwin Kennath b. 27 Jan 1920. d. 30 Jun 1973. m. Wilma C. **Conway** 1925-1989.
        1 child:
           Tracy 1956-2016

512. Gustav **KLESS** born 1882 in Tupikai (near Aštriakalnis). Son of Friedrich Kless and Marie **Neubacher**. Baptized at Wischainy Evangelical Lutheran Church. Immigrated June 1901 via New York aboard the S.S. *Pennsylvania*. Married Wilhelmine "Minnie" **Karnowski** (1887-1956) 5 May 1906 at St. Paul's Evangelical Independent Church . Died 24 Aug 1958. Interment at Whitehaven Memorial Park in Mayfield, Ohio.

    513.   i. Arthur F. Kless b. 21 Oct 1907. d. 21 Apr 1998. m. Adele M. **Petraitis** 1911-2001.
        1 child:
           Artur 1939-

    514.   ii. Elmer Kless b. 13 Jan 1910. d. 6 Aug 1967. m. Eleanor **Spreitzer** 1915-2011.
        2 children:
           Eleanor 1944-

Elmer 1947-

515. iii. Mildred Dorothy Kless b. 15 Jun 1912. d. 18 Jul 2007. m. Walter John **Plesko** 1909-1983.
> 2 children:
> Richard 1946-
> Audrey 1948-

516. iv. Robert Kless b. 4 Apr 1920. d. 3 Dec 2012. m. Mildred A. **Conaway** 1921-2009. m. Shirley L **Pressly** 1933-.
> 3 children:
> Jack R. 1944-
> Diane L. 1946-
> Robert Jr.

517. Wilbert William Kless b. 4 Apr 1920. d. 29 Jan 2009. m. Margaret Eva **Jackson** 1922-2009.
> 3 children:
> Dennis O. 1944-
> Donald J. 1948-
> Debra A.

518. Adolf "Adam" **KLESS** born 1884 in Tupikai (near Aštriakalnis). Son of Friedrich Kless and Marie **Neubacher**. Baptized at Wischainy Evangelical Lutheran Church. Immigrated April 1903 via Baltimore. Married Ottilie **Kinat**[485] (1891-1965) 22 Jul 1911 at Christus Kirche Evangelical Lutheran Church. Died 5 Dec 1968. Interment at Crown Hill Cemetery and Mausoleum, Twinsburg, Ohio.

519. i. Eugene Kless b. 8 Mar 1915. d. 5 Feb 2006. m. Celeste **Falce** 1913-1999.
> 2 children:
> Cynthia 1942
> William D. 1944-

520. ii. Malvern Kless b. 22 May 1913. d. 19 May 1980. m. Josephine **Dugar** 1917-1984.
> 1 child:
> Laverne 1936-

521. iii. Adeline Kless b. 21 May 1920. d. 2 May 1999. m. Franklin J. **Bradley** 1913-????.
> 1 child:
> Lynn A.

522. iv. Elisabeth Kless b. 29 Dec 1922. d. 30 Jan 2008. m. Barry Vincent **Rhodes** 1923-1990.

    1 child:
      Robert Allen 1950-2005

523. v. Robert Charles Kless b. 10 Jan 1929. d. 3 Apr 2004. m. Marsha **?**.
    2 children:
      Adam
      Kurt

524. Friedrich **KLESS** born 1887 in Tupikai (near Aštriakalnis). Son of Friedrich Kless and Marie **Neubacher**. Baptized at Wischainy Evangelical Lutheran Church. Immigrated April 1909 via New York aboard the S.S. *Amerika*. Married Esther **Kinat**[489] (1897-1983) 31 Dec 1926 in Cleveland by a Justice of the Peace. Died 5 Jan 1964 in Geneva, Ohio. Interment in North Madison Cemetery, North Madison, Ohio.

  525. i. Nancy L. Kless b. 28 Mar 1934. m. John W. **Bennie** 1932-????. m. Blanton Kenneth **Perkins**.
    1 child:
      Patricia Lynne 1953-

667. Bertha **KLESS (SCHARFETTER)** born 1893 in Tupikiai (near Auštriakalnis). Daughter of Johann Kless and Auguste **Schiller**. Baptized at Wischainy Evangelical Lutheran Church. Married Friedrich **Scharfetter**[663] (1887-1984) 27 Jun 1914 at Bethlehem Evangelical Lutheran Church. Died 17 Feb 1956. Interment at Whitehaven Memorial Park, Mayfield, Ohio. For list of children, see husband Friedrich Scharfetter.

KLEIN

283. Mathilde "Tillie" **KLEIN** (**ESSEL**) born 27 Feb 1878 in Rudwaliszki (no longer exists; was near Liudvinavas). Daughter of Friedrich Klein and Karoline **Giersch**. Baptized and confirmed at Mariampol Lutheran Church. Married Eduard **Essel**[279] (1877-1919) 7 Jul 1901 at St. Paul's Evangelical Lutheran Church. Married Josef **Perrey** (1866-1941) 5 Sep 1922 at St. Paul's Evangelical Lutheran Church. Died 20 Mar 1979 (aged 101). Interment at Lutheran Cemetery. For list of children, see husband Eduard Essel.

KLOTZHOBER / GLOTZOBER

380. Matthias Martin **KLOTZOBER** born 20 Oct 1887 in Kregždžiai. Son of Johann Klotzober and Anna **Kremer**. Baptized and confirmed at Wischtiten Evangelical Lutheran Church. Immigrated April 1905 via Baltimore aboard the S.S. *Brandenburg*. Married Bertha **Günther**[386] (1887-1916) 17 Oct 1908 at Zion Evangelical Lutheran Church. Married Fanny **Jutoff** (sp?) 1887-1923. Died 10 Jan 1958 in Detroit, Michigan. Interment unknown.

    381.   i. Emma Klotzober b. 8 Aug 1909. d. 15 Sep 1909.

    382.   ii. Marjorie Martha Klotzober b. 14 Jul 1910. d. 3 Oct 1976. m. William A. **Martin** 1905-1974.

    383.   iii. Albert August Klotzober b. 14 May 1912. d. 17 Nov 1987. m. Dorothy L. **Rassler** 1913-1983. m. Anna Sylvia **Grigas** 1910-2004. m. Edith May **Rupert** 1918-????.

    384.   iv. Florence Wanda Klotzober b. 15 Mar 1916. d. 24 Jun 1997. m. Calvin C. **York** 1912-1956. m. Andrew J. **Dziob** 1916-1984.
        2 children:
            David F. 1936-1994
            Barbara Ann 1938-2007

    385.   v. Arthur Klotzober b. 15 Nov 1918. d. 10 Dec 1977. m. Ethel Flora **Schultz** 1919-1984.

    386.   vi. Infant Klotzober b. 10 Sep 1923. d. 12 Sep 1923.

1361. Helene **KLOTZHOBER (DOCZKIS)** born 30 Mar 1887 in Lankupėnai. Daughter of Josef Klotzhober and Catherine **Neff**. Baptized and confirmed at Wischtiten Evangelical Lutheran Church. Married Georg **Doczkis**[1360] (1886-1954) likely in Pennsylvania. Died 6 Feb 1934. Interment at Lutheran Cemetery. For list of children, see husband Georg Doczkis.

1365. Bertha **KLOTZHOBER (DOCZKAT)** born 18 Nov 1883 in Lankupėnai. Daughter of Josef Klotzhober and Catherine **Neff**. Baptized and confirmed at Wischtiten Evangelical Lutheran Church. Married Johann **Doczkat**[96] (1883-1953) 30 Sep 1903 at First St. Paul's Evangelical Lutheran Church, Pittsburgh, Pennsylvania. Died 6 Nov 1965. Interment at Knollwood Cemetery, Mayfield Heights, Ohio. For list of children, see husband Johann Doczkat.

KOKOSCHKA / KOKOSKY / KOKOSKI

364. Friedrich **KOKOSCHKA** born 28 Mar 1894 in Měčiūnai. Son of Gustav Heinrich Kokoschka (1849-1945) and Marianna **Duchowski** (1860-1893.) Baptized at Serey Lutheran Reformed Church. Immigrated October 1910 via New York aboard the S.S. *Potsdam*. Married Anna **Schnell**[368] (1894-1922) 19 Apr 1913 at Zion Evangelical Lutheran Church. Married Albina **Lang** (1891-1981) 16 Jan 1926 at Zion Evangelical Lutheran Church. Died 27 Feb 1962 in Lyndhurst, Ohio. Interment at Lutheran Cemetery.

    365.   i. Helene Anna Kokoschka b. 19 Mar 1914. d. 28 May 1996. m. Albert **Hillenbrand** 1916-1976.
        3 children:
            Albert 1938-
            Carl 1942-
            Mary Ann 1944-

    366.   ii. Lydia Kokoschka b. 21 Feb 1916. d. 27 Aug 1998. m. William **Haase** 1910-1973.
        5 children:
            William F. 1935-
            Lynda Lee 1937-2020
            David 1942-
            Lindsey C 1945-
            Carl 1948

    367.   iii. Edwin Frederick Kokoschka b. 3 Mar 1928. d. 10 Sep 2006. m. Helen Marion **Ibos** 1928-2004.
        4 children:
            Susan
            Edwin Jr.
            Frederick
            Edwina

KONRAD / CONRAD

588. Ludwig "Louis" **KONRAD** (***CONRAD***) born 30 Mar 1874 in Degučiai. Son of Johann Julian Konrad and Justine **Albat** (**Urbat**). Baptized and confirmed at Mariampol Evangelical Lutheran Church. Immigrated June 1895 via New York aboard the S.S. *Weser*. Married Christine **Jurgeleit**[596] (1875-1949) 14 May 1898 at German Evangelical Lutheran Church in McKeesport, Pennsylvania. Died 9 Aug 1956. Interment at Lutheran Cemetery.

    589.   i. Emma E. Conrad b. 9 Feb 1899. d. 7 Oct 1980. m. William Oscar **Perry**[411] 1894-1978.
        2 children:
            Evelyn Wilhelmina 1916-2000
            Dorothy C. 1920-2013

    590.   ii. Louis Christ Conrad b. 8 Jul 1902. d. 29 Mar 1999. m. Anna **Philipps** 1903-1994.
        1 child:
            Ruth 1923-

    591.   iii. Gustave Michael Conrad b. 5 Jan 1905. d. 22 Sep 1980. m. Pauline Elsa **Reily** 1915-1982.
        2 children:
            Cheryl L. 1940-
            Wendy 1946-

    592.   iv. Herman Gustave Conrad b. 29 Mar 1907. d. 1999. m. Wanda M. **Weber** 1916-1954.
        1 child:
            James A. 1949-

    593.   v. Helen M. Conrad b. 3 Nov 1909. d. 3 May 1911.

    594.   vi. Theodore Conrad b. 27 Feb 1912. d. 9 Apr 1987.

    595.   vii. Walter Leo Conrad b. 31 Jan 1915. d. 25 Feb 1993.

707. Amalie **KONRAD** (**HAASE**) born 1868 in Degučiai. Daughter of Johann Julian Konrad and Justine **Albat** (**Urbat**.) Baptized and confirmed at Mariampol Evangelical Lutheran Church. Married August **Haase**[697] (1869-1946) 1888 at Kalwaria Evangelical Lutheran Church. Immigrated June 1895 via New York aboard the S.S. *Normannia*. Died 2 Mar 1943. Interment at Lutheran Cemetery. For list of children, see husband August Haase.

KRAMER / KRÄMER

1105. Ludwig "Louis" Friedrich **KRAMER** born 1884 in Polesie (near Pagiriai). Son of August Kramer and Henriette **Pritzkat**. Baptized at Goddlau Evangelical Lutheran Church. Immigrated June 1898 via New York aboard the S.S. *Bismarck*. Married Anna **Perry**[1104] (1888-1946). Died 17 Jul 1966. Interment at Lutheran Cemetery.

    1106. i. Walter Adolf Kramer b. 2 Feb 1908. d. 5 Jul 1987. m. Ella Margret **Rankin** 1930-2002.
> 4 children:
> Shirley Mae 1930-1992
> Jane 1933-
> Phyllis Gail 1934-2014
> Linda 1947-2018

    1107. ii. Doris Ann Kramer b. 1912. d. 1966.

    1108. iii. Ruth Kramer b. 27 Feb 1910. d. 15 May 1975. m. Harry James **Hendron** 1910-1983.

    1109. iv. Marian C. Kramer b. 1916. d. ????. m. Jack S. **Curtiss** 1916-1985.
> 3 children:
> Jack Jr. 1938-
> Jill A. 1940-
> James L. 1942-

    1110. v. Richard Louis Kramer b. 7 Jan 1922. d. 16 May 1998. m. Rita Ann **Koch** 1921-1992.
> 3 children:
> Kathleen A. 1945-
> Richard Jr. 1948-
> Mary E. 1950-

    1111. vi. Kenneth C. Kramer b. 27 May 1924. d. 19 Jan 1973. m. Lois J. **Dillenbeck** 1924-2001.
> 1 child.
> Karen A. 1947-

    1112. vii. Harriet Kramer b. 23 Apr 1926. d. 14 Sep 2006. m. Arthur R. **May** 1919-2003.
> 3 children:
> Susan
> John
> Bonnie

    1113. viii. David Arthur Kramer b. 24 Jun 1933. d. 11 Sep 2010.

LACKNER / LACHNER / LOCKNER

387. Bertha **LACKNER** (**WELZ**) born 27 Jan 1886 in Skardupiai. Daughter of Josef Lackner and Wilhelmine **Hubert**. Baptized and confirmed at the Wischtiten Evangelical Lutheran Church. Immigrated September 1906 via New York aboard the S.S. *Hamburg*. Married Georg **Welz** (1883-1943) 26 Dec 1908 at Zion Evangelical Lutheran Church. Died 13 May 1965. Interment at Knollwood Cemetery, Mayfield Heights, Ohio.

    388.   i. Norma Welz b. 7 Nov 1910. d. 23 Dec 1992. m. Vernon C. **James** II 1916-2013.
        3 children:
            Vernon C. III 1942-
            Rolland T. 1945-

    389.   ii. Arthur Erich Welz b. 17 Mar 1912. d. 26 Dec 1987. m. Virginia **Brown** ????-1968.

    390.   iii. Harold Leonard Welz b. 12 Oct 1918. d. 1 Aug 1998. m. Laura May **Baker** 1917-2007.

391. Georg **LACKNER** (*LOCKNER*) born 30 Sep 1884 in Skardupiai. Son of Josef Lackner and Wilhelmine **Hubert**. Baptized and confirmed at the Wischtiten Evangelical Lutheran Church. Immigrated May 1905 via New York aboard the S.S. *Graf Waldersee*. Married Anna **Neubacher** (1887-1947) 16 Apr 1911 at St. Paul's Evangelical Lutheran Church. Married Frances J. **Dahlke** (1895-1981) 18 Jul 1950 in Stark County, Ohio. Died 23 Feb 1959 in Clearwater Beach, Florida. Interment unknown.

    392.   i. Norma Lockner b. 11 Nov 1912. d. 14 Aug 1992. m. Harry Wendell **Bestgen** 1911-2005.
        1 child:
            Janis K. 1948-

    393.   ii. Mildred Lockner b. 21 Jul 1916. d. 22 Jun 1998. m. **Hoffman**.

LANG / LANGE

368. Albine **LANG** (**SCHWELGIN**) (**KOKOSCHKA**) born 15 Nov 1891 in Pažėlsviai. Daughter of Karl Leopold Lang and Bertha **Lukat**. Baptized and confirmed at Mariampol Evangelical Lutheran Church. Married Adolf **Schwelgin**[369] (1891-1948) 22 Aug 1914 at St. Paul's Evangelical Lutheran Church. Divorced 1925. Married Friedrich **Kokoschka**[364] (1894-1962) 16 Jan 1926 at Zion Evangelical Lutheran Church. Died 20 Mar 1981 in Tiffin, Ohio. Interment at Lutheran Cemetery. For list of children, see husbands Adolf Schwelgin and Friedrich Kokoschka.

395. Ludwig "Louis" **LANG** born 16 Nov 1875 in Bambiniai. Son of Julius Lang and Karoline **Schnell**. Baptized and confirmed at Mariampol Evangelical Lutheran Church. Immigrated September 1906 via Baltimore aboard S.S. *Rhein*. Married Berta **Jurgelewitz**[397] (1893-1962) 31 May 1913 at St. Paul's Evangelical Lutheran Church. Died 24 Feb 1962. Interment at Crown Hill Cemetery in Twinsburg, Ohio.

    396.   i. Emma Lang b. 5 Mar 1914. d. 5 Mar 2004. m. William Julius **Schwed** 1912-1988.
              1 child:
                  Donald 1937-2009

817. Adeline "Nellie" **LANG** (**LUKAT**) born 24 Jan 1891 in Randiškė. Daughter of Gustav Lang and Pauline **Duchowski**. Baptized at Serey Reformed Lutheran Church. Married Eduard **Lukat**[814] (1884-1918) 21 Nov 1909 at Zion Evangelical Lutheran Church. Married Eduard's brother Gustav **Lukat**[813] (1871-1953) 7 Feb 1920 at Third Reformed Lutheran Church. Died 10 Mar 1954. Interment at Lutheran Cemetery. For list of children, see husband Eduard Lukat.

926. Karl **LANG** born 1895 in Trakėnai. Son of Karl Lang and Bertha **Lukat**. Baptized and confirmed at Kalwaria Evangelical Lutheran Church. Immigrated April 1913 via Philadelphia aboard the S.S. *Breslau*. Married Bertha **Gerulat**[930] (1894-1989) 26 Jan 1920 at Zion Evangelical Lutheran Church. Died 7 Mar 1971. Interment at Lutheran Cemetery.

    927.   i. Irvin Carl Lang b. 26 Apr 1925. d. 9 Aug 1985. m. Esther L. **Davis** 1924-????.
              2 children:
              Richard
              Laura 1956-2000

    928.   ii. Alma Edna Lang b. 1930. d. Apr 2022. m. Ray C. **Miller** ????-????.
              2 children:

>Ray
>Glenn

929. iii. Lillian Ruth Lang b. 4 Sep 1933. d. 3 Oct 2018. m. David **Brueggemann** 1930-2017.
>2 children:

1278. Ferdinand **LANG** born 28 Mar 1878 in Bambininkai. Son of Julian Lang and Karoline **Schnell**. Baptized and confirmed at Mariampol Evangelical Lutheran Church. Married Emma **Jurgelewitz**[1279] (1887-1959) in 1906 at Mariampol Evangelical Lutheran Church. Immigrated June 1910 via New York aboard the S.S. *Bremen*. Died 21 Aug 1960 in Ashtabula, Ohio. Interment at Crown Hill Cemetery and Mausoleum, Twinsburg, Ohio.

> 1280. i. Waler Lang b. 10 Nov 1911. d. 9 Jan 1987. m. Dorothy **Miller** 1911-????. m. Julia **Yasko** 1917-1972.
>> 1 child:
>>> Kenneth 1939-

> 1281. ii. Alfred Lang b. 9 Aug 1913. d. 27 Oct 1966. m. Sophia **?** ????-????.
>> 2 children:
>>> Marline Janet 1936-
>>> Danny Mitchell 1946-

> 1282. iii. William Lang b. 10 May 1919. d. 15 Apr 1997.

> 1283. iv. Harold Ferdinand Lang b. 1 Jan 1921. d. 29 Apr 2007. m. Jean Mavis **Sainsbury** 1925-2013.
>> 1 child:
>>> Alan 1948-

> 1284. v. Erwin Earl Lang b. 11 Jun 1923. d. 15 Dec 2010. m. Ellen Jane **Poponak** 1928-2023.
>> 2 children:
>>> Lynn
>>> Jackie

1380. Auguste **LANG (NEUMANN)** born 1874 in Bukta. Daughter of August Lang and Anna **Kesslau**. Baptized and confirmed at Kalwaria Evangelical Lutheran Church. Married Karl Adolf **Neumann**[1379] (1866-1953) 24 Jun 1894 at Zion Evangelical Lutheran Church. Died 3 Feb 1960 in Maple Heights, Ohio. Interment at Knollwood Cemetery, Mayfield Heights, Ohio. For list of children, see husband Karl Adolf Neumann.

1384. Heinrich Robert Karl **LANGE** born 26 Oct 1874 in Bukta. Son of August Lange and Anna **Kesslau**. Baptized and confirmed at Mariampol Evangelical Lutheran Church. Married Louise **Schieman** (1881-1960) 6 Aug 1901 at St. Paul's Evangelical Lutheran Church. Died 8 Nov 1925. Interment at Knollwood Cemetery, Mayfield Heights, Ohio.

> 1385. i. Carl "Charles" Lange b. 29 Jun 1902. d. 1962. m. Esther A. **Fink** 1903-????.
> > 1 child:
> > > Henry 1925-1984
>
> 1386. ii. Hannah Elisabeth Lange b. 2 Nov 1903. d. 10 Apr 1996. m. Ewald **Heinrich**[1399] 1901-1957.
> > 4 children:
> > > Lois Ann 1923-2004
> > > Elaine Doris 1927-1931
> > > Charles Edwin 1932-2022
> > > Judith 1939-
>
> 1387. iii. Ella Louise Lang b. 30 Sep 1906. d. 29 Feb 2012. m. Lawrence Elmer **Hobbs** 1902-1985.
> > 2 children:
> > > Eileen L. 1928-2009
> > > Roy J. 1944-1986

1388. Albert **LANG** born 23 Nov 1871 in Bukta. Son of August Lange and Anna **Kesslau**. Baptized and confirmed at Mariampol Evangelical Lutheran Church. Married Wilhelmine **Metzdorf**[1389] (1878-1916) 26 Sep 1894 at Zion Evangelical Lutheran Church. Married Antonette H. **Templin** (1881-1945) 18 Oct 1917 at Lakewood Presbyterian Church in Lakewood, Ohio. Died 22 Dec 1945. Interment at Knollwood Cemetery, Mayfield Heights, Ohio.

> 1390. i. Albert F. Lang b. 24 Jan 1895. d. 28 Feb 1895.
>
> 1391. ii. Ida Lang b. 20 Feb 1896. d. 27 Jun 1976. m. August Oskar **Berwing**[252] 1891-1946.
> > 3 children:
> > > Dorothy Ida[260] 1915-1992
> > > Robert A.[261] 1917-1970
> > > Pauline J.[262] 1933-2017
>
> 1392. iii. Edward A. Lang b. 22 Nov 1898. d. 8 Jan 1948.
>
> 1393. iv. Emma Martha Lang b. 2 May 1903. d. 24 Mar 1989. m. Christian H. **Smith** 1902-1968.

2 children:
> Elaine 1925-
> Norman 1930-2012

1394. v. Ella Amelia Lang b. 20 Nov 1905. d. Mar 1980. m. Elmer Peter Leonard **Peterson** 1897-1978.
> 2 children:
>> Phyllis Anna 1921-1998
>> Shirley Anna 1939-2004

1395. vi. Arthur Carl Heinrich Lang b. 16 Jan 1905. d. 30 Jan 1973. m. Elsie **Schanz** 1900-1993.
> 1 child:
>> Katherine 1940-

1396. vii. Albert Leroy Lang b. 15 Feb 1920. d. 20 Apr 1920.

1450. Gustav Ludwig "August" **LANG** born around 1861 in Metelytė. Son of Julius Lang and Karoline **Schnell**. Baptized and confirmed at Mariampol Evangelical Lutheran Church. Married Pauline **Dukowski**[1451] (1862-1938) 1886 at Serey Reformed Lutheran Church. Died 30 Dec 1948 North Olmsted, Ohio. Interment at Lutheran Cemetery.

1451. i. Emilie Lang b. 1887. d. bef. 1889.

1452. ii. Amelia Lang b. 1889. d. 11 Jun 1916. m. Johann **Pohl** 1876-1942.
> 2 children:
>> Amelia "Millie"[1457] 1909-????
>> Helen[1458] 1913-1975

817. iii. Adeline "Nellie" Lang[817] b. 24 Jan 1891. d. 10 Mar 1954. m. Gustav **Lukat**[814] 1871-1953.
> 2 children:
>> Artur Eduard[815] 1914-1961
>> Harold Leonard[816] 1917-1970

1453. iii. Adolf Lang b. 1894. d. 1894.

1454. iv. Helene Lang b. 1895. d. 1977. m. August **Günther**[622] 1890-1926. m. Leroy Lovden **Barton** 1897-1958.
> 3 children:
>> Howard Walter[623] 1915-1918
>> Leonard Earl[624] 1917-2010
>> Raymond Arthur[625] 1920-1988

1455. Adolf Eduard Lang b. 17 Sep 1899. d. 11 Sep 1951. m. Lenora **Conrad** 1902-1968.
> 1 child:
>> Ruth 1921-2011

1452. Amelia **LANG (POHL)** born 1889 in Randiškė. Daughter of Gustav Ludwig "August" Lang[1450] (1861-1948) and Pauline **Dukowski**[1451] (1862-1938). Baptized at Serey Reformed Lutheran Church. Immigrated Oct 1904 via Philadelphia aboard the S.S. *Haverford*. Married Johann **Pohl**[1456] (1876-1942) 3 Jan 1907 at Zion Evangelical Lutheran Church. Died 11 Jun 1916. Interment at Lutheran Cemetery. For list of children, see husband Johann Pohl.

1455. Adolf Eduard **LANG** born 17 Sep 1899 in Randiškė. Son of Gustav Ludwig „August" Lang[1450] (1861-1948) and Pauline **Dukowski**[1451] (1862-1938). Baptized at Serey Reformed Lutheran Church. Immigrated Oct 1904 via Philadelphia aboard the S.S. *Haverford*. Married Lenora May **Conrad** (1902-1968) 12 Apr 1920 in East Cleveland, Ohio, by a Justice of the Peace. Died 11 Sep 1951. Interment at Hillcrest Cemetery, Bedford Heights, Ohio.

> 1460. i. Ruth Lang b. 23 Feb 1921. d. 10 May 2011. m. Stanley **Sherwin** 1914-????.
>> 5 children:
>>> Mary
>>> Kathy
>>> Mona
>>> Christian
>>> Nina

LAUKS

1091. Marie **LAUKS (GLEICHFORSCH)** born 1904 in Ramanavas. Daughter of Julius Luaks and Karoline **Telgas**. Baptized at Mariampol Evangelical Lutheran Church. Married Adolf **Gleichforsch**[1090] (1896-1968) 26 Dec 1924 at Mariampol Evangelical Lutheran Church. Immigrated April 1955 via Pan American Airways. Died 29 Sep 1972. Interment at Lake View Cemetery. For list of children, see husband Adolf Gleichforsch.

LEHMANN

82. Mathias **LEHMANN** born 20 Nov 1886 likely near Marijampolė. Son of Matthias Lehmann and Anna **Kruopkat**. Possibly the same person as Julius Lehmann[84]. Married Pauline **Kirschner (Kroschnewski)**[40] (1881-1942) 4 May 1907 at Zion Evangelical Lutheran Church. Divorced 1919. Married Auguste **Hirsch**[957] (1891-1985) 14 Jan 1922 at Zion Evangelical Lutheran Church. Died 28 Dec 1942. Interment at Lutheran Cemetery. For list of children with Pauline Kirschner[40] see her listing.

    83.   i. Eleanor Augusta Lehman b. 28 Oct 1922. d. 13 Dec 2005. m. Donald Edward **Affeldt** 1920-1915. m. Russell **Affeldt**; **Bortz. M.** Robert F. **Howell** 1916-1977. m. William H. **McDowell** 1928-1994.

84. Julius **LEHMANN** born 1887 in Gižai. Son of Matthias Lehmann and Anna Kruopkat. Baptized at Mariampol Evangelical Lutheran Church. Possibly the same person as Mathias Lehmann[82.]

85. Anna **LEHMANN (KAIRAT)** born 1890 in Gižai. Daughter of Matthias Lehmann and Anna **Kruopkat**. Baptized at Mariampol Evangelical Lutheran Church. Immigrated Nov 1907 via Baltimore aboard S. S. *Breslau*. Married Christof "Christ" **Kairat** 5 May 1919 at Zion Evangelical Lutheran Church. Died 28 Aug 1969. Interment at Lutheran Cemetery.

    86.   i. Lillian Ann Kairait b. 1922 d. 21 May 1942.

87. Emilie **LEHMANN (SCHWED)** born 1893 in Rūda. Daughter of Matthias Lehmann and Anna **Kruopkat**. Baptized at Mariampol Evangelical Lutheran Church. Married Heinrich **Schwed** (1889-1942) 18 Feb 1912 at Zion Evangelical Lutheran Church. Died 25 Dec 1960. Interment at Lutheran Cemetery.

    88.   i. William Julius Schwed b. 1 Dec 1912. d. 21 Apr 1988. m. Emma **Lang** 1914-2004. m. Helen **Roll** 1918-1995.
           1 child:
                Donald 1937-2009

    89.   ii. Emma Schwed b. 22 Jun 1914. d. 24 Jun 1914.

    90.   iii. Lydia Amelia Schwed b. 23 Sep 1915. d. 23 Jun 1994. m. Wilber A. **Beal**.
           1 child:
                Janice

91. Emma **LEHMANN (KALWEIT)** born 1896 in Rūda. Daughter of Matthias Lehmann and Anna **Kruopkat**. Baptized at Mariampol Evangelical Lutheran Church. Married Karl "Charles" **Kalweit** (1890-1979) 5 Sep 1915 at Zion Evangelical Lutheran Church. Died 24 Oct 1918. Interment at Lutheran Cemetery.

    92.   i. Helen E. Kalweit b. 22 Jun 1916. d. 16 Oct 1997. m. Heber James **Litt**le 1911-1981. 1 child: Joan Carol 1938-1950.

93. Luise "Elizabeth" **LEHMANN (SCHWED)** born 1898 in Rūda. Daughter of Matthias Lehmann and Anna Kruopkat. Baptized at Mariampol Evangelical Lutheran Church. Immigrated Sept 1913 via New York aboard S.S. *Großer Kurfurst*. Married Julius **Schwed** (1896-1966) 27 Oct 1917 at Zion Evangelical Lutheran Church. Died 2 Apr 1982 in Brunswick, Ohio. Interment at Lutheran Cemetery.

    94.   i. Alma L. Schwed b. 6 Jul 1918. d. 6 Jun 2008. m. John Walter **Dutchcot**[101] 1913-2006.
          1 child:
                Judy A 1947-

    95.   ii. Arthur W Schwed b. 1920. d. 10 Feb 1964. m. Irene E. 1921-1988.

1304. Bernhardt **LEHMANN** born 1889 in Gulbiniškiai. Son of Wilhelm Lehmann and Karoline **Blum**. Baptized and confirmed at Mariampol Evangelical Lutheran Church. Immigrated September 1910 via New York aboard the S.S. *Kaiser Wilhelm II*. Married Ernestine **Romanowski**[1305] (1898-1959) 2 Oct 1915 at St. Paul's Evangelical Lutheran Church. Died 12 Dec 1954. Interment at Knollwood Cemetery, Mayfield Heights, Ohio.

    1306.   i. Erna Lydia Lehman b. 23 Nov 1916. d. 24 Aug 2003. m. Glenn M. **Gahan** 1909-????.

LEICHERT

788. Magdalene Helene **LEICHERT** (**BALTRUNAT**) born about 1872 likely in Patilčiai. Daughter of Johann Leichert and Henriette Hedwig **Reder**. Likely baptized at Mariampol Evangelical Lutheran Church. Married Karl **Baltrunat**[779] (1871-1943) 1896 at Mariampol Evangelical Lutheran Church. Immigrated November 1902 via Baltimore aboard the S.S. *Neckar*. Died 24 Oct 1941. Interment at Lutheran Cemetery. For list of children, see husband Karl Baltrunat.

789. Christine **LEICHERT** (**NEITZEL**) born 1874 in Patilčiai. Daughter of Johann Leichert and Henriette Hedwig **Reder**. Baptized at Kalwaria Evangelical Lutheran Church. Married Ferdinand Karl **Neitzel**[790] (1878-1955) 7 Apr 1901 at Zion Evangelical Lutheran Church. Died 5 Apr 1950. Interment at Lutheran Cemetery. For list of children, see husband Ferdinand Karl Neitzel.

LIER / LEAR

742. August **LIER (LEAR)** born 14 Jun 1869 in Virbalis. Son of Friedrich Lier and Anna **Reichenberger**. Baptized at Wirballen Evangelical Lutheran Church. Name of first wife, date of marriage, and place unknown. Immigrated March 1896 via New York aboard the S.S. *Stuttgart*. Married Amelia **Hein**[741] (1877-1948) 18 Aug 1898 at German Reformed Church in Plymouth, Pennsylvania. Died 23 Mar 1939. Interment at Hillcrest Cemetery, Bedford Heights, Ohio.

 743. i. Anna Lear b. 13 May 1899. d. 23 Dec 1983. m. Max **Doinwick** 1899-1987.

 744. ii. Amelia "Mildred" Lear b. 26 Dec 1900. d. 16 Apr 1980.

 745. iii. Bertha Lear b. 10 Dec 1902. d. 27 Dec 1907.

 746. iv. Frederick Adolph Lear b. 26 Dec 1904. d. 26 Sep 1970. First wife unknown. m. Anne **Smith** 1916-1981. m. Ann G. **Pevens** 1897-????.

 747. v. Emil Leopold Lear b. 19 Jan 1907. d. 1 Jul 1955. m. Adeline **Isetts Jensen** 1895-1962.

 748. vi. John Albert Lear b. 17 Feb 1909. d. 12 Jun 1988. m. Margaret Ellen **Hoge** 1904-1974.
   4 children:
    Marlene Edna 1932-2015
    Shirley Jean 1933-2012
    Phyllis M. 1935-
    Beverly A. 1939-

 749. vii. Edna Lear b. 7 Jul 1911. d. 21 Mar 1989. m. Louis W. **Medved** 1909-1991.
   2 children:
    Richard Louis 1939-2000
    Louis 1942-

 750. viii. Lillian Lear b. 1914. d. 1972. m. Dillard G. **Bowles** 1904-1956. m. Vincent **Reo**.

 751. ix. Herman Karl Lear b. 2 Apr 1916. d. 11 Apr 1986. m. Pauline F. **Hudnall** 1917-1959. m. Julia **Krusec** 1919-1958.
   1 child:
    Deborah Lynn 1951-1985

752. x. Lucille Ruth Lear b. 3 Oct 1917. d. 14 May 2002. m. Frank Philip **Grimshaw** 1915-1980.

753. xi. Dorothy Mariam Lear b. 3 Dec 1921. d. 24 Dec 2000. m. Paul Henry **Sanner** 1912-1979.
    2 children:
        Jeffrey 1947-2002
        Jill Cheryl 1948-

754. xii. Florence Loretta Lear b. 13 Sep 1923. d. 8 Jan 2001. m. Albert James **Adams** 1918-1979.

LINDHAMMER

863. Henriette **LINDHAMMER (TETMEIER)** born 21 Oct 1853 in Liukiai. Daughter of Friedrich Lindhammer and Anna **Schestokat**. Baptized and confirmed at Wischtiten Evangelical Lutheran Church. Married Ferdinand Christof **Tetmeier**[848] (1857-1935) 1877 at Wischtiten Evangelical Lutheran Church. Died 18 Jul 1935. Interment at Lutheran Cemetery. For list of children, see husband Ferdinand Christof Tetmeier.

LOGIES

343. Karl Franz **LOGIES** born 1887 in Mickai. Son of Gustav Logies and Marie **Rebner**. Baptized at Schaken Evangelical Lutheran Church. Immigrated June 1907 via Baltimore aboard the S.S. *Rhein*. Married Auguste **Gudat** (1880-1918) 10 Sep 1910 Third Reformed Lutheran Church. Married Ottilie **Kaptein**[342] (1895-1983) 14 Feb 1919 at Zion Evangelical Lutheran Church. Died 23 Nov 1975. Interment at Lutheran Cemetery.

    344.   i. Ruth Logies b. 5 Oct 1916. d. 17 Dec 1999. m. Carl **Delemater** 1910-1961.
        3 children:
            Carole Ruth 1939-
            Kenneth C 1943-1997

    345.   ii. Raymond Logies b. 28 Jan 1924. d. 23 Dec 2017. m. Joan Rose **Pishnery** 1929-2002.
        4 children:
            Mark 1953-
            Matthew 1958-2010
            Martin 1960-
            Thomas 1963-

    346.   iii. Leona Ottilie Logies b. 1 Oct 1927. d. 18 Oct 2006. m. Joseph Ernest **Konery** 1927-2007.
        5 children:
            Joseph 1953-
            Robert 1955-
            Patricia 1958
            Barbara 1961-
            John 1968-

354. Gustav **LOGIES** born around 1883 likely in Mickai. Son of Gustav Logies and Marie **Rebner**. Likely baptized at Schaken Evangelical Lutheran Church. Immigrated April 1913 via New York. Married Auguste **Puschkat** (1889-1981) 27 Oct 1906 at Third Reformed Lutheran Church. Died 22 Oct 1939. Interment at Knollwood Cemetery, Mayfield Heights, Ohio.

    355.   i. Adelia Logies b. 20 Jan 1908. d. 14 Sep 1988. m. Eric **Muehl** 1905-1986.
        4 children:
            Robert 1931-
            Marilyn 1936-
            Karen Marie 1941-2005
            Diana 1946-

356. ii. Ruth Logies b. 3 Sep 1912. d. 4 Feb 1946.

LUKAT

408. Leopoldine "Tina" **LUKAT (PETERS)** born 1 Nov 1881 in Balaikai. Daughter of Adolf Lukat and Wilhelmine **Hess**. Baptized and confirmed at Mariampol Evangelical Lutheran Church. Immigrated March 1906 via New York aboard the S.S. *Pennsylvania*. Married Karl **Peters**[182] (1880-1955) 15 Jun 1910 at Zion Evangelical Lutheran Church. Died 1 Sep 1929. Interment at Lutheran Cemetery. For list of children, see husband Karl Peters.

813. Gustav **LUKAT** born 1871 in Balaikai. Son of Adolf Lukat and Wilhelmine **Hess**. Baptized and confirmed at Mariampol Evangelical Lutheran Church. Immigrated April 1904 via New York aboard the S.S. *Pretoria*. Married Adeline "Nellie" **Lang**[817] (1891-1954) 7 Feb 1920 at Third Reformed Lutheran Church. Died 16 Feb 1953. Interment at Lutheran Cemetery.

814. Eduard **LUKAT** born 6 Nov 1884 in Balaikai. Son of Adolf Lukat and Wilhelmine **Hess**. Baptized and confirmed at Mariampol Evangelical Lutheran Church. Immigrated November 1906 via Baltimore aboard the S.S. *Cassel*. Married Adeline "Nellie" **Lang**[817] (1891-1954) 21 Nov 1909 at Zion Evangelical Lutheran Church. Died 15 May 1918. Interment at Lutheran Cemetery.

    815.   i. Arthur Edward Lukat b. 1 Aug 1914. d. 14 Apr 1961. m. Helen E. **Bechberger** 1914-1995. m. Ruth A. **McGarr** 1914-1971.
            1 child:
                 Cuvier Lee 1937-

    816.   ii. Harold Leonard Lukat b. 11 Sep 1917. d. 15 Mar 1970. m. Arlene **Schollmeyer** 1921-1982.
            3 children:
                 Harold Edward 1942-1948
                 Diane L. 1946-
                 Gary L.

818. Albine **LUKAT (ZIGANDER)** born 14 Mar 1886 in Balaikai. Daughter of Adolf Lukat and Wilhelmine **Hess**. Baptized and confirmed at Mariampol Evangelical Lutheran Church. Immigrated June 1908 via Baltimore aboard the S.S. *Neckar*. Married Franz **Zigander** (1889-1966) 11 Feb 1912 at Zion Evangelical Lutheran Church. Died 27 Mar 1983 in Laguna Hills, California. Interment unknown.

    819.   i. Lydia H. Zigander b. 22 Nov 1912. d. 4 Feb 1995. m. Leo **Garrett** 1913-????.

820. ii. Walter W. Zigender b. 14 Nov 1913. d. 29 Jun 1968. m. Helen Ida **Bloom** 1908-1991.

821. iii. Ernest Frank Zigander b. 17 May 1915. d. 19 Oct 1973. m. Elizabeth Katherine **Hermann** 1915-1983.
    2 children:
        Carol 1941-
        Noreen 1947-

822. iv. Ruth M. Zigander b. 13 Dec 1916. d. 2 Mar 1988. m. Arthur **Krause** 1914-1972. m. Gilbert **Blase** 1907-1988.
    2 children:
        Judith 1942-2014
        Donna Lee 1943-2016

823. Johann **LUKAT** born 1893 in Balaikai. Son of Adolf Lukat and Wilhelmine **Hess**. Baptized and confirmed at Mariampol Evangelical Lutheran Church. Immigrated September 1913 via New York aboard the S.S. *Kaiser Wilhelm der Große*. Married Minnie **Rom** (1894-1992) 22 May 1920 in Cleveland by a Justice of the Peace. Died 6 Dec 1972 in Garfield Heights, Ohio. Interment at St. John Lutheran Cemetery, Garfield Heights, Ohio.

824. i. Lillian Ruth Lukat b. 16 Oct 1921. d. 29 July 1998. m. Robert **Teschke** 1923-1992.
    2 children:

825. ii. Dorothy M. Lukat b. 4 Dec 1923. d. 14 Aug 2009. m. Dale Richard **Goebelt** 1923-2012.
    2 children:
        Robert R. 1945-
        Donna Lynn 1956-2004

826. iii. Irvin John Lukat b. 22 Apr 1926. d. 16 Sep 1990. m. Norine **Moore** 1930-????.
    2 children:
        Pamela D.
        Keith H.

831. Amalie "Mollie" **LUKAT** (**JONAT**) born 18 Mar 1897 in Balaikai. Daughter of Adolf Lukat and Wilhelmine **Witlieb**. Baptized and confirmed at Mariampol Evangelical Lutheran Church. Married Johann **Jonat**[827] (1892-1960) 21 Nov 1915 at Zion Evangelical Lutheran Church. Married John H. **Remington** (1898-1985) 6 Dec 1950. Died 14 Dec 1972. Interment at Sunset Memorial Park Cemetery, North Olmsted, Ohio. For list of children, see husband Johann Jonat.

MAI / MAY

397. Alexander **MAI** (*MAY*) born 1883 in Balbieriškis. Son of Gustav Mai and Julia **Kurwoder** (sp?). Baptized at Prenen Evangelical Lutheran Church. Immigrated June 1901 via New York aboard the S.S. *Darmstadt*. Married Albertine "Bertha" **Hirsch**[402] (1882-1963) in Pittsburgh, Pennsylvania. Died 2 January 1942. Interment at Lutheran Cemetery.

    398.   i. Gustave May b. 29 Feb 1908. d. 15 Mar 1982. m. Lydia **Schmidt** 1911-1963.

    399.   ii. Wanda May b. 11 Jul 1910. d. 17 Nov 1994. m. Richard Dallas **Myers** 1911-1988.
            2 children:
                Elaine 1940
                Sharon L 1948-

    400.   iii. Oswald May b. 12 Sep 1912. d. 26 Feb 1983. m. Elisabeth Jane **Chamberlain** 1915-1998.
            3 children:
                Susan J. 1941-
                Roger D. 1946-
                Linda N.

    401.   iv. Richard Otto May b. 13 Jun 1915. d. 5 Sep 1980. m. Jane Eleanor **Kubes** 1924-1979.

    402.   v. Walter Emil May b. 29 Apr 1920. d. 4 Jul 1983. m. Sarah M. **Browne** 1923-2008.
            1 child:

404. Leopold "Leo" Witold **MAI** ("**MAY**") born 20 Jun 1892 in Balbieriškis. Son of Gustav Mai and Julia **Kurwoder** (sp?). Baptized at Prenen Evangelical Lutheran Church. Immigrated September 1910 via New York aboard the S.S. *Potsdam*. Married Gottliebe **Heldke** (1894-1970) 23 May 1915 at St. Paul's Evangelical Lutheran Church. Died 14 Jul 1961. Interment unknown.

    405.   i. Rudolph Walter May b. 16 May 1916. d. 19 May 1980. m. Alma **Johanns** 1915-1988.
            3 children:
                Judy 1941-
                Janet 1944-
                Joyce 1947-

406. ii. Eugene Arthur May b. 19 Apr 1919. d. 21 Jun 1994. m. Lena M. **Swarens** 1908-1994.
    1 child:
        Beatrice L. 1925-1994
407. iii. Harold May b. 13 Mar 1925. d. 14 Apr 1998.

MAURUSCHAT / NAURUSCHAT / NAURUSCHAITIS

1073. Eduard **MAURUSCHAT** (*NAURUSCHAT*) born 1887 in Poluńce (Poland). Son of Karl Nauruschat and Eva **Neumann**. Baptized at Seine Evangelical Lutheran Church. Immigrated August 1907 via New York aboard the S.S. *Main*. Married Johanna **Burke**[1072] (1886-1969) 16 Jul 1911 at Zion Evangelical Lutheran Church. Died 24 Feb 1941. Interment at Lutheran Cemetery.

    1074. i. Walter Carl Mauruschat b. 21 Jun 1913. d. 30 Aug 1978. m. Treva Eldora **Everstine** 1919-2011.

    1075. ii. Bertha (Joan?) Mauruschat b. 25 Jul 1915. d. ????.

METT

889. Auguste Pauline **METT** (**PETERS**) born 1870 in Kumečiai. Daughter of Friedrich Franz Mett and Pauline **Pudimat**. Baptized and confirmed at Mariampol Evangelical Lutheran Church. Married Karl **Peters** (1867-????) 1891 at Mariampol Evangelical Lutheran Church. Died 15 Sep 1958. Interment at Lutheran Cemetery.

    890.   i. Karl Peter b. 1892. d. ????.

    891.   ii. Otto Peter b. 1895. d. ????.

    892.   iii. Anna Beter b. 1896. d. 16 Dec 1977. m. Michael **Gergely** 1902-1975.
              2 children:
                    Arthur Walter[895] 1928-1989
                    Robert[896] 1935-1997

    893.   iv. August Johann Peter b. 1898. d. ????.

    894.   v. Adeline Peter b. 1899. d. ????.

897. Josef **METT** born 1886 in Kumečiai. Son of Friedrich Franz Mett and Pauline **Pudimat**. Baptized and confirmed at Mariampol Evangelical Lutheran Church. Died 29 Jan 1942. Interment at Lutheran Cemetery.

898. Eva **METT** (**ZORKIS**) born 1889 in Kumečiai. Daughter of Friedrich Franz Mett and Pauline **Pudimat**. Baptized and confirmed at Mariampol Evangelical Lutheran Church. Immigrated 1905 via Baltimore. Married Walter **Zorskis** (1892-1959) in Cleveland by a Justice of the Peace. Died 27 Mar 1974. Interment at Lake View Cemetery.

METZDORF

1389. Wilhelmine **METDORF (LANG)** born 28 Feb 1878 in Krosna. Daughter of Friedrich Metzdorf and Justine **Bernutat**. Baptized and confirmed at Mariampol Evangelical Lutheran Church. Married Albert **Lang**[1388] (1871-1945) 26 Sep 1894 at Zion Evangelical Lutheran Church. Died 16 Feb 1916. Interment at Knollwood Cemetery, Mayfield Heights, Ohio. For list of children, see husband Albert Lang.

MÜLLERSZOWSKI / MILLERSKOWSKI / MILLERSKOFSKI / MILLER

1327. Adolf **MILLERSKOFSKI** (**MILLER**) born 1883 in Antakalnis. Son of Friedrich Müllerszkowski and Ottilie **Hasenheit**[1338] (1859-1935). Baptized at Goddlau Evangelical Lutheran Church. Immigrated July 1902 via New York aboard the S.S. *Friesland*. Married Agatha **Fricke** (1887-1926) at St. John's Evangelical Lutheran Church. Died 23 Mar 1960. Interment unknown.

    1328. i. Karoline Elma Millerskofski b. 16 Apr 1907. d. 31 May 1967. m. Rudolf C. **Sipan** 1902-1963.

    1329. ii. Erna Anna Millerskofski b. 3 Jan 1909. d. 19 Jul 1977. m. George Edward **Wills** 1908-1969.
        1 child:
            Carol Lynn 1950-

    1330. iii. Roland Millerskofski b. 6 May 1911. d. 1 May 1992. m. Fern Marie **Dennis** 1911-1991.
        2 children:
            Beth Ann 1941-2023
            Cheryl L.

    1331. iv. Gertrude Millerskofski b. 13 Oct 1917. d. 12 May 1975. Harold **Parker** 1910-????.
        1 child:
            Richard 1936-

1332. Wilhelm Albert **MILLERSKOFSKI** (*MILLER*) born 12 Nov 1887 in Degim (current location unknown; located near Panemunė). Son of Friedrich Müllerszkowski and Ottilie **Hasenheit**[1338] (1859-1935). Baptized at Goddlau Evangelical Lutheran Church. Married Wilhelmine "Minne" **Bring** (1895-1950) 30 May 1914 at St. John's Evangelical Lutheran Church. Died 2 Aug 1955. Interment at St. John Lutheran Cemetery, Garfield Heights, Ohio.

    1333. i. William Albert Miller b. 12 Nov 1914. d. 10 Apr 1996. m. Irma Dorothy **Karl** 1919-2008.
        3 children:
            William III
            Janice
            Gail

1334. ii. Theodore Friedrich Miller b. 15 Nov 1915. d. 5 Sep 1997. m. Laura Esther **Borges** 1913-1991.
       2 children:
            Dale R.
            Neil 1948-

1335. iii. Herman Edward Miller b. 27 Aug 1920. d. 28 Aug 2001. m. Margaret **Hrin** 1926-2009.
       4 children:
            Jill Ann
            Scott Robert
            Mark Allan
            Glenn Michael

1336. iv. Donald Franklin Miller b. 21 Jun 1926. d. 25 Dec 1973. m. Norma Lillian **Bohning** 1929-2003.
       2 children:
            Donald J.

1337. v. Lawrence Miller b. 8 Dec 1928. d. 28 Dec 2008.

MISSUN

224. Christian "Christ" **MISSUN** born 23 Dec 1870 in Lankupėnai. Son of Josef Missun and Christine **Schwed**. Baptized and confirmed at Wischtiten Lutheran Church. Immigrated May 1896 via Baltimore. Married Anna **Schack** (1886-1960) 21 Nov 1897 at Zion Evangelical Lutheran Church. Died 9 Sep 1960. Interment in Lutheran Cemetery.

    225.   i. Carl Missun b. 9 Sep 1898. d. 7 Aug 1921.

    226.   ii. Lucille Missun b. 23 May 1900. d. 2 Jul 1997. m. Albert Henry **Tessman** 1898-1973.

    227.   iii. Oswald Missun b. 24 Nov 1900. d. 3 Jun 1922.

    228.   iv. Alma Missun b. 3 May 1909. d. 25 Jul 2002. m. Oskar **Aukschun**[212] 1898-1945.
        2 children:
            Loretta Jean 1931-2006
            Richard L. 1933-

229. Anna **MISSUN (REITER)** born 1864 in Grzybina (Poland). Daughter of Josef Missun and Christine **Schwed**. Baptized at Wischainy Evangelical Lutheran Church. Married Andreas Heinrich **Reiter**[230] (1869-1933) 1887 at Wischainy Evangelical Lutheran Church. Died April 1951. Interment at Lutheran Cemetery. For list of children, see husband Andreas Heinrich Reiter.

MITTAG

1067. Auguste **MITTAG (WORM)** born 1873 in Dotamai. Daughter of August Mittag and Marie **Naujokat**. Baptized at Kalwaria Evangelical Lutheran Church. Married Karl **Worm**[1066] (1870-1934) 1894 at Kalwaria Evangelical Lutheran Church. Died 9 Mar 1941. Interment at Lutheran Cemetery. For list of children, see husband Karl Worm.

MURANKO / MURANKE / MURANKI

769. Alexander **MURANKO** (*MURANKE*) born 1893 in Poluńce (Poland). Son of Jakob Muranko and Henriette **Engelhardt**. Baptized at Seine Evangelical Lutheran Church. Immigrated December 1912 via New York aboard the S.S. *Lapland*. Married Julianna **Podgis**[768] (1894-1945) 24 July 1920 in Naugatuck, Connecticut. Died 11 Jan 1958. Interment at Lutheran Cemetery.

    770.   i. Walter Muranke b. 1 Jun 1921. d. 4 May 2006.

    771.   ii. Raymond Richard Muranke b. 23 Jul 1922. d. 10 Sep 1955. m. Norma **Buettner** 1922-2014.
           1 child:
                  Diane L. 1949-2008

    772.   iii. Lillian Ester Muranke b. 21 Apr 1924. d. 19 Feb 2015. m. Edward Earl **Negenborn** 1919-1956.
           2 children:

MUSCHINSKI

576. Adolf **MUSCHINSKI** born 1883 in Leipalingis. Son of Theodor Muschinski and Julianna **Pfeifer**. Baptized at Leipalingis Roman Catholic Church. Married Natalia **Weinschröder**[575] (1874-1968) 1910 at Serey Reformed Lutheran Church. Immigrated July 1910 via New York aboard the S.S. *Fatherland*. Died 8 Mar 1956. Interment at Lutheran Cemetery.

> 577. i. Natalie Muschinski b. 26 Feb 1911. d. 31 Oct 1915.
>
> 578. ii. William Muschinski b. 20 Oct 1913. d. 19 Jul 1999. m. Frances May **Lucas** 1922-2000.
>
> 579. iii. Adolf Alwin Muschinski b. 27 Nov 1916. d. ????.

1439. Josef **MUSCHINSKI** born 1874 in Barkūniškis. Son of Teodor Muschinski and Julianna **Pfeifer**. Baptized at Serey Reformed Lutheran Church. Married Anna **Kühlmann** (1862-1957) 1893 at Serey Reformed Lutheran Church. Immigrated April 1900 via New York aboard the S.S. *Graf Waldersee*. Died 1 Nov 1937. Interment at Lutheran Cemetery.

> 1440. i. Anna Muschinski b. 14 Apr 1894. d. 20 Feb 1988. m. Fredrick Ferdinand George **Telatko** 1891-1955. m. John Jacob **Adler** 1875-1958.
> 5 children:
> Alexander George 1911-1966
> Edward Frederick 1911-1978
> Dorothy 1913-1913
> Howard 1914-1979
> Delores Ann 1932-2010
>
> 1441. ii. Marianna "Marie" Muschinski b. 10 Apr 1897. d. 30 Dec 1995. m. Gustav **Dikheiser**[968] 1895-1963.
> 2 children:
> Lillian Dorotha 1918-1963
> Alfred G. 1920-1997

1440. Anna **MUSCHINSKI (TELATKO) (ADLER)** born 14 Apr 1894 in Seirijai. Daughter of Josef Muschinski[1439] (1874-1937) and Anna **Kühlmann** (1862-1957). Baptized at Serey Reformed Lutheran Church. Married Fredrick Ferdinand George **Telatko** (1891-1955) 28 Jan 1911 at Zion Evangelical Lutheran Church. Divorced. Married John Jacob **Adler** (1875-1958). Died 20 Feb 1988 in Middleburg Heights, Ohio. Interment at West Park Cemetery.

> 1442. i. Alexander George Telatco b. 3 Jul 1911. d. 7 May 1966. m. Mildred Violet **Runyon** 1907-1972.

> 3 children:
>> Marjorie Carl 1936-2022
>> June Marie 1937-1995
>> Thomas Alexander 1940-2011

1443. ii. Edward Frederick Telatco b. 3 Jul 1911. d. 25 Aug 1978. m. Mildred D. **Young** 1919-1939. m. Marian **Carson** 1913-1996. m. Onita Pauline **Pool** 1892-1988.
> 2 children:
>> Geraldine Ann 1935-2018
>> Baby Boy 1937-1937

1444. iii. Dorothy Telatko b. 29 Mar 1913. d. 5 May 1913.

1445. iv. Howard Telatko b. 24 Apr 1914. d. 1 Jul 1979. m. Margaret Cecelia **Runyon** 1919-2020.

1446. v. Dolores Ann Adler b. 28 Mar 1932. d. 26 Mar 2010. m. John Anthony **Yurchenko** 1933-2015.
> 3 children:
>> Bruce Michael 1958-2007

1447. Marianna "Marie" **MUSCHINSKI** (**DICKHEISER**) born 10 Apr 1897 in Seirijai. Daughter of Josef Muschinski[1439] (1874-1937) and Anna **Kühlmann** (1862-1957). Baptized at Serey Reformed Lutheran Church. Married Gustav **Dikheiser**[968] (1895-1963) 19 Sep 1917 in Cleveland by a Justice of the Peace. Died 30 Dec 1995 in Willoughby, Ohio. Interment at Forest Lawn Memorial Park, Cypress, California.

1448. i. Lilliam Dorothy Dickheiser b. 22 Jun 1918. d. 18 Oct 1963. m. Melvin Walter **Gee** 1916-1985.
> 1 child:
>> Shirley M.

1449. ii. Alfred G. Dickheiser b. 1 Jan 1920. d. 21 Apr 1997. m. Dorothy **Miles** 1924-1972.
> 1 child:
>> Wayne W. 1947-

NAUSNER / NOS

145. Bertha **NAUSNER (WESTFAL) (SLITER)** born 1887 in Balbieriškis. Daughter August Nausner (1861-????) and Anna **Pollak**[144] (1866-1952). Baptized at Prenen Evangelical Lutheran Church. Married Carl J. **Westfal** (1880-????) 1909 in Pittsburgh, Pennsylvania. Married ? **Sliter** in Cleveland. Died 29 Dec 1986 in Painesville, Ohio. Interment at Willoughby Village Cemetery, Willoughby, Ohio.

    146.   i. Arthur C. Westfal b. 5 May 1910. d. 14 Mar 1990. m. Viola **Toghill** 1913-1992.

    147.   ii. Lillian Wesfall b. 8 Jul 1912. d. 12 Aug 1994. m. Harvey Maurice **Groll** 1911-1973.

148. Emilie **NAUSNER (MIELKE)** born 1891 in Balbieriškis. Daughter of Wilhelm August Nausner (1861-????) and Anna **Pollak**[144] (1866-1952). Baptized at Prenen Evangelical Lutheran Church. Married Adolf **Mielke** (1888-1966) 18 May 1912 at Immanuel Evangelical Lutheran Church. Died 29 Dec 1958 in Medina, Ohio. Interment at Brooklyn Heights Cemetery, Brooklyn Heights, Ohio.

    149.   i. Leda "Lydia" Emilie Mielke b. 17 Feb 1913. d. 22 Aug 2004. m. William Adolph Mielke 1909-1967. m. Jack **Bawolak**. m. Warren **Forbes**.
        3 children:
            Linda 1942-
            Judith E. 1947-
            William

    150.   ii. Lucille Martha Mielke b. 1 Nov 1914. d. 22 Jun 1998. m. Joseph J. **Pergl** 1910-1981.

    151.   iii. Adolph E. Mielke b. 17 Dec 1916. d. 6 Mar 1959. m. Anna Ruth **Gapinski** 1918-2001.

152. Alexander-Edmund „Edward" **NAUSNER** born 12 Dec 1893 in Balbieriškis. Son of Wilhelm August Nausner (1861-????) and Anna **Pollak**[144] (1866-1952). Baptized at Prenen Evangelical Lutheran Church. WWI veteran. Died 30 Mar 1944. Interment at Brooklyn Heights Cemetery, Brooklyn Heights, Ohio.

153. Natalie-Martha "Martha" **NAUSNER (HALLER)** born 11 November 1895 in Balbieriškis. Daughter of Wilhelm August Nausner (1861-????) and Anna **Pollak**[144] (1866-1952). Baptized at Prenen Evangelical Lutheran Church. Emigrated September 1912 via Baltimore aboard the S.S. *Rhein*. Married Filipp "William" **Haller** (1894-1955) 8 November 1919 at Friedenskirche Evangelical Lutheran Reformed Church. Died 8 May 1980 in Barberton, Ohio. Interment in Brooklyn Heights Cemetery, Brooklyn Heights, Ohio.

    154.   i. Ruth Haller b. 6 Dec 1922. d. 1 Aug 1976. m. William **Guth** 1919-1983.

155. "Carl" Rudolf **NAUSNER** (*NOS*) born 3 Aug 1899 in Balbieriškis. Son of Wilhelm August Nausner (1861-????) and Anna **Pollak**[144] (1866-1952). Baptized at Prenen Evangelical Lutheran Church. Immigrated May 1923 via Boston aboard S.S. *Passenger*. Listed as a "stowaway." Also recorded as crossing Canadian border to Buffalo 17 Aug 1923. Married Louise Auguste **Witner Wittkowski** (1909-1991) in Brooke, West Virginia. Died 19 May 1987. Interment at Brooklyn Heights Cemetery, Brooklyn Heights, Ohio.

    156.   i. Rudolph William Nos b. 23 Dec 1927. d. 30 Jun 2013. m. Florence Eleanor **Lassafare** 1926-2008.
            2 children:

    157.   ii. Carl Alfred Nos b. 13 Jul 1929. d. 18 Jun 1995. m. Nancy Jean **Margo** 1936-2007.
            5 children:
                Janice Lynn 1959-
                Darin Michael 1962-1995

158. Olga **NAUSNER (DENGLER)** born 21 Nov 1905 in Balbieriškis. Daughter of Wilhelm August Nausner (1861-????) and Anna **Pollak**[144] (1866-1952). Married August **Dengler** (1896-????) in Europe. Divorced before 1945. Owned a restaurant in Prenen. Emigrated June 1949 via New York aboard U.S.S. *General Howze*. Died 31 Jan 1981. Interment at Brooklyn Heights Cemetery, Brooklyn Heights, Ohio.

    159.   i. Siegfried Dengler b. 13 May 1927. d. 18 Jul 2008. m. Aldona **Welz** 1928-2025.
            2 sons:
                Arnold Brian Siegfried 1953-
                Errol W. 1957-

    160.   ii. Erwin Dengler b. 30 Jul 1929. d. 9 Feb 1989. m. Dorothea **Roth** 1929-2002.

161. Emma **NAUSNER (JANSSEN)** born 10 Jun 1907 in 1905 in Balbieriškis. Baptized at Prenen Evangelical Lutheran Church. Daughter of Wilhelm August Nausner (1861-????) and Anna **Pollak**[144] (1866-1952). Immigrated via Detroit May 1928. Married George **Janssen**. Died 2 May 1995 in Kirtland, Ohio. Interment at Whitehaven Memorial Park, Mayfield, Ohio.

    162.   i. Jane Emma Janssen b. 30 Apr 1934. d. 28 Dec 2000. m. ? **Heavilin**. m. ? **Fellner**.

    163.   ii. Richard "Dick" G. Janssen b. 19 May 1936. d. 19 Jan 2019. m. Virginia **?**.

    164.   iii. Walter F. Janssen b. 12 Jan 1944. d. 28 Jun 1994. m. Barbara **Porter**.
        4 children:
            Cynthia
            Brad
            Brian
            Deborah

165. Adeline **NAUSNER (HEIN)** born 11 Dec 1889 in Butrimiškės. Daughter of Alexander **Nausner** and Marianna **Hausrath**. Baptized at Prenen Evangelical Lutheran Church. Married Gustav **Hein** (1885-1971) 26 Jan 1910 at Zion Evangelical Lutheran Church. Died 19 Feb 1983 in St. Johns County, Florida. Interment in Evergreen Cemetery, Saint Augustine, Florida.

    166.   i. Elinore M. Hein b. 11 Nov 1910. d. 29 Dec 2005. m. William Carl **Sonnie** (1913-1984).
        2 children:
            John Ray 1937-2003
            William Allan 1940-2003

    167.   ii. Raymond Gustav Hein Sr. b. 10 Sep 1912. d. 17 Nov. 1978. m. Dorothy Mae **Jackson** (1916-1963).
        2 children:
            David 1943-2012

    168.   iii. Alexander Hein b. 8 Dec 1914. d. 13 May 1993. m. Elsie Virginia **Pepke** 1920-2008. m. Eunice C. **Fendley**.

169. Karoline **NAUSNER (DREITZLER)** born 1891 in Butrimiškės. Daughter of Alexander **Nausner** and Marianna **Hausrath**. Baptized at Prenen Evangelical Lutheran Church. Immigrated June 1913 via New York aboard the S.S. *Barbarossa*. Died 26 Jul 1963. Interment unknown.

199. Emilie **NAUSNER (ACKERMANN)** born about 1860, likely in Balbieriškis. Daughter of Andreas Heinrich Nausner and Ernestine **Rentel**. Married Adolf Franz **Ackermann**[188] 1882 in Prenen Evangelical Lutheran Church. Immigrated August 1902 via Baltimore aboard the S.S. *Breslau*. Died 23 Jun 1942 in Maple Heights, Ohio. Interment at Lake View Cemetery. For list of children, see husband Adolf Franz Ackermann.

1287. Reimund "Raymond" **NAUSNER** born 5 Feb 1905 in Seirijai. Son of Alexander Nausner and Marianna **Hausrath**. Baptized at Serey Reformed Lutheran Church. Immigrated June 1928 via Halifax, Canada aboard the S.S. *Karlsruhe*. Immigrated July 1940 via Detroit-Windsor Tunnel by automobile. Married Bernice **Finch** (1910-1995) 28 Dec 1939 at Newport, Kentucky. Died 24 Dec 1986 in Saint Augustine, Florida. Interment at Forest Lawn Cemetery, Beaufort, South Carolina.

    1288.   i. Carolyn R. Nausner b. 27 Jan 1943. d. 9 Nov 2017.

    1289.   ii. Janic L. Nausner b. 1945-

    1290.   iii. Barbara E. Nausner b. 1949-

NEITZEL / NETZEL / NECEL

790. Ferdinand Karl **NEITZEL** born 1878 in Wojtokiemie (Poland). Son of Karl Neitzel and Karoline **Cipolowski**. Baptized at Seine Evangelical Lutheran Church. Immigrated March 1898 via New York. Married Christine **Leichert**[789] (1875-1950) 7 Apr 1901 at Zion Evangelical Lutheran Church. Died 8 Mar 1955 in Garrettsville, Ohio. Interment at Lutheran Cemetery.

    791.   i. Adolf Georg Neitzel b. 26 Jan 1901. d. 18 Nov 1986. m. Helena W. **Sokolik**[1044] 1906-1985.
            2 children:
                Mildred Loretta 1924-2015
                Eleanore Louise 1925-2013

    792.   ii. Anna Emilie Neitzel b. 3 Apr 1903. d. 20 Sep 1995. m. George Dale **Goodhart** 1902-1965. m. Gene William **MacFarland** 1903-????.
            2 children:
                Marguerite 1923-2016
                Infant son 1925-1925

    793.   iii. Auguste Christine Neitzel b. 13 Aug 1904. d. ????. m. Charles W. **Scott** 1899-????. m. Arthur **Fielitz** 1905-????.
            1 child:
                Charles 1925-

    794.   iv. Ferdinand Karl Neitzel Jr. b. 7 Apr 1906. d. 15 Aug 1979. m. Etta Edith **Schara** 1910-1987.
            3 children:
                Gearldine 1932-
                Shirley M. 1933-1979
                Leroy

    795.   v. Friedrich Julius Neitzel b. 24 Feb 1908. d. 3 Jan 1914.

    796.   vi. Emma Helen Neitzel b. 11 Nov 1910. d. 24 Aug 2010. m. Wayne Elton **Craver** 1913-1984.
            3 children:
                Donald Wayne 1939-2018
                Dorothy Eileen 1941-
                Glenn A 1943-

797. Adolf Otto **NEITZEL** born 1882 in Wojtokiemie (Poland). Son of Karl Neitzel and Karoline **Cipolowski**. Baptized at Seine Evangelical Lutheran Church. Died 23 Apr 1914. Interment at Lutheran Cemetery.

1238. Ernst Friedrich **NETZEL** born 2 Aug 1890 in Garliava. Son of August Adolf Netzel and Amelia **Hermann**. Baptized at Goddlau Evangelical Lutheran Church. Married Emma **Balsat** (1892-1930). Married Gertrude R. **Olnhausen** (1890-1969) 17 Sep 1932 at the Evangelical Church, Fostoria, Ohio. Married Luise **Zimmermann** (1895-1986) 25 May 1935 at the Evangelical Lutheran Church, Fostoria, Ohio. Died 24 Aug 1947. Interment at Fountain Cemetery, Fostoria, Ohio.

NEUBACHER

394. Anna **NEUBACHER** (**LACKNER**) (*LOCKNER*) born 18 Nov 1887 in Lankupėnai. Daughter of Georg Neubacher and Anna **Kalwait**. Baptized and confirmed at Wischtiten Evangelical Lutheran Church. Married Georg **Lackner**[391] (1884-1959) 16 Apr 1911 at St. Paul's Evangelical Lutheran Church. Died 11 Oct 1947 in Euclid, Ohio. Interment at Knollwood Cemetery, Mayfield Heights, Ohio. For list of children, see husband Georg Lackner.

1567. Gustav Emil **NEUBACHER** born about 1883 likely in Dubiany (no longer exists; was located south of Būdviečiai). Son of Adolf Neubacher and Helene **Friedrichsdorf**. Probably baptized at Mariampol Evangelical Lutheran Church and confirmed at Kalwaria Evangelical Lutheran Church. Immigrated March 1916 via New York aboard the S.S. *Orduna*. Married Valentine **Nicholas**(?) (1891-1928). Married Helen **Moisef** (1899-????) 27 June 1931 by a Justice of the Peace in Shaker Heights, Ohio. Divorced 1935. Married Stanisława **Pieknik** 29 Apr 1939 by a Justice of the Peace in Cleveland. Died 15 Sep 1943. Interment at Knollwood Cemetery, Mayfield Heights, Ohio.

    1568. i. Eugena "Jenny" „Jeanne" Neubacher b. 1 Jan 1913. d. 2 Dec 2003. m. John Jacob **Henderson** 1909-2009.

    1569. ii. Emma Neubacher b. 6 Nov 1918. d. 12 Aug 2010. m. Vito **Cusumano** 1914-2012.
        1 child:
            Paul J. 1944-

799. Johann **NEUBACHER** born 5 Aug 1881 in Żelazkowizna (Poland). Son of Johann Neubacher and Justine **Kausch**. Baptized at Wischainy Evangelical Lutheran Church. Confirmed at Wischtiten Evangelical Lutheran Church. Married Auguste **Baltrunat**[798] (1880-1915) 2 Nov 1904 at Zion Evangelical Lutheran Church. Married Ernestine **Klepatz** (1883-1946) 29 Apr 1916 at Christus Kirche Evangelical Lutheran Church. Married Wilhelmine **Griwatsch** (1890-1973). Died 20 Aug 1957. Interment at Lutheran Cemetery.

    800. i. John Gerhardt Neubacher b. 16 Aug 1905. d. 16 May 1967. m. Luella Adeline Gatz 1909-1989.

    801. ii. Erich Karl Neubacher b. 25 Oct 1906. d. 20 Apr 1983. m. Elsye Vošmik 1903-2003.
        2 children:
            Carol 1942-2013

    802. iii. Rudolph Carl Neubacher b. 19 Sep 1908. d. 6 Aug 1985. m. Audrey Josephine Bourne 1909-2008.

        1 child:
                Arlyn Ruth 1936-2004

803.   iv. Wilhelm Adolf Neubacher b. 11 Nov 1910. d. 22 Jun 1989. m. Irene Kleinfelt 1918-2004.
        3 children:
                William 1938-2013
                Nancy R. 1942-
                Jane L. 1948-

804.   v. Ottilie Neubacher b. 19 May 1911. d. 19 Sep 1993. m. John D. Grange 1913-????.
        2 children:
                Timothy 1944-
                James 1948-

805.   vi. Emil August Neubacher b. 6 Aug 1913. d. 23 Mar 1999. m. Ruth Gladys Anderson 1920-????.
        2 children:
                Robert G. 1943-
                Jack E. 1946-2018

806.   vii. Lydia Auguste Neubacher b. 4 Nov 1914. d. 9 May 2003. m. Harry Gustav Berntson 1915-2004.
        2 children:
                Lynn 1943-
                Carolyn M. 1947-

NEUMANN / NEIMANN / NIEMANN

479. Bertha **NEUMANN** (*NIEMAN*) (**SCHNEIDER**) born 1892 in Marijampolė. Daughter of Rudolf Neumann and Pauline **Nausner**. Baptized and confirmed at Mariampol Evangelical Lutheran Church. Married Adolf **Schneider**[473] (1889-1973) 16 Aug 1913 at Zion Evangelical Lutheran Church. Died 9 Feb 1973. Interment at Acacia Masonic Memorial Park Cemetery, Mayfield Heights, Ohio. For list of children, see husband Adolf Schneider.

480. Emilie **NEUMANN** (*NIEMAN*) (**SCHNEIDER**) born 12 Mar 1898 in Marijampolė. Daughter of Rudolf Neumann and Pauline **Nausner**. Baptized and confirmed at Mariampol Evangelical Lutheran Church. Married Julius **Schneider**[470] (1894-????) 5 Sep 1915 at Zion Evangelical Lutheran Church. Divorced 1929. Married Albert J. M. **Knick** (1902-1986) 17 May 1929 in Cleveland by a Justice of the Peace. Died 17 Sep 1990. Interment unknown. For list of children, see husband Julius Schneider.

1016. Gustav **NEUMANN** (*NEIMAN*) born 13 Feb 1887 in Sosnowo (no longer exists; was a neighborhood in southern Marijampolė). Son of Rudolf Neumann and Pauline **Nausner**. Baptized and confirmed at Mariampol Evangelical Lutheran Church. Immigrated June 1912 via Baltimore aboard the S.S. *Neckar*. Married Marie **Radezki** (1892-1920) 22 May 1915 at Zion Evangelical Lutheran Church. Married Anna **Dengelat**[1022] (1902-1994) 15 Jul 1922 at Zion Evangelical Lutheran Church. Died 22 Oct 1975 in Mayfield Heights, Ohio. Interment unknown.

    1017. i. Martha Neiman b. 13 Mar 1916. d. 7 Oct 1999. m. Oscar Oswald **Tiedman**[447] 1916-1994.
        1 child:
           Ronald 1937-

    1018. ii. Arthur Carl Neiman b. 17 Feb 1918. d. 9 Jan 1980.

    1019. iii. Howard W. Neiman b. 14 Oct 1923. d. 2 Mar 1993.

    1020. iv. Eddy Neiman b. 5 May 1937.

1230. Karl **NEUMANN** born 13 Feb 1895 in Poluńce (Poland). Son of Ferdinand Neumann and Julianna **Juknat**. Baptized at Seine Evangelical Lutheran Church. Married Emilie **Gudat**[1231] 16 Oct 1915 at Zion Evangelical Lutheran Church. Died 19 Dec 1976. Interment at Lutheran Cemetery.

    1232. i. Gertrude Neumann b. 12 Sep 1916. d. 28 Jun 2012. m. Eugene W. **Newnes** 1914-2002.
        1 child:

Duane E. 1948-

1233. ii. Harold L. Neumann b. 22 Aug 1918. d. 29 Jan 1985. m. Hilda **Roll** 1915-1995.
>   3 children:
>   Harold C. 1945-
>   Thomas 1946-
>   Dineen E. 1948-

1234. iii. Loretta Velma Neumann b. 14 Apr 1920. d. 25 Feb 1993. m. John **Benedict**.
>   1 child:
>   Deborah E.

1235. iv. Doris Neumann b. 20 Mar 1923. d. 14 Nov 2011.

1236. v. Janet Neumann b. 11 Nov 1925. d. 14 May 2017. m. Walter F. **Teras** 1923-1967.
>   2 children:
>   Donna 1947-
>   Darrel

1337. vi. Eleanor C. Neumann b. 29 Jun 1929. d. 26 Oct 2017. m. Frank V. **Gallo** 1928-2015.
>   3 children:
>   Paul R.
>   Sandra J.
>   Judy L.

1379. Karl Adolf **NEUMANN** born 1866 in Ungurinė. Son of Friedrich Neumann and Marianna **Jurkschat**. Baptized and confirmed at Mariampol Evangelical Lutheran Church. Immigrated June 1892 via Baltimore aboard the S.S. *Stuttgart*. Married Auguste **Lang**[1380] (1874-1960) 24 Jun 1894 at Zion Evangelical Lutheran Church. Died November 1953. Interment at Knollwood Cemetery, Mayfield Heights, Ohio.

1381. i. Emma Neumann b. 12 Mar 1896. d. 4 May 1980. m. Theodore Edward **Essel**[294] 1894-1966.
>   3 children:
>   Betty A. 1924-1926
>   Albert Edward 1925-1976
>   Edith 1927-

1382. ii. Augusta Neumann b. 19 May 1897. d. 7 Jan 1987. m. Aaron Millard **Albert** 1897-1989.
>   2 children:

     Harvey Carl 1920-2000
     Robert Edward 1923-1926

1383. iii. Henry C. Neumann b. 13 Dec 1902. d. 9 Dec 1973. m. Mary Louise **Hurley** 1906-1978.
    4 children:
     Ella Louise 1926-2018
     Vivian R. 1927-2019
     Carl Edward 1930-1994
     Robert C. 1934-2001

NIEDERSTRASS / NIEDERSTRASSE / NIEDER

1240. Georg **NIEDERSTRASS** born 1874 likely in Krosna. Son of Karl Niederstrass and Eva **Richter**. Likely baptized at Mariampol Evangelical Lutheran Church. Married Christine **Schultz**[1239] 30 May 1909 at Zion Evangelical Lutheran Church. Died 19 May 1949. Interment at Lutheran Cemetery.

    1241. i. Carl W. Niederstrasse b. 13 Mar 1912. d. 21 May 1935.

    1242. ii. Emil George Niederstrasse b. 11 Aug 1913. d. 28 May 1989. m. Beatrice **Sorbes** 1918-2008.
        2 children:
            Caroline 1937-2016
            Mary Jane 1939-2018

    1243. iii. Lillian P. Niederstrasse b. 28 May 1915. d. 11 Dec 1997. m. Earl J. **White** 1912-1963. Married Charles **Stuntz** ????-????.
        4 children:
            Jean 1934-
            Constance 1938-
            Earl R. 1941-
            Carl D. 1943-

    1244. iv. Gertrude Alma Niederstrasse b. 18 Feb 1917. d. 23 Jul 2002. m. Helmut Martin **Kebbel** 1913-2001.
        3 children:
            Carl 1938-
            Joyce 1940-
            Daniel 1948-

1245. Julius **NIEDERSTRASSE (*NIEDER*)** born 26 Jul 1870 likely in Krosna. Son of Karl Niederstrass and Eva **Richter**. Likely baptized at Mariampol Evangelical Lutheran Church. Married Martha Wilhelmine Henriette **Brockob** (1872-1936) 13 Jan 1898 at St. Mary's Edge Hill (Church of England) in Liverpool, England. Immigrated May 1903 via New York aboard the S.S. *Campania*, from Liverpool. Died 20 Jan 1943. Interment at Lutheran Cemetery.

    1246. i. Eduard Julius Nieder b. 10 Oct 1898. d. 27 Jul 1959. m. Catherine E. **Mitchell** 1899-1937. m. Louise **Ramsdalle** 1912-1998.

    1247. ii. Marie Nieder b. 14 Jun 1900. d. 12 Mar 1979. m. James Raymond **Dysert** 1899-1964.

1248. iii. Anna Nieder b. 17 Apr 1902. d. 19 Jan 1994. m. Edward M. **McNaughton** 1888-1965.

1249. iv. Elsie Nieder b. 18 Mar 1904. d. 27 Oct 1990.

1250. v. Paul Alfred Nieder b. 16 Sep 1906. d. 3 May 1972. m. Helen M. **Smith** 1906-1958.
    1 child:
        John Richard 1936-2020

1251. vi. Margaret Nieder b. 4 Jul 1908. d. 25 Mar 2004. m. Fredrick Daniel **Hartmann** 1905-1980.
    2 children:
        Fredrick 1935-
        Leonard J. 1943-

1252. vii. Lillian Nieder b. 18 Feb 1911. d. 17 Apr 1994. m. Edward Frank **Rowland** 1909-1983.

1253. viii. Leonard Nieder b. 6 Feb 1914. d. 25 Nov 1980. m. Vera Irma **Russell** 1922-2014.
    2 children:
        Patricia Lee 1947-
        James Robert 1949-2003

1254. Karl **NIEDERSTRASSE** (*NIEDER*) born 1875 in Krosna. Son of Karl Niederstrass and Eva **Richter**. Baptized at Serey Reformed Lutheran Church. Married Auguste **Krom** (1886-1959) 10 Apr 1910 at Zion Evangelical Lutheran Church. Died 4 May 1953. Interment at Lutheran Cemetery.

    1255. i. Edith Nieder b. 18 Feb 1914. d. 7 Oct 1999. m. Clarence A. **Schönbeck** 1913-1985.
        2 children:
            Kenneth 1942-
            Glen

    1256. ii. Leonard Arthur Nieder b. 23 Jan 1917. d. 1 Aug 1996. m. Lucille E. **Neu** 1917-2010.
        3 children:
            Carl L
            Leonard M.
            LuAnne

NIESS / NEISS

1147. Gustav **NIESS** born 1848 in Kybartai. Son of Gottlieb Niess and Christine **Bridzun**. Baptized and confirmed at Wirballen Evangelical Lutheran Church. Married Anna **Schulz**[1148] (1855-1935) 1876 at Wirballen Evangelical Lutheran Church. Died 8 Feb 1915. Interment at Lake View Cemetery.

    1149. i. Gustav Eduard b. 23 Mar 1877. d. ????.

    1150. ii. August Niess b. 1880. d. 2 Nov 1949. m. Margaret Sara **Burns** 1882-????.
           1 child:
                Raymond Francis 1906-1973

    1151. iii. Hermann Eduard Niess b. 29 Oct 1882. d. 1 Sep 1977.

    1152. iv. Martha Marie Niess b. 4 Sep 1884. d. 9 July 1944. m. Friedrich G. **Krause** 1872-1940.
           7 children:
                Fred Reinhart 1899-1979
                Agnes Lydia 1900-1970
                Arthur Watler 1901-1986
                Edna Alma 1902-1998
                Erma 1913-1916
                Leona Louise 1916-1917
                Mildred 1919-2007

    1153. v. Adolph Niess b. 1885. d. 20 May 1958. m. Margaret **McFadden** 1894-????.

    1154. vi. Olga Niess b. 1887. d. 5 Sep 1977. m. William Henry **Gray** 1880-1942.
           4 children:
                Evelyn M. 1903-2000
                Mildred Anna 1905-1952
                Gwendolyn Olga 1908-1973
                Martha Lillian 1913-2002

    1155. vii. Auguste Niess b. 1889. d. 4 Apr 1936. m. Owen J. **Bready** 1865-1936.

    1156. viii. Anna Niess b. 1891. d. 1956. m. Louis Otto **Eckert** 1892-1975.
           3 children:
                Louis Hermann 1914-1977
                Clarence 1917-????

Howard 1919-????

1157. ix. William Niess. 27 May 1893. d. 13 Feb 1960. m. Esther **Kaase** 1893-????.
2 children:
Robert William 1914-1978
Ralph Frederick 1919-1956

1158. x. Lydia Niess b. 13 Feb 1898. d. 18 Apr 1972. m. Carl Grimes **Beck** 1896-1964.
2 children:
Russell Carl 1919-????
Dorian L. 1921-????

NOWIAK / NAUJOK / NOWJACK

55. Eva **NOWIAK** (**WEIER**) (*WEIHER*) born about 1864 in Ungurinė. Daughter of Johann Nowiak and Christine **Reges**. Baptized at Mariampol Evangelical Lutheran Church. Married August **Weier** (1859-1918) 1885 at Mariampol Evangelical Lutheran Church. Died 2 Oct 1935. Internment at Lutheran Cemetery.

    56.   i. Pauline Weier b. 18 Dec 1886. d. 18 Aug 1953. m. Emil **Witzke** 1883-????.
            5 children:
                Beatrice 1907-1983
                Edith 1909-1991
                Lillian "Lydia"
                Martha 1912-1988
                Helen Mildred 1918-1998

    57.   ii. Helene "Edna" Weier b. 1888. d. ????. m. ? **Wallace.**

    58   iii. August Karl Weier b. 14 Dec 1889. d. 15 Aug 1965. m. Margory **Immel** 1893-1965.

    59.   iv. Albert Weier b. 1893. d. 1976.

    60.   v. Bertha Weier b. 28 Sep 1896. d. 23 Jan 1969. m. Fred Jennings **Dees** 1898-1989.
            1 child:
                Dr. Marvin F. 1922-2010

    61.   vi. Leonard Weiher b. 2 Apr 1907. d. 2 Mar 1960.

62. Georg **NOWIAK** born 23 Apr 1873 in Lucyanow? (sp.) probably near Marijampolė. Son of Johann Nowiak and Christine **Reges**. Immigrated July 1902 via Baltimore aboard S.S. *Chemnitz*. Married Auguste Kirschner.[32] Died 12 Apr 1959. Internment at Lutheran Cemetery. For list of children, see wife Auguste Kirschner[32]

82. Emilie **NOWIAK** (**HEINRICH**) born about 1863 in Degučiai. Daughter of Karl Nowiak (????-1911) and Luise **Urbat**. Baptized at Mariampol Evangelical Lutheran Church. Married August **Heinrich**[67] (1855-1916) 31 Aug 1879 at Wirballen Evangelical Lutheran Church. Died 22 Feb 1945. Interment at Lutheran Cemetery. For list of children, see husband August Heinrich.

111. Gustav Emil **NOWJAK** (*NOWIAK*) born 20 Mar 1881 in Kvietiškis. Son of Ludwig Nowiak (1862-????) and Amelia **Tetmeier** (1862-1949). Baptized at Mariampol Evangelical Lutheran Church. Immigrated August 1906 via Baltimore aboard S.S. *Breslau*. Married Marie **Galinat** (1892-1969) 23 May 1913 at Zion Evangelical Lutheran Church. Died 12 March 1975 in Lyndhurst, Ohio. Interment at Knollwood Cemetery, Mayfield Heights, Ohio.

    112.   i. Ida Emily Nowjak b. 5 Jan 1914. d. 2 May 2008. m. Arnold Carl **Gronert** 1914-2007.
        1 child:
            Alan Rodger 1944-2016

    113.   ii. Lucia M. Nowjak b. 13 Jul 1915. d. 13 Jul 2009. m. Karl Henry **Grisard** 1913-1988.
        2 children:
            Kathleen Marie 1942-1984
            Raymond Carl 1947-2019

    114.   iii. Robert Gustave Nowjak b. 20 Mar 1917. d. 28 Aug 1988. m. Pearl Marie **Enges** 1917-2003.
        2 children:
            Sherrill 1939-
            Nancy L. 1946-

    115.   iv. Adele Marie Nowjak b. 08 Jul 1918. d. 29 Jul 2013. m. John V. **Kirsch** 1920-1977.
        1 child:
            Lynn Marie 1947-2004

    116.   v. Olga Natalie Nowjak b. 25 Oct 1920. d. 15 Nov 1988. m. Charles A. **Hall** 1921-1960.
        1 child:
            Joyce ????-2018

    117.   vi. Walter Emil Nowjak b. 9 Feb 1923. d. 26 Sep 1963. m. Jean Rose **DiLauro** 1920-1995.

118. Richard **NOWJACK** (*NOWIAK*) born 30 Jul 1888 in Degučiai. Son of Ludwig Nowiak (1862-????) and Amelia **Tetmeier** (1862-1949). Baptized and confirmed at Mariampol Evangelical Lutheran Church. Immigrated June 1907 via Baltimore aboard S.S. *Main*. Married Wanda **Dickheuser**[967] (1892-1918) 25 August 1915 at Zion Evangelical Lutheran Church. Married Elsie **Wachtler** 7 June 1922 by Pastor Armin Egli, possibly at a Scandinavian Lutheran Church in Cleveland. Died 9 Feb 1980 in Rice Lake, Wisconsin. Interment at Sunset Memorial Park, North Olmsted, Ohio.

119.   i. Alert "Albert" Nowjack b. 18 Nov 1916. d. 18 Dec 2012. m. Margaret Jane **McDonald** 1922-1998.
      4 children:
        Amy
        Ruth
        David
        James

120.   ii. Ella Johanna Nowjack b. 4 Apr 1918. d. 31 July 2008. m. Martin Theodore William **Rose** 1917-2001.
      4 children:
        Lois
        Karl A.
        Susan; Judith

121. Hugo **NOWJACK** (*NOWIAK*) born 4 Feb 1896 in Degučiai. Son of Ludwig Nowiak (1862-????) and Amelia **Tetmeier** (1862-1949). Baptized and confirmed at Mariampol Evangelical Lutheran Church. Emigrated June 1910 via Baltimore aboard S.S. *Rhein*. Married Theresa Gladys **Steierlein** (1913-1981) 14 September 1932 in Wellsburg, West Virginia. Died 6 Aug 1944 in Phoenix, Arizona. Interment at Lutheran Cemetery.

    122.   i. Lucille A. Nowjack b. 30 Jun 1934. d. 19 May 2017. m. ? **Owad**.

    123.   ii. Irma June Nowjack b. 5 Jun 1938. d. 3 Sep 1994. m. Richard A **Sajovec** 1935-1994. m. Harvy D. **Rush** 1938-2011. m. Terrance K. **Owad** 1936-1999.

124. Albin "Alvin" Friedrich Wilhelm **NOWJACK** (*NOWIAK*) born 17 May 1898 in Degučiai. Son of Ludwig Nowiak (1862-????) and Amelia **Tetmeier** (1862-1949.) Baptized and confirmed at Mariampol Evangelical Lutheran Church. Immigrated June 1910 via Baltimore aboard S.S. *Rhein*. Married Wilhelmine Leokadia "Lottie" **Knut** (1900-1980) 26 Feb 1922 at Zion Evangelical Lutheran Church. Married Katherine Carmella **Kacic** (1922-2013) 13 May 1944. Died 7 July 1984 in El Monte, California. Interment at Live Oak Memorial Park, Los Angeles, California.

    125.   i. Betty Alice Nowjack b. 20 Feb 1924. d. 10 Feb 2015. m. Leonard Charles **Jarvis** Jr. 1922-2001.

    126.   ii. Alvin Lee Nowjack b. 20 Mar 1931. d. 26 Jan 2017. m. Aphrodite **Patisteas** 1932-2007.
        3 children:

127. Ludwig "Louis" **NOWJACK** (*NOWIAK*) born 17 Sep 1905 in Tarpučiai. Son of Ludwig Nowiak (1862-????) and Amelia **Tetmeier** (1862-1949). Baptized and confirmed at Mariampol Evangelical Lutheran Church. Immigrated via Baltimore June 1910. Married Florence **Knuth** (1911-2000) 12 October 1935 at Zion Evangelical Lutheran Church. Died 1 Apr 1993 in Chardon, Ohio. Interment at Maple Hill Cemetery, Munson Township, Ohio.

128. Irene **NOWJACK** (*NOWIAK*) born 10 Mar 1909 likely near Marijampolė. Daughter of Ludwig Nowiak (1862-????) and Amelia **Tetmeier** (1862-1949). Immigrated via Baltimore June 1910. Died 1 Dec 1917. Interment at Lutheran Cemetery.

PASEKEL

103. Ludwig „Louis" **PASEKEL** born 5 Nov 1871 in Potilsch (near Bartininkai). Son of Ludwig Pasekel and Anna **Becker**. Baptized and confirmed at Wilkowischken Evangelical Lutheran Church. Married Emilie **Grigat** 1873-1953 in 1894 at Kalwaria Evangelical Lutheran Church. Immigrated via Baltimore June 1905 aboard S.S. *Chemnitz*. Died 14 Nov 1955. Interment in Knollwood Cemetery, Mayfield Heights, Ohio.

    104.   i. Leopold Pasekel b. 10 Nov 1895. d. 18 Aug 1939. m. Emma A. **Kuhn** 1890-1979.
                2 children:
                      Geraldine Willa 1920-2002
                      Howard Leo 1927-2014

PAMPUS / PEMPUS

647. Gustav **PAMPUS** born 23 Jun 1893 in Marijampolė. Son of Wilhelm Pampus and Auguste **Schmidt**. Baptized and confirmed at Mariampol Evangelical Lutheran Church. Immigrated January 1913 via Baltimore aboard the S.S. *Necker*. Married Anna **Jurkschat**[646] (1874-1944) 10 Jan 1914 at Zion Evangelical Lutheran Church. Died 15 Apr 1922. Interment at Lutheran Cemetery.

    648.   i. Gustave Pampus b. 16 Jun 1904. d. 27 Oct 1939. m. Norma **Sommer** 1907-1980.
            1 child:
                Lois Helen 1928-2010

    649.   ii. Oscar Pampus b. 9 Oct 1914. d. 10 Dec 1961. m. Margaret **Brazofsky** 1916-1986.

PERREY / PERRY / PERREI / PERREJ / BAREIG

284. Josef **PERREY (PERRY)** born 5 Mar 1866 in Lankeliškiai. Son of August Perrey and Henriette **Weber**. Baptized at Wirballen Evangelical Lutheran Church. Married Berta **Schnieder** (1870-1920) 18 Jul 1891 at Zion Evangelical Lutheran Church. Married Mathilde **Klein**[283] (1878-1979) 5 Sep 1922 at St. Paul's Lutheran Church. Died 28 Sep 1941. Interment at Lutheran Cemetery.

285.   i. Martha Perry b. Jul 1891. d. ????. m. William **Zins** 1884-????. m. Harry R. **Williams** 1888-????. m. Albert W. Fischer 1890-????.
   1 child:
   Elenore Williams 1913-????.

286.   ii. Edward Perry b. 4 Nov 1896. d. 10 May 1965. m. Catherine **Zahler** 1891-1984.

287.   iii. Rose Perry b. 12 Nov 1897. d. 7 Jan 1930. m. Wesley **Fowler** 1893-1933.
   4 children:
   Wesley Jr. 1912-1929
   June 1916-1917
   Warren P. 1918-1980
   Barbara R 1925-2017

288.   iv. Arthur Perry b. 6 Sep 1898. d. 21 Sep 1950. m. Versa Goldia **Duncan** 1889-1938. m. Jean Frances **Ruthledge**.
   4 children:
   Wynn
   Ban
   Paul
   Michelle

289.   v. Irving Perry b. 13 Jan 1903. d. 19 Jan 1971. m. Edna M. **Kirby** 1907-1999.
   2 children:
   Gloria Louise 1932-2001
   Andreas 1940-1922

290.   vi. Berta Perry b. 1908. d. 1910.

291.   vii. Henry Warren Perry b. 23 Jun 1905 d. 22 Apr 1960. m. Marie **Wehner** 1903-????. m. Elizabeth **?**. m. Catherine Helene **Phister** 1903-2003.

409. Adolf "Adam" **PERREJ** (*PERRY*) born around 1868 in Maszymietischken (current name and location unknown.) Son of Jakob Perrej and Amelia **Keller**. Baptized and confirmed at Wilkowischken Evangelical Lutheran Church. Immigrated via New York aboard the S.S. *Amalfi* March 1889. Married Karoline **Herr** (1873-1955) 11 Feb 1893 at Zion Evangelical Lutheran Church. Died 24 Jun 1961. Interment at Lutheran Cemetery.

   410.   i. Emma Parry b. 1 Dec 1893. d. 5 Apr 1964. m. August **Spei**[417] 1887-1971.
   2 children:
   Herbert Harry[418] 1918-2000
   Howard Perry[419] 1923-2010

   411.   ii. William Oscar Perry b. 29 Dec 1894. d. 29 Oct 1978. m. Emma **Conrad**[589] 1899-1980.
   2 children:
   Evelyn Wilhelmine 1916-2000
   Dorothy C. 1920-2013

   412.   iii. Albert Perry b. 15 Apr 1899. d. 7 Feb 1973. m. Wanda **Wachhaus**[558] 1905-1987.
   2 children:
   Albert D 1929-1929
   Ronald Lee 1933-2015

   413.   iv. Minnie Perry b. 7 Jun 1900. d. 22 Feb 1929. m. Adam **Wachhaus** 1902-1967.

   414.   vi. Herman Perry b. 7 Nov 1903. d. 29 Mar 1977. m. Edith **Brandt** 1907-1989.
   2 children:
   Florence June 1926-2006
   Doris 1931-2011

   415.   v. Alma Perry b. 1905. d. 18 Oct 1967.

   416.   vi. Walter Albert Perry b. 6 Jun 1912. d. 1957. m. Anne B. **Clische** 1913-????.
   1 child:
   Sandra 1939-

1096. Thomas **PERRY** born 20 Oct 1870 in Slibinai. Son of Josef Perrey and Marie **Hasebein**. Baptized at Neustadt Evangelical Lutheran Church. Married Anna **Hubert**[1102] (1876-1942) likely at Wirballen Evangelical Lutheran Church. Immigrated Jun 1903 via New York aboard the S.S. *Pretoria*. Died 23 Jan 1955. Interment at Lutheran Cemetery.

> 1097. i. Thomas Perry Jr. b. 1898. d. 25 Oct 1964. m. Eleanor **Oppenheimer** 1867-1973.
>> 4 children:
>>> Carol Ann 1926-2002
>>> Harriet Jean 1930-2007
>>> Thomas III 1934-201
>>> Phyllis 1937-2009
>
> 1098. ii. Josef Perry Sr. b. 29 Mar 1900. d. 7 Jun 1971. m. Maude A. **Henderson** 1899-1988.
>> 3 children:
>>> Virginia 1922-2007
>>> Doris H. 1924-????
>>> Joseph D. Jr. 1929-2009
>
> 1099. iii. August Perry b. 1903. d. ????.
>
> 1100. iv. Anna Perry b. 1904. d. 2 Aug 1965.
>
> 1101. v. Mathilde Bertha Perry b. 1909. d. 11 Oct 1962. m. Erwin Ferdinand **Stettin** 1899-1961.

1103. Matthias "Max" **PERRY** (***BAREIG***) born 8 Oct 1867 in Slibinai. Son of Josef Perry and Anna **Greiczuweit**. Baptized at Neustadt Evangelical Lutheran Church. Married Luise Elisabeth **Essert** (1866-1955) 10 Dec 1888 at Zion Evangelical Lutheran Church. Died 17 Dec 1915. Interment at Lutheran Cemetery.

> 1104. i. Anna Perry b. 10 Dec 1888. d. 12 Sep 1946. m. Ludwig Friedrich **Kramer**[1105] 1884-1966.
>> 7 children:
>>> Walter Adolf[1106] 1908-1987
>>> Ruth[1107] 1910-1975
>>> Doris Ann[1108] 1912-1966
>>> Marian[1109] 1917-????
>>> Richard Louis[1110] 1922-1998
>>> Kenneth[1111] 1924-1973
>>> Harriett[1112] 1926-2006
>>> David Arthur[1113] 1933-2010

1114. ii. Albert Perry b. 19 Mar 1890. d. 12 Jun 1942. m. Mable **Holzberger** 1891-1948.
> 6 children:
>> Elizabeth Hannah 1912-2004
>> Vivian 1915-????
>> Willus Hugh 1917-1930
>> June Arlene 1920-1999
>> Virginia 1923-2007
>> Norman 1925-????

1115. iii. William C. Perry b. 22 Nov 1891. d. 6 May 1973. m. Hedwig "Hattie" **Hirsch**[946] 1896-1937.
> 3 children:
>> William Arthur 1913-????
>> Thomas Donald 1921-2006
>> Dorothy Ruth 1925-2016

1116. iv. Bertha Perry b. 10 Jan 1894. d. 12 Jul 1964. m. Georg **Boeing** 1885-????. m. Georg **Schaak** 1894-????.

1117. v. Arthur Charles Perry b. 16 Nov 1900. d. 18 Nov 1971. m. Leona **Ames** 1899-1982.
> 1 child:
>> Joanne 1930-2006

1118. Christof Adam "Christian" **PERRY** born 13 Feb 1877 in Slibinai. Son of Josef Perry and Marie **Hasebein**. Baptized at Neustadt Evangelical Lutheran Church. Married Marie **Kalchert** (1888-1979) 2 Feb 1907 at Zion Evangelical Lutheran Church. Died 17 Apr 1938 in Painesville, Ohio. Interment at Evergreen Cemetery, Painesville, Ohio.

1119. i. Walter Johann Perrey b. 13 Aug 1908. d. 14 Dec 1989. m. Marion **Woodworth** 1908-1996.
> 4 children:
>> Grace 1936-
>> LeGrand John 1937-1943
>> Marylyn C. 1941-
>> Walter Ernst 1942-2003

1120. ii. Anna Bertha Perry b. 6 Mar 1910. d. 1 Oct 2002. m. Otto George **Nerad** 1896-1976.

1121. iii. Dorothy Margaret Perry b. 21 Nov 1914. d. 27 Aug 1994. m. Kenneth **Waterman** 1909-1990.
> 1 child:
>> Joyce 1933-2000

1122. Josef **PERREY** born 31 May 1863 in Slibinai. Son of Josef Perry and Anna **Greiczuweit**. Baptized at Neustadt Evangelical Lutheran Church. Married Ida **Kirst** (1871-1957) 6 Jun 1891 at St. Paul's Evangelical Independent Church. Died 25 Apr 1942 in Mentor, Ohio. Interment at Lutheran Cemetery.

    1123. i. Friedrich Perrey b. 1891. d. 11 Nov 1951. m. Margaret **Mayer** 1897-????.
           2 children:
                Frederick Charles 1915-2000
                Margaret M. 1917-1986

    1124. ii. Max W. Perrey b. 28 Mar 1892. d. 28 Jun 1905.

    1125. iii. Oskar Perrey b. 16 Aug 1893. d. 26 Jan 1977.

    1126. iv. Joseph Hermann Perry b. 9 Feb 1895. d. 19 Jun 1972. m. Charlotte Margaret **Owens** 1895-1973.

    1127. v. Olga Helene Perrey b. Feb 1897. d. 4 Aug 1906.

    1128. vi. Adolf Perrey b. 5 Jun 1899. d. 28 Feb 1989. m. May Anna **Wachhaus** 1910-2000.
           4 children:
                Ralph 1934-
                Donald 1937-
                Leroy Joseph 1941-2022
                David 1960-1977

    1129. vii. Elisabeth Perrey b. 1901. d. ????.

PETER / PETERS

179. Olga **PETER** (**KRAFT**) born 1901 in Vartai. Daughter of Adolf Peters and Julianna **Kinat**. Baptized at Mariampol Evangelical Lutheran Church. Immigrated November 1923 via New York aboard the S.S. *Tyrrhenia*. Married Philipp **Kraft** (1901-1990) 14 May 1927 at Zion Evangelical Lutheran Church. Died 16 Apr 1987. Internment at Maple Hill Cemetery, Munson Township, Ohio.

    180.   i. Robert Lee Kraft b. 30 Jun 1928. d. 25 Nov 2000. m. Cora Mae **Worley** 1923-.
            1 child:

    181.   ii. Ralph Kraft b. 30 Nov 1930. d. 10 Jan 2009. m. Shirley **Willett**.
            1 child:
                Susan

182. Karl "Carl" "Charles" **PETERS** (*PETER*) born 31 Dec 1880 in Vartai. Son of Adolf Peters and Julianna **Kinat**. Baptized at Mariampol Evangelical Lutheran Church. Married Leopoldine **Lukat**[408] (1881-1929) 15 Jun 1910 at Zion Evangelical Lutheran Church. Died 22 Apr 1936. Interment at Lutheran Cemetery.

    183.   i. Martha Amelia Peters b. 5 Apr 1911. d. 14 Oct 1983. m. Fred **Moss** 1900-????.
            1 child:
                Carolyn

    184.   ii. Adeline Josephine Peters b. 21 Jun 1913. d. 7 Jun 2003. m. Kenneth J. **Soules** 1908-1973.
            1 child:
                Kenneth J. Jr. 1935-2004

    185.   iii. Ewald Carl Peters b. 19 Mar 1915. d. 14 Jan 2000. m. Erna Olga **Zeitz** 1918-2007.
            2 children:
                Linda J 1943-
                Kathleen R. 1949-

    186.   iv. Harry W. Peters b. 9 Aug 1918. d. 11 Nov 1988. m. Joan **Burdick** 1924-????.
            1 child:
                Sharon Lee 1950-

187. Ludwig "Louis" **PETERS** born 1889 in Vartai. Son of Adolf Peters and Julianna **Kinat**. Baptized at Mariampol Evangelical Lutheran Church. Immigrated March 1910 via Philadelphia aboard the S.S. *Frankfurt*. Married Wilhelmine **Schindel** (1892-1993) 5 Sep 1914 at Zion Evangelical Lutheran Church. Divorced 1917. Married each other again in Cleveland by a Justice of the Peace 27 Dec 1917. Divorced again. Married Olga **Kroll** (1904-1976) 20 Nov 1941 at St. John's Evangelical Lutheran Church. Died 22 Nov 1974. Interment at Lutheran Cemetery.

    884.   i. Natalie Peters b. 4 Jun 1915. d. 22 Jul 2010. m. Walter V. **Schramm** 1912-1998.
            2 children:
                Barbara L. 1939-
                Karen L. 1942-

    885.   ii. Eleanor Peters b. 23 Oct 1917. d. 23 Sep 2018. m. Oswald **Brauer**[900] 1917-1981.
            1 child:
                Cheryl L. 1949-

    886.   iii. Ruth Alice Peters b. 20 Feb 1922. d. 21 Jul 1996. m. Walter Elmer **Davidson** 1989-1959.

887. Adolf **PETER** born 1891 in Zailiai. Son of August Peter and Albertine **Gerulat**. Baptized at Mariampol Evangelical Lutheran Church. Immigrated Oct 1912 via New York aboard the S.S. *Cincinnati*. Married Emilie **Tennebor**[996] (1895-1952) 16 Jun 1923 at Zion Evangelical Lutheran Church. Married Bertha **Myet** (1894-1977). Died 6 Sep 1973 in Medina, Ohio. Interment at Lutheran Cemetery.

    888.   i. Ralph Arnold Peters b. 17 Mar 1927. d. 10 Jun 1999. m. Bernice **Sobol** 1925-2000.

892. Anna **PETER (GERGELY)** born 1896 in Nowopól (no longer exists; located near Danieliškiai). Daughter of Karl Peter (1867-????) and Auguste Pauline **Mett**[889] (1870-1958). Married Michael **Gergely** (1902-1975) 24 Sep 1927 in Cleveland by a Justice of the Peace. Died 16 Dec 1977 in Middleburg Heights, Ohio. Interment at Lutheran Cemetery.

    895.   i. Arthur Walter Gergely b. 12 Jan 1929. d. 27 Dep 1989. m. Gloria Jean **Anderson** 1920-2019.
            1 child:
                Michael

    896.   ii. Robert Gergely b. 10 May 1935. d. 8 Feb 1997. m. Carolyn J. **Eidenmiller**.

1 child:
: Rebecca Grace 1959-

1051. Adolf Ferdinand **PETERS** born 1890 in Vartai. Son of Ferdinand Peters and Julia **Gersch**. Baptized and confirmed at Mariampol Evangelical Lutheran Church. Immigrated March 1910 via Philadelphia aboard the S.S. *Frankfurt*. Married Anna **Reder**[1052] (1889-1975) 15 Oct 1913 at Bethlehem Evangelical Lutheran Church. Died 8 Jan 1959 in Geauga County, Ohio. Interment unknown.

    1053. i. Alma Helen Peters b. 15 Aug 1914. d. 15 Jan 2015. m. Richard Carl **Plietchwait** 1910-1986.
: 1 child:
: : Janice Eleanor 1936-2018

    1054. ii. Herman P. Peters b. 14 Nov 1915. d. 8 Jun 2016. m. Vera **Burke**[1081] 1922-2005.
: 2 children:
: : Sanrda 1942-
: : Kathleen 1947-

    1055. iii. Adolph Howard Peters b. 30 Apr 1919. d. 23 Oct 2010. m. Evelyn Hannah **Yurkschat**[1059] 1921-1970.

    1063. iv. Eleanor Amelia Peters b. 31 Oct 1921. d. 8 Feb 2011. m. Howard William **Gutman**[1050] 1922-1998.
: 1 child:
: : Richard Howard 1947-1994

    1065. v. Arnold Louis Peters b. 7 May 1924. d. 31 Aug 2020. m. Betty Lou **Logelin** 1929-2018.
: 2 children:
: : Gary
: : Jayne

1291. Albert Ewald **PETERS** born 3 Oct 1893 in Seirijai. Son of Ludwig Peters and Leokadia **Blazek**. Baptized at Serey Reformed Lutheran Church. Married Albertine **Schnell**[1292] (1897-1983) 24 Apr 1915 at Zion Evangelical Lutheran Church. Died 14 May 1975. Interment at Lutheran Cemetery.

    1293. i. Walter Albert Peters b. 28 Apr 1916. d. 7 Aug 2000. m. Anna Belle **Scheamer** 1922-1983.
: 2 children:
: : Eleanor 1943-1943
: : David T. 1945-2016

1294. ii. Harvey Edwin Peters b. 5 Apr 1924. d. 4 Sep 2011. m. Harriet Theresa **Plona** 1924-2007. Twin of Harry Edwin Peters.[1295]
   3 children:
   Don
   Hattie
   Debbie

1295. iii. Harry Edwin Peters b. 5 Apr 1924. d. 22 Mar 1997. Twin of Harvey Edwin Peters.[1294.] Married Eileen **Young**.
   1 child:
   Infant Girl 1973-1973

1297. Emilie Mathilde **PETER** (**SCHÜTZ**) (*SCHULTZ*) born 24 Dec 1913 in Kermušinė. Daughter of Adolf Peter and Eva **Pudimat**. Baptized and confirmed at Mariampol Evangelical Lutheran Church. Married Johann **Schütz**[1296] (1912-2001). Immigrated via New York November 1951 aboard the U.S.S. *General Greeley*. Died 18 May 1989 in Parma, Ohio. Interment at Lutheran Cemetery. For list of children, see husband Johann Schütz.

1366. Johann Josef **PETER** (*PETERS*) born 1894 in Vartai. Son of Ferdinand Peter and Julianna **Gersch**. Baptized and confirmed at Mariampol Evangelical Lutheran Church. Immigrated June 1913 via Baltimore aboard the S.S. *Eisenach*. Married Adele **Harbart** (1892-1997) 28 Oct 1920 by a Justice of the Peace in Warrensville, Ohio. Died 30 May 1961. Interment at Lutheran Cemetery.

1367. i. Doris A. Peters b. 2 Mar 1921. d. 21 Oct 2017. m. ? **Pgulas**.

PODZIS / PODGIS / PODGIES

765. Adeline **PODZIS** (**HEIN**) born 1891 Poluńce (Poland). Daughter of Georg Podzis and Pauline **Herbst**. Baptized at Seine Evangelical Lutheran Church. Married Julius **Hein**[761] (1890-1970) 24 May 1913 at St. Paul's Evangelical Lutheran Church. Died 15 Nov 1963. Interment at Lutheran Cemetery. For list of children, see husband Julius Hein.

766. Alexander **PODGIS** (**PODZIS**) born 1892 in Poluńce (Poland). Son of Georg Podzis and Pauline **Herbst**. Baptized at Seine Evangelical Lutheran Church. Married Julia **Kinat** (1893-1980). Married Margaret **Farron**. Died 14 Feb 1950. Interment at Lutheran Cemetery.

> 767. i. Alfred Kenneth Karl Podgis b. 12 Feb 1924. d. 5 Jul 1982. m. Twila Hope **Parker** 1926-2019. m. Rosemary **Franz** 1926-1982.
> 1 child:

768. Julianna **PODZIS** (**MURANKE**) born 1894 in Poluńce (Poland). Daughter of Georg Podzis and Pauline **Herbst**. Baptized at Seine Evangelical Lutheran Church. Married Alexander **Muranke**[769] (1894-1958) 24 Jul 1920 in Naugatuck, Connecticut. Died 15 Dec 1945. Interment at Lutheran Cemetery. For list of children, see husband Alexander Muranke.

POLLAK / PAULAK

144. Anna **POLLAK (NAUSNER)** born about 1866 in Liepajojai. Daughter of Julius Pollak and Hedwig Richter. Baptized and confirmed at Mariampol Evangelical Lutheran Church. Married Wilhelm August **Nausner** (1861-????) 1884 at Mariampol Evangelical Lutheran Church. Died in Willoughby, Ohio, May 1952. Interment in Brooklyn Heights Cemetery.

1456. Johann **POHL** (*POLAK*) born 1876 in Jackonys. Son of Julius Polak and Jakobine **Pfeifer**. Baptized at Prenen Evangelical Lutheran Church. Married Amelia **Lang**[1452] (1889-1916) 3 Jan 1907 at Zion Evangelical Lutheran Church. Married Clara **Reiter** (1892-1978) 3 Feb 1917 at Zion Evangelical Lutheran Church. Died 27 Mar 1942 in Jefferson, Ohio. Interment at Lutheran Cemetery.

    1457. i. Amelia "Millie" Pohl b. 30 Mar 1909. d. ????. m. Eric Walter **Selneit** (1904-1948). m. James P. Campbell 1913-1962.

    1458. ii. Helen Pohl b. 12 Jun 1913. d. 30 Mar 1975. m. Joseph **Seidman** 1907-1986.

    1459. iii. Elizabeth Pohl b. 31 Oct 1917. d. 12 Dec 2009. m. Edward A. **Begalke** Sr. 1913-2003.
        2 children:
            Edward A. Jr. 1942-
            John C. 1946-

PUDIMAT / PUDIM / PUDIMAITIS

740. Adeline **PUDIMAT** (**HEIN**) born 1876 in Poluńce (Poland). Daughter of Heinrich Pudimat and Christine **Podzis**. Baptized at Seine Evangelical Lutheran Church. Married Andreas "Heinrich" **Hein**[730] (1875-1949) 1896 at Seine Evangelical Lutheran Church. Died 30 July 1956. Interment at Lutheran Cemetery. For list of children, see husband Andreas "Heinrich" Hein.

760. Marie **PUDIMAT** (*PUDIM*) (**HEIN**) born 1887 in Jiestrakis. Daughter of Wilhelm Pudimat and Christine **Domschat**. Baptized at Prenen Evangelical Lutheran Church. Immigrated July 1899 via New York aboard the S.S. *Southwark*. Married Leopold **Hein**[755] (1885-1936) 10 May 1913 at St. Peter's Evangelical Lutheran Church. Died 28 Oct 1995 (at age 108) in Auburn, California. Interment at New Auburn Cemetery, Auburn, California. For list of children, see husband Leopold Hein.

1415. Heinrich **PUDIMAT** born 1879 in Poluńce (Poland). Son of Heinrich Pudimat and Christine **Podzis**. Baptized at Seine Evangelical Lutheran Church. Immigrated May 1900 via New York aboard the S.S. *Phoenicia*. Married Pauline Bertha **Franulewicz**[1416] (1887-1921) 20 Aug 1904 at Zion Evangelical Lutheran Church. Married Julia **Migowitz** (1892-1952) 28 Aug 1922 in Shaker Heights, Ohio, by a Justice of the Peace. Divorced. Died 6 Jun 1942. Interment at Lutheran Cemetery.

    1426. i. Elizabeth Pudimat b. 1906. d. 11 Jul 1914.

    1427. ii. Alma Pudimat b. 9 Aug 1907. d. May 1984. Twin of Lillian Pauline Pudimat.[1428] m. Julius Card **Sharpe** Jr. 1906-1972.
        1 child:
            Sedate Alma 1935-2003

    1428. iii. Lillian Pauline Pudimat b. 9 Aug 1907. d. 15 Jul 2003. Twin of Alma Pudimat.[1427] m. Howard W. **Lowrance** 1909-1992.
        2 children:
            Howard D. 1932-2008
            Joy Nash 1936-1998

    1429. iv. Olga Marie Pudimat b. 15 Feb 1909. d. 1 Feb 2011. m. Thomas **Caraffi** 1907-1997.

    1430. v. Albert Arnold Pudimat b. 24 Apr 1917. d. 4 Sep 1996.

    1431. vi. Eduard Julius Pudimat b. 9 May 1919. d. 26 Oct 2001. m. Gertrude Frances **?** (1918-1964).

1432. vii. Wilber Erich Pudimat (Hein) b. 10 Feb 1921. d. 15 Aug 1999. Adopted by Julius Hein[761] and Adeline Lena Podgis.[765]

1433. viii. Carl Heinrich Pudimat b. 20 Oct 1922. d. 4 May 2000. m. Laverne **Moennich** 1924-2007.
> 4 children:
>> William H. 1943-
>> Sandra L. 1945-
>> Mary F. 1946-
>> Robert W. 1949-

1434. ix. Ruth Pudimat b. 10 Apr 1926. d. 6 Dec 2007. m. Charles **Thomas** 1926-2010.
> 1 child:
>> Charlotte R. 1948-

PUSHKAT / PUSKAT

776. Auguste **PUSHKAT (LOGIES) (BUDNIK)** born 1889 in Bakšiškiai. Daughter of Karl Puschkat and Helene **Geschwandtner**. Baptizied at Wischainy Evangelical Lutheran Church. Married Gustav **Logies** (1884-1939) 27 October 1906 at Third Reformed Lutheran Church. Married Friedrich **Budnik** (1883-1972) 17 Nov 1953 at St. John's Evangelical Lutheran Church. Died 10 Apr 1981. Interment unknown.

    777.   i. Adelia Logies b. 20 Jan 1908. d. 14 Sep 1988. m. Erich **Miehl** 1905-1986.
>
> 4 children:
> Robert 1931-
> Marilyn J. 1936-
> Karen Marie 1941-2005
> Diana R. 1946-

    778.   ii. Ruth Logies b. 3 Sep 1911. d. 4 Feb 1948. m. George H. **Dolch** 1907-1986.
>
> 2 children:
> Douglas 1941-
> Karen 1941-

1404. August **PUSCHKAT (PUSKAT)** born 25 Nov 1880 in Lauckaimis. Son of Karl Puschkat and Marie Anna **Kakstein**. Baptized and confirmed at Neustadt Evangelical Lutheran Church. Married Malwine **Frenkel**[1407] (1882-1951) 17 May 1902 at Third Reformed Lutheran Church. Died 27 Jul 1950. Interment at Hillcrest Cemetery, Bedford Heights, Ohio.

    1405.   i. Arthur Ethan Puskat b. 13 Aug 1906. d. 3 Jun 1998. m. Adelia Komar 1910-1939. m. Lillian Ruth **Kaptein**[340] (1923-1987).
>
> 2 children:
> Beverly A. 1936-
> Ralph A. 1949-

    1406.   ii. Leona A. Puskat b. abt. 1904. d. 2 Jan 1982. m. August **Holecsek** 1905-????. m. Gustave **Rebell** 1892-????.

PUTNAT / PUTNOT / PUTNAITIS

1143. Julianna Auguste **PUTNAT (BUSCHAR)** born 2 Feb 1858 in Trakiškiai. Daughter of Christof Putnat and Karoline **Müller**. Baptized at Kalwaria Evangelical Lutheran Church. Married Georg **Buschar**[1142] (1856-1916) 1884 at Kalwaria Evangelical Lutheran Church. Died 25 Nov 1952. Interment at Lutheran Cemetery. For list of children, see husband Georg Buschar.

REBNER

1257. Marta **REBNER (GOTTSCHALK)** born 1 Feb 1902 near Sakiai. Daughter of Rudolf Rebner and Emilie **Kalweit**. Likely baptized at Schaken Evangelical Lutheran Church. Married Otto **Gottschalk** (1890-1974) 8 July 1937 in Toronto, Canada. Immigrated April 1938 via Buffalo, New York, on the Peace Bridge. Died 27 Jan 1971. Interment at Sunset Memorial Park, North Olmsted, Ohio.

REDER / RÄDER

978. Gustav **REDER** born 1893, likely near Virbalis. Son of Ludwig Reder and Christine **Klibingat**. Likely baptized at Wirballen Evangelical Lutheran Church. Immigrated April 1910 via New York aboard the S.S. *President Grant*. Married Marie **Heinrich**[982] (1891-1960) 4 Jul 1914 at Zion Evangelical Lutheran Church. Died 1972 in Albion, Pennsylvania. Interment at Albion Cemetery, Albion, Pennsylvania.

> 979. i. Oscar Henry Reder b. 8 May 1915. d. 26 May 1971. m. Helen Leona **Howard** 1920-1997.
> 2 children:
> Richard Howard 1941-2009
> April G. 1948-

> 980. ii. Arthur Gustave Reder b. 26 Oct 1917. d. 17 Jul 1982. m. Elizabeth **Pancis** 1921-1999.
> 2 children:
> Elaine M. 1942-
> Arthur D. 1947-

> 981. iii. Lillian Marie Reder b. 21 Oct 1919. d. 11 Nov 1992. m. Richard Merle **Osterberg** 1916-2009.

1052. Anna **REDER** (**PETERS**) born 1889 in Atesninkai. Daughter of Julius Reder and Emilie **Gleichforsch**. Baptized at Kalwaria Evangelical Lutheran Church. Married Adolf Ferdinand **Peters**[1052] (1890-1959) 15 Oct 1913 at Bethlehem Evangelical Lutheran Church. Died 18 Mar 1975. Interment unknown. For list of children, see husband Adolf Ferdinand Peters.

REICHEL / REJCHEL

328. Anna **REICHEL (HARTIG)** born 1888 in Prienai. Daughter of Josef Reichel and Julia **Kinder**. Baptized at Prenen Evangelical Lutheran Church. Immigrated September 1913 via New York aboard the S.S. *Kronprinz Wilhelm*. Married Julius Karl **Hartig**[325] (1883-1956) 15 Oct 1913 by a Justice of the Peace. Died 21 Jun 1973. Interment at Lakeview Cemetery. For list of children, see husband Julius Karl Hartig.

REINECKER

832. Richard Johann **REINECKER** born 9 Apr 1932 in Vilkaviškis. Son of Ewald Hugo Reinecker (1893-????) and Ida-Antonie **Schiller**[843] (1893-1968). Baptized and confirmed at Wilkowischken Evangelical Lutheran Church. Immigrated February 1957 via New York. Married Magdalena Maria **Czich** (1938-2013) 6 Feb 1965 at St. Francis Roman Catholic Church in Cleveland. Died 22 Apr 2005 in Macedonia, Ohio. Interment at Crown Hill Cemetery and Mausoleum, Twinsburg, Ohio. Meisterbäcker and founder of Reinecker's Bakery in Macedonia, Ohio.

    833.   i. Richard Johann Reinecker Jr. b. 12 Aug 1967.

    834.   ii. Heidi Susan Reinecker b. 9 Nov 1968.

    835.   iii. Monika Magdalena Reinecker b. 16 Oct 1970.

    836.   iv. Christina Anneliese Reinecker b. 7 Jul 1973.

    846.   v. Caroline.

837. Hildegard Erna **REINECKER (KRÜGER)** born 12 Feb 1930 in Vilkaviškis. Daughter of Ewald Hugo Reinecker (1893-????) and Ida-Antonie **Schiller**[843] (1893-1968). Baptized and confirmed at Wilkowischken Evangelical Lutheran Church. Married Reinhold Paul Friedrich **Krüger** (1928-1998). Immigrated December 1956 via New York. Died 3 Mar 2020 in Northfield Center, Ohio. Interment unknown.

    838.   i. Roland Erwin Krueger b. 9 Jul 1951. m. Debra M. **Babey** 1958-.

    839.   ii. Astrid Krueger b. 1 Mar 1954. m. Joseph **Hrovat** 1952-.

    840.   iii. Norbert Kurt Krueger b. 19 Mar 1959. m. Kimerley Kay **Workman** 1970-.
        1 child:
            Andrew John Paul 1989-

    841.   iv. Reinhold Herbert Krueger b. 1 Jul 1969. m. Susan V. **Poindexter** 1969-.

    842.   v. Krim Krueger b.????. d. ????. m. ? **Hart**.

REINKE / RENKE / RENK

170. Adolf Julius **REINKE** (*RENKE*) born 1876 in Noragėliai. Son of Karl Reinke and Freida **Franulewitz**. Baptized at Serey Reformed Lutheran Church. Emigrated February 1902 via New York aboard the S.S. *Patricia*. Married Henriette **Bender**[174] (1883-1961) 26 April 1903 at Zion Evangelical Lutheran Church. Died 25 January 1951 in Homerville Township, Ohio. Interment at Lutheran Cemetery.

    171.   i. Adolph Renke b. 13 Jul 1904. d. 27 Dec 1990. m Lillian Ruth **Polenschat**[1011] 1912-1991.

    172.   ii. Marie Renke b. 16 Oct 1905. d. 27 Feb 2003. m. Michale **Fehlan** 1905-1976.
        3 children:
            Michael Adolph 1932-2005
            Richard H. 1938-
            Raymond A. 1939-

    173.   iii. Hugo Renke b. 2 Oct 1911. d. 4 Sep 1974. m. Dorothy M. **Snyder** 1917-2017.
        1 child:
            Roberta 1939-

965. Anna **REINKE** (**DIKHEISER**) born 1861 in Kalvarija. Daughter of Emil Reinke and Karoline **Thiel**. Married Adolf Luis **Dikheiser**[964] (1863-1946) 1885 at Mariampol Evangelical Lutheran Church. Died 6 Oct 1942. Interment at Lutheran Cemetery. For list of children, see husband Adolf Luis Dikheiser.

1031. Angeline **REINKE** (**DILL**) born 1880 in Noragėliai. Daughter of Johann Karl Reinke and Freida **Franulewitz**. Baptized at Serey Reformed Lutheran Church. Married Karl **Dill**[1025] (1870-1943) 5 Oct 1900 at Zion Evangelical Lutheran Church. Died 29 Apr 1969. Interment at Lutheran Cemetery. For list of children, see husband Karl Dill.

1032. Anna **REINKE** (**MILLER**) born 1888 in Pilokalnie (no longer exists; southeast of Seirijai). Daughter of Johann Karl Reinke and Freida **Franulewitz**. Baptized at Serey Reformed Lutheran Church. Married Georg Rudolf **Miller** 28 Apr 1912 at Zion Evangelical Lutheran Church. Died 5 Dec 1975 in Middletown, Ohio. Interment at Lutheran Cemetery.

    1033.   i. Rudolph George Miller b. 11 Feb 1917. d. 29 Jan 1996. m. Margaret Alberta **Schmidt** 1918-2010.
        2 children:
            Rudolph George Jr. 1944-

        Marlene A. 1946-

1034. ii. Walter Robert Miller b. 4 Jul 1926. d. 20 Mar 2013. m. Patsy Ruth **Bunch**.
        5 children:

1035. Johann Karl **REINKE** born 1844 in Seirijai. Son of Karl Reinke and Anna Marianna **Hirsch**. Baptized at Serey Evangelical Lutheran Church. Married Franciszka "Freida" **Franulewitz** (1855-1907) 1876 at Serey Reformed Lutheran Church. Died 13 Oct 1927 in Freedom Township, Ohio. Interment at Lutheran Cemetery.

170. i. Adolf Julius Reinke b. 1876. d. 25 Jan 1951. m. Henriette **Bender**[174] 1883-1961.
        3 children:
            Adolf 1904-1990
            Marie 1905-2003
            Hugo 1911-1974

1036. ii. Karl Reinke b. 1878. d. 1879.

1031. iii. Angeline Reinke b. 1880. d. 29 Apr 1969. m. Karl **Dill**[1025] 1870-1943.
        5 children:
            Henry J.[1026] 1901-1985
            Pauline[1027] 1906-1975
            Gustave[1028] 1909-1995
            Regina Wanda[1029] 1911-1983
            Lydia[1030] 1916-2002

1037. iv. Bronislawa Reinke b. 1883. d. 1894.

1038. v. Marianna Reinke b. 1886. d. 5 Mar 1956. m. Adolf **Sokolek**[1043] 1883-1934. m. August **Fretke** 1892-1966.
        5 children:
            Helene W. 1906-1985
            Marie R. 1908-1989
            Adolph Carl 1911-1978
            Emil R. 1913-1990
            Gustave W. 1916-1995

1032. vi. Anna Reinke b. 1888. d. 5 Dec 1975. m. Georg Rudolf **Miller** 1888-1967.
        2 children:
            Rudolf Jr. 1917-1996
            Walter R. 1926-2013

1039. vii. Karl Reinke b. 1893. d. ????.

1040. viii. Pauline Reinke b. 26 May 1895. d. 2 May 1987. m. Karl Johann **Gutmann**[1049] 1894-1966.
2 children:
Howard W. 1922-1998
Edna 1924

1041. Helene Reinke b. 1897. d. ????.

1042. Marianna **REINKE (SOKOLEK)** (*FRETKE*) (*FREIDKE*) born 1886 in Obelija. Daughter of Johann Karl Reinke[1035] (1844-1927) and Franciszka **Franulewitz** (1855-1907). Baptized at Serey Reformed Lutheran Church. Married Adolf **Sokolek**[1043] (1883-1934) 6 Aug 1905 at Zion Evangelical Lutheran Church. Married August **Fretke** (1892-1966). Died 5 Mar 1956, Fremont, California. Interment at Lutheran Cemetery. For list of children, see husband Adolf Sokolek.

1040. Pauline **REINKE (GUTMAN)** born 26 May 1895 in Kibyšiai. Daughter of Johann Karl Reinke[1035] (1844-1927) and Franciszka **Franulewitz** (1855-1907). Baptized at Serey Reformed Lutheran Church. Married Karl Johann **Gutmann**[1049] (1894-1966) 27 Apr 1921 in Cleveland by a Justice of the Peace. Died 2 May 1987. Interment unknown. For list of children, see husband Karl Johann Gutmann.

REITER

230. Andreas Heinrich **REITER** born 1867 in Bolcie (Poland). Son of Andreas Reiter and Karoline Elmer. Baptized at Wischainy Evangelical Lutheran Church. Married Anna **Missun**[229] (1864-1951) at Wischainy Evangelical Lutheran Church 1887. Died 21 Sep 1933. Interment at Lutheran Cemetery.

    231.   i. August Reiter b. 28 Feb 1888. d. 7 May 1955. m. Mable Rose **Kepke** 1894-1926. m. Fannie **Yates** (1897-1988).
>   2 children:
>>Louis Henry 1919-1987
>>Alan W. 1936-2000

    232.   ii. Heinrich Reiter b. 1 Oct 1889. d. 4 Mar 1969. m. Kathryn **Klingman** 1903-1971.

    233.   iii. Emma Reiter b. 20 Mar 1893. d. Dec 1968. m. Edward O. **Fischer** 1892-????.

    234.   iv. Edward Arthur Reiter b. 6 Mar 1895. d. 19 Apr 1976. m. Mildred Ida Caroline **Mortensen** 1901-1978.
>   1 child:
>>Edward Arthur 1921-1996

    235.   v. Harold Oskar Reiter b. 16 Aug 1898. d. 10 May 1992. m. Ernestine **Eberle** 1901-1946. m. Henriette "Yeta" **Goldberg** 1909-1987.

    236.   vi. Rudolph Oswald Reiter b. 16 Aug 1989. d. 21 Jul 1957. m. Mary A **?**.

    237.   vii. Edna Reiter b. about 1900. d. ????. m. Charles W **Pittman** 1896-????.

    238.   viii. Lillian Reiter b. 20 Aug 1906. d. 6 Feb 1995. m. Nicholas **D'Amico** 1902-1956.
>   2 children:
>>Franklin A 1926-2005
>>Donaleen 1931-

    239.   ix. Elenore Reiter b. 1 Apr 1918. d. 31 Dec 1983. m. Carl J. **Fischer** 1916-1997.
>   3 children:
>>Loretta A. 1936-2014
>>Gary C. 1939-2021
>>Charles H. 1941-

504. August **REITER** born 1866 in Bolcie (Poland). Son of Karl Reiter and Dorothea **Raschpichler**. Baptized at Wischainy Evangelical Lutheran Church. Married Christine **Zaborowski** (????-1890) 1890 at Wischainy Evangelical Luthrean Church. Married Marie **Kless**[503] (1873-1962) at Wischainy Evangelical Lutheran Church. Died 1 Mar 1947. Interment Knollwood Cemetery, Mayfield Heights, Ohio.

    505.   i. Oskar Adolf Reiter b. 26 Sep 1899. d. 28 Mar 1995. m. Catherine **Goeppert** (1900-????). m. Olga **Knisely** 1895-1983.

    506.   ii. Bertha Marie Reiter b. 30 Jun 1904. d. 11 Feb 1991. m. Bruce A. **Knapp** 1908-1935. m. Norman Odell **Morris** 1895-1970.
        1 child:
            Betty Jean 1933-2008

847. Matthias „Max" **REITER** born 1869 in Bolcie (Poland). Son of Karl Reiter and Dorothea **Raschpichler**. Baptized at Wischainy Evangelical Lutheran Church. Immigrated April 1901 via New York aboard the S.S. *Bulgaria*. Married Anna **Tetmeier**[849] (1879-1958) October 1905. Died 29 Jun 1956. Interment at Lutheran Cemetery.

ROMANOWSKI

1305. Ernestine **ROMANOWSKI (LEHMANN)** born 1898 in Kineryszki (no longer exists; near Aleksotas). Daughter of Wilhem Romanowski and Berta **Filipp.** Baptized at Goddlau Evangelical Lutheran Church. Immigrated December 1913 via Baltimore aboard the S.S. *Wittekind*. Married Bernhardt **Lehmann**[1304] (1889-1954) 2 Oct 1915 at St. Paul's Evangelical Lutheran Church. Died 19 Oct 1959. Interment at Knollwood Cemetery, Mayfield Heights, Ohio. For list of children, see husband Bernhardt Lehmann.

ROSEKEIT

1317. Emilie **ROSEKEIT (SCHÜTZ)** born 1866 in Gižai. Daughter of Friedrich Franz Rosekeit and Karoline **Feitusch**. Baptized and confirmed at Mariampol Evangelical Lutheran Church. Married Georg **Schütz**[1316] 1884 at Mariampol Evangelical Lutheran Church. Immigrated July 1907 via Baltimore aboard the S.S. *Main*. Died 29 Jun 1927 in Warrensville, Ohio. Interment at Lutheran Cemetery. For list of children, see husband Georg Schütz.

SALEKER / SALECKER

1. Johann Andreas "Heinrich" SALEKER born 4 June 1866 in Liukiai. Baptized and confirmed at Wischtiten Evangelical Lutheran Church. Son of Andreas Saleker and Marie **Renkiewicz**. Married Emilie **Wiemert**[21] 21 May 1893 at Zion Evangelical Lutheran Church. Died 7 Feb 1945. Interment at Lutheran Cemetery. Great-great-grandfather of IAGL co-founder Owen M. McCafferty II.

- 2\.   i. Friedrich "Fred" Heinrich Saleker b. 28 Apr. 1894. d. 15 Feb 1948. m. Rose **Peterson** 1902-1921.
    - 1 child:
        - Edmond Raymond 1920-2002

- 3\.   ii. Emma Salecker b. 5 Jul. 1896. d. 5 Jul 1896.

- 4\.   iii. Gustav Saleker b. 1 Sep. 1897. d. 22 Nov. 1965. m. Julianna **Dauksza** (*Dickson*) 1901-1929.
    - 4 children:
        - Richard 1921-1993
        - Mary Julia 1923-2001
        - Henry Edward 1924-1967
        - Walter Allen **Schultz** (adopted by Lydia Saleker[7] and Kurt Sachwitz) 1927-1974

- 5\.   iv. Eduard "Ed" Saleker b. 24 Feb. 1900. d. 9 May 1985.

- 6\.   v. Walter Richard Saleker b. 1 Oct 1906. d. 18 Jul. 1912.

- 7\.   vi. Lydia Emilie Saleker b. 29 Dec 1908. d. 8 Feb 1994. m. Kurt Gerhardt Sachwitz (*Schultz*) 1905-1968.
    - 3 children:
        - Wilma Esther 1928-1928
        - Dolores 1930-2010
        - Walter Allen 1927-1974

- 8\.   vii. Anna Esther Saleker b. 23 Jul 1913. d. 26 Mar 1997. m. John "Jack" Robert **Warner** 1905-1989.

9. Anna SALEKER (OTTO) born 28 Feb 1881 in Liukiai. Baptized and confirmed at Wischtiten Evangelical Lutheran Church. Daughter of Andreas Saleker and Marie **Renkiewicz**. Immigrated via Baltimore May 1896 aboard S.S. *Crefeld*. Married Wilhelm Adolf **Otto** 26 Aug 1902 Zion Evangelical Lutheran Church. Died 13 Nov 1956. Interment at Riverside Cemetery.

10.   i. William George Otto b. 30 Mar 1903. d. 15 Apr 1951.

11.   ii. Walter Edward Otto b. 21 Jun 1904. d. 25 Nov 1958. m. Mildred Ann **Reitz** 1905-1990.
> 3 children:
>> Dorothy 1939-
>> Ruth 1943-
>> William

12.   iii. Eleanor Dorothea Otto b. 4 May 1906. d. 21 Sep 1910.

13.   iv. Elsie Anna Otto b. 30 May 1913. d. 10 Jan 1939.

14. Justine Auguste **SALEKER (WIEMERT)** (*WIMMERT*) **(HEINRICH)** (*HENRY*) born 7 Aug 1883 in Liukiai. Baptized and confirmed at Wischtiten Evangelical Lutheran Church. Daughter of Andreas Saleker and Marie **Renkiewicz**. Immigrated Feb 1900 via Baltimore aboard S.S. *München*. Married Friedrich **Wiemert**[22] 2 Jun 1904 at Schifflein Christi Evangelical Lutheran Church. Married Adolf Edward **Heinrich** 28 Jan 1911 at Zion Evangelical Lutheran Church. Died 29 Dec 1969 in Cleveland Heights, Ohio. Interment at Lakewood Park Cemetery, Westlake, Ohio.

15.   i. Ida Edith Wiemert (*Henry*) b. 21 Mar 1905. d. 29 Aug 1924.

16.   ii. Wilma Leone Henry b. 13 Nov 1912. d. 31 Jul 1983.

17. Gustav Adolph **SALEKER** born 2 Jan 1886 in Liukiai. Baptized and confirmed at Wischtiten Evangelical Lutheran Church. Son of Andreas Saleker and Marie **Renkiewicz**. Immigrated via Baltimore Apr 1904 aboard S.S. *Brandenburg*. Married Jeanette **Kirschner**[47] 10 Dec 1908 at Schifflein Christi Evangelical Lutheran Church. Married Marie **Gregori (Gregory) Wonnerth Balogh Auner** 27 Feb 1943 at St. John's Lutheran Church (Eddy Rd.). Died 7 July 1956. Interment at Lutheran Cemetery.

18.   i. Albert Victor Saleker b. 28 Jun 1909. d. 6 Dec 1960. m. Catherine A. **Uniak** 1912-1985.
> 2 children:
>> Edith 1932-1995
>> Marianne 1938-

19.   ii. Gustave Adolph Saleker Jr. b. 25 Mar 1911. d. 27 Dec 1976. m. Mildred **Hrudka** 1917-1991.
> 2 children:
>> Albert Dale Saleker 1941-
>> Ronald L. Saleker 1949-

20. iii. Edith Jeanette Saleker b. 1 Apr 1913. d. 28 May 1978. m. Herbert Franklin **Lawrence** 1908-1981.
  2 children:
   Herbert Strange Lawrence II 1949-2021
   Jeanette Lawrence

SCHAAK / SZAK / SCHACK

856. Georg **SCHAAK** (*SCHACK*) born 1887 in Ungurinė. Son of August Heinrich Schaak (1855-1921) and Anna **Domin** (1851-1924). Baptized at Mariampol Evangelical Lutheran Church. Married Louise **Zemke** (1894-1921) 14 Oct 1911 at St. John's Evangelical Lutheran Church. Married Marie **Vogt** (1902-????) 16 Oct 1923 in Cleveland by a Justice of the Peace. Died 14 Feb 1934 in Los Angeles, California. Interment at Forest Lawn Memorial Park, Glendale, California.

    857.   i. Dorothy Schack b. 17 Mar 1913. d. 10 Apr 1922.

    858.   ii. George Benson Schack b. 1 Oct 1916. d. 26 May 1993. m. Hazel Marie **Swan** 1907-????.

859. Josef **SCHAAK** (*SCHACK*) born 1890 in Bukta. August Heinrich Schaak (1855-1921) and Anna **Domin** (1851-1924). Baptized at Mariampol Evangelical Lutheran Church. Church. Married Henriette Karoline Marie **Linnert** (1893-1988) 28 Aug 1912 at St. John's Evangelical Lutheran Church. Died 20 Jun 1936 in Madison, Ohio. Interment at Middle Ridge Cemetery, Madison, Ohio.

    860.   i. Amanda Henriette Schack b. 10 Nov 1913. d. 20 Aug 2006. m. Raymond L. **Neff** 1910-1972.
        2 children:
            Susan H. 1948-
            Douglas 1949-

    861.   ii. Robert Joseph Schack b. 16 Mar 1915. d. 21 May 1994. m. Maude **Fell** 1913-2013.
        2 children:
            Marcia J. 1937-
            Patricia K.

    862.   iii. Joseph Schack b. 30 Jan 1919. d. 27 Aug 1983. m. Doris E. **Kimmy** 1922-1998.
        3 children:
            Doreen 1943-
            Jerry 1947-
            Barbara 1948-

SCHARFETTER

663. Friedrich Wilhelm **SCHARFETTER** born 1887 in Matuliškiai. Son of Georg Scharfetter and Auguste **Rogal**. Baptized and confirmed at Wilkowischken Evangelical Lutheran Church. Immigrated 1908 via Baltimore aboard the S.S. *Main*. Married Bertha A. **Klees**[667] (1893-1956) 27 Jun 1914 at Bethlehem Evangelical Lutheran Church. Died 14 Apr 1984 in Seffner, Florida. Interment at Whitehaven Memorial Park, Mayfield, Ohio.

    664.   i. Albert E. Scharfetter b. 16 Nov 1914. d. 7 Mar 1969. m. Eleanore Frieda **Hausrath**[660] 1913-1989.
        2 children:
            Sandra W. 1939-
            Greogry P. 1949-

    665.   ii. Edna Auguste Scharfetter b. 17 Oct 1917. d. 30 Jul 2005.

    666.   iii. Harold F. Scharfetter b. 3 Dec 1924. d. 6 Feb 2002. m. Shirley **Blake** 1929-.
        1 child:
            Harold F. 1949-

SCHILLER

843. Ida Antonie **SCHILLER (REINECKER)** born 30 Nov 1893 in Miknaičiai. Daughter of Ludwig Schiller and Johanna **Wingendorf**. Baptized and confirmed at Neustadt Evangelical Lutheran Church. Married Ewald Hugo **Reinecker** (1893-????) 11 Feb 1922 at Wilkowischken Evangelical Lutheran Church. Immigrated February 1957 via New York. Died 27 Mar 1968. Interment at Crown Hill Cemetery and Mausoleum, Twinsburg, Ohio.

    843.   i. Erwin Reinecker b. 30 Jun 1923. d. 21 Nov 1943.

    844.   ii. Ewald Reinecker b. 15 Jun 1935. d. ????.

    845.   iii. Waldemar Reinecker b. 1927. d. ????.

    837.   iv. Hildegard Erne Krueger b. 12 Feb 1930. d. 3 Mar 2020. m. Reinhold Paul **Krüger** 1928-1998.
> 5 children:
> - Roland Erwin R. 1951-
> - Astrid 1954-
> - Norbert Kurt 1959-
> - Reinhold Herbert 1969-
> - Krim

    832.   v. Richard Johann Reinecker b. 9 Apr 1932. d. 22 Apr 2005. m. Magdalena Marie **Czich** 1938-2013.
> 5 children:
> - Monika Magadalena 1970-
> - Christina
> - Heide
> - Richard Johann
> - Caroline

SCHMIDT / SZMIDT

1212. August **SCHMIDT** born 1862 in Didžioji Kirsna. Son of Martin Schmidt and Eva **Greff**. Baptized and confirmed at Serey Reformed Lutheran Church. Married Marianna **Bumblis**[1208] (1862-1942) 16 Nov 1884 at Mariampol Evangelical Lutheran Church. Died 3 Feb 1917. Interment at Lutheran Cemetery.

    1213. i. Anna Schmidt b. 1886. d. 17 Mar 1919. m. Adolf **Luther** 1884-1952.
          2 children:
               Lillian Ruth 1907-1997
               Walter Leonard 1916-1970

    1214. ii. August Schmidt b. 16 Jul 1888. d. 5 Sep 1921.

    1215. iii. Albert Ferdinand Schmidt b. 23 Mar 1890. d. 3 Dec 1939. m. Alice **Haas** 1906-1968.

    1216. iv. Eduard Karl "Charles" Schmidt b. 12 Mar 1892. d. 19 Sep 1973. m. Josephine „Shopia" **Pucel** 1893-1985.
          3 children:
               Edward Jr. 1916-1967
               William Frank 1919-2001
               Eileen Josephine 1922-1988

    1217. v. Friedrich Schmidt b. 30 Jul 1893. d. 1942. m. Hilda J. **Stalder** 1898-1978.
          1 child:
               Kenneth Fred 1921-1993

    1218. vi. Lillian Schmidt b. 30 May 1895. d. 15 Feb 1966. m. William Rudolph **Ritz** 1892-1960.

    1219. vii. Elmer Schmidt b. 3 May 1900. d. 16 Jun 1970. m. Estelle M. **Cunningham** 1889-1973.

1213. Anna **SCHMIDT (LUTHER)** born 1886 in Seimeniškiai. Daughter of August Schmidt[1212] (1862-1917) and Marianna **Bumblis**[1208] (1862-1942). Baptized at Kalwaria Evangelical Lutheran Church. Married Adolf **Luther** (1884-1952) 28 Oct 1905 at Zion Evangelical Lutheran Church. Died 17 Mar 1919. Interment at Woodland Cemetery.

    1220. i. Lillian Ruth Luther b. 21 May 1907. d. 19 Jun 1997. m. John J. **Smith** 1903-1969.
          2 children:

Ann Marie 1931-1996
Dorotha E. 1943-1997

1221.   ii. Walter Leonard Luther b. 26 May 1916. d. 30 Nov 1970.

1340. Adolf Franz **SCHMIDT** born 12 Dec 1904 in Valavičiai. Son of Georg Schmidt and Emilie **Peters**. Baptized and confirmed at Mariampol Evangelical Lutheran Church. Married Anna Marie **Schütz**[1341] (1913-1995). Immigrated April 1952 via New York aboard the U.S.S. *General R. M. Blatchford*. Died 14 Jun 1977. Interment at Lutheran Cemetery.

> 1342.   i. Hedwig Schmidt b. 14 Apr 1933. d. 2014. m. Helmut **Arndt** 1931-2006.
> 4 children:
> James Alan
> Lillie
> Linda R.
> Helmut O.
>
> 1343.   ii. Erna Schmidt b. 1934. m. Willie Dee **Kent** 1929-2023.
> 5 children:
> William
> Daniel
> Linda
> Lisa
> Steve
>
> 1344.   iii. Erika Schmidt b. 1944. m. Vitold **Schnell** 1938-2017.
> 3 children:
> Kathy Marie 1966-
> Karen Lisa 1966-
> Steven Victor 1970-
>
> 1345.   iv. Trudy Schmidt b. 1950. m. Gregory A. **Johns** 1947-
>
> 1346.   v. Marilyn Schmidt b. 1955. m. Celesti **DiBiasio** 1944-
>
> 1347.   vi. Arthur Schmidt

SCHNEIDER

470. Julius **SCHNEIDER** born 11 Nov 1894 in Kvietiškis. Son of Ludwig Schneider and Friedrike **Günther**. Baptized and confirmed at Mariampol Evangelical Lutheran Church. Married Emilie **Neumann**[480] (1898-1990) 5 Sep 1915 at Zion Evangelical Lutheran Church. Divorced 1929. Unconfirmed death date 6 Jul 1972. Interment unknown.

    471.   i. Edward Schneider b. 8 Jun 1916. d. 13 Aug 1994. m. Mary **Christenson** 1919-1969.
        1 child:
            Linda 1941-

    472.   i. Julius Schneider Jr. b. 28 Mar 1918. d. 8 Feb 2004. m. Violet **Tiedman**[449] 1920-1995.
        3 children:
            Nancy Charlene 1939-2005
            Kenneth M 1942-
            Gary B. 1947

473. Adolf **SCHNEIDER** born 1889 in Pagerniavė. Son of Ludwig Schneider and Friedrike **Günther**. Baptized at Wilkowischken Evangelical Lutheran Church. Confirmed at Mariampol Evangelical Lutheran Church. Immigrated July 1910 via New York aboard the S.S. *Main*. Married Bertha **Neumann**[479] (1892-1970) 16 Aug 1913 at Zion Evangelical Lutheran Church. Died 9 Feb 1973. Interment at Acacia Masonic Memorial Park Cemetery, Mayfield Heights, Ohio.

    474.   i. Walter Schneider b. 21 Jul 1915. d. 9 Jan 1992. m. Dorothy Josephine **Jehlicka** 1916-1988.
        1 child:
            Joyce Lynn 1940-2017

    475.   ii. Edna Schneider b. 5 Dec 1916. d. 30 May 2013. m. Roy Wilson **Davis** 1914-1994.
        4 children:
            Kirk
            Randall
            Fay
            Debra

    476.   iii. Ruth Schneider b. 9 Jul 1919. d. 28 Feb 2002. m. Robert G. **Armstrong** 1910-1987.

477. Karl **SCHNEIDER** born 1891 in Pagerniavė. Son of Ludwig Schneider and Friedrike **Günther**. Baptized at Wilkowischken Evangelical Lutheran Church. Confirmed at Mariampol Evangelical Lutheran Church. Married Emma **Hein**[731] (1896-1990) 26 Sep 1914 at St. Peter's Lutheran Church. Died 1 Nov 1961, Saint Cloud, Florida. Interment at Osceola Memory Gardens, Kissimmee, Florida.

    478.   i. Leonard Carl Schneider b. 24 Nov 1915. d. 3 Sep 1990. m. Olga **Greco** 1916-1998.
              2 children:
                      Joyce Lynne 1940-2017
                      Gayle Lenore 1944-2016

SCHNELL

368. Anna **SCHNELL (KOKOSCHKA)** born 17 March 1894 on the Ivoniškio dvaras (Folwark Iwoniszki) near Gudeliai. Daughter of Julius Schnell and Marianna **Pollock**. Baptized and confirmed at Mariampol Evangelical Lutheran Church. Married Friedrich **Kokoschka**[364] (1894-1962) 19 Apr 1913 at Zion Evangelical Lutheran Church. Died 19 Dec 1922. Interment at Lutheran Cemetery. For list of children, see husband Friedrich Kokoschka.

1292. Albertine **SCHNELL (PETERS)** born 17 Jan 1897 in Krokialaukis. Daughter of Julius Schnell and Marianna **Pollock**. Baptized at Serey Reformed Lutheran Church. Immigrated July 1914 via Baltimore aboard the S.S. *Rhein*. Married Albert Ewald **Peters**[1291] 24 Apr 1915 at Zion Evangelical Lutheran Church. Died 8 Jul 1983. Interment at Lutheran Cemetery. For list of children, see husband Albert Ewald Peters.

1291. Friedrich **SCHNELL** born 8 July 1872 in Krosna. Son of Wilhelm Schnell and Karoline **Hess**. Baptized and confirmed at Mariampol Evangelical Lutheran Church. Married Bertha **Weber** 12 Oct 1895 at Zion Evangelical Lutheran Church. Divorced. Married Auguste **Buknat**[1292] (1889-1991) 24 Oct 1910 in Cleveland by a Justice of the Peace. Died 13 Apr 1964. Interment unknown.

SCHÖNRANK / SCHÖNRANG

1348. Karl **SCHÖNRANK** born 24 Nov 1925 near Marijampolė. Son of August Schönrank (1872-????) and Emilie **Peters** (1883-????). Baptized at Mariampol Evangelical Lutheran Church. Immigrated September 1951 via New York aboard the U.S.S. *General R.M. Blatchford*. Married Sigrid Helga Anneliese **Treptow** (1933-2016) 13 Mar 1953. Died 15 Apr 1988 in Chesterland, Ohio. Interment at Western Reserve Memorial Gardens, Chesterland, Ohio.

1349.   i. Bernd Schönrank

1350. ii. Klaus Schönrank

SCHRÖDER

455. Henriette **SCHRÖDER** (**KIRSTEIN**) (**GÜNTHER**) born 7 Oct 1874 in Lankupėnai. Daughter of Jakob Schröder (1848-1916) and Marie **Wallner**. Baptized and confirmed at Wischtiten Evangelical Lutheran Church. Married Friedrich **Kirstein** (1870-1922) 9 Feb 1901 at Zion Evangelical Lutheran Church. Married Julius **Günther** (1867-1956) 5 Jan 1925 at Zion Evangelical Lutheran Church. Died 11 Feb 1957. Interment at Lutheran Cemetery.

    456.   i. Arthur Fred Kirstein b. 25 Jul 1906. d. 20 Aug 1956. m. Lydia **Soller** 1912-1981.
          1 child:
              Natalie 1940-

1180. Gottlieb **SCHRÖDER** born 23 Feb 1876 in Lankupėnai. Son of Jakob Schröder (1848-1916) and Marie **Wallner**. Baptized at Wirballen Evangelical Lutheran Church. Confirmed at Wischtiten Evangelical Lutheran Church. Married Ernestine **Friedrich**[1179] (1871-1942) 12 Jan 1901 at Zion Evangelical Lutheran Church. Died 1961. Interment at Lutheran Cemetery.

    1181.   i. Otto Schröder b. 11 Nov 1901. d. 16 Jan 1988. m. Helen **Samplinski** 1907-1928. m. Violet Irene **Hamilton** 1934-1988.

    1182.   ii. Marie Schröder b. 12 Feb 1903. d. 24 Aug 1994. m. Otto Hermann **Kolke** 1898-1975.
          3 children:
              Harland Adam 1919-2005
              Kenneth Marvin 1930-2017
              Audrey S. 1932-

    1183.   iii. Walter Schröder b. 30 Jul 1907. d. 6 Aug 1990. m. Dorothy P. **Ferguson** 1909-1970.

    1184.   iv. Albert Schröder b. 25 Aug 1910. d. 8 Apr 1911.

    1185.   v. Arthur Schröder b. 15 Sep 1912. d. 15 Oct 1979. m. Sylvia Madow **Chesley** 1916-2003.
          1 child
              Barbara 1942-

1187. Amelia **SCHRÖDER (FRIEDRICH)** born 1 Feb 1865 in Lankupėnai. Daughter of Jakob Schröder (1848-1916) and Marie **Wallner**. Baptized and confirmed at Wischtiten Evangelical Lutheran Church. Married Karl **Friedrich**[1186] (1873-1950) 24 Sep 1892 at Bethlehem Evangelical Lutheran Church, Detroit, Michigan. Died 16 Sep 1900. Interment at Monroe Street Cemetery. For list of children, see husband Karl Friedrich.

1188. Helene "Lena" **SCHRÖDER (FRIEDRICH)** born 9 Apr 1878 in Lankupėnai. Daughter of Jakob Schröder (1848-1916) and Marie **Wallner**. Baptized and confirmed at Wischtiten Evangelical Lutheran Church. Married Karl **Friedrich**[1186] (1873-1950) 27 Oct 1900 at Zion Evangelical Lutheran Church. Died 19 Apr 1933. Interment at Lutheran Cemetery. For list of children, see husband Karl Friedrich.

SCHULZ / SCHULTZ / SCHÜTZ / SCHITZ

1021. Albine **SCHULTZ (DANGELEIT) (KINAT) (SALEWSKI)** born 1882 in Krejwiany (Poland). Daughter of Andreas Schultz and Pauline **Worm**. Baptized at Kalwaria Evangelical Lutheran Church. Married Ludwig **Dangeleit** (1873-1904) in 1901 at Kalwaria Evangelical Lutheran Church. Married Ferdinand **Kinat**[484] (1867-1926) 22 Aug 1914 at Zion Evangelical Lutheran Church. Married Franz **Salewski** (1881-1959) 8 Oct 1927 at Zion Evangelical Lutheran Church. Died 28 Dec 1970. Interment at Lutheran Cemetery. For list of children, see husband Ferdinand Kinat.

    1022. i. Anna Dangelat b. 2 Jul 1902. d. 19 Jul 1994. m. Gustav **Neumann (Neiman)**[1016] 1887-1975.
           2 children:
                Howard[1019] 1923-1993
                Eddy[1020] 1935-

    1023. ii. Ludwig Dangelat b. 1904. d. 26 Nov 1987. m. Pauline **Dill** 1906-1975.
           1 child:
                Ruth 1928-1934

1148. Anna **SCHULZ (NIESS)** born 1855 in Kybartai. Daughter of August Schulz and Anna **Kalweit**. Baptized and confirmed at Wirballen Evangelical Lutheran Church. Married Gustav **Niess**[1147] 1876 at Wirballen Evangelical Lutheran Church. Died 6 Mar 1935. Interment at Lake View Cemetery. For list of children, see husband Gustav Niess.

1239. Christine **SCHULTZ (NIEDERSTRASS) (TIEDMANN)** born 20 Aug 1889 in Svidiškiai. Daughter of Andreas Schultz and Pauline **Wurm**. Baptized and confirmed at Kalwaria Evangelical Lutheran Church. Immigrated August 1907 via New York aboard the S.S. *Amerika*. Married Georg **Niederstrass**[1240] (1875-1949) 30 May 1910 at Zion Evangelical Lutheran Church. Married Eduard **Tiedemann**[422] 23 Jun 1910, Cleveland, Ohio. Died 6 Apr 1989 in Westlake, Ohio. Interment at Lutheran Cemetery.

1296. Johann **SCHÜTZ (SCHULTZ)** born 12 Mar 1912 in Skirptiškė. Son of August Schütz and Helene **Henkel**. Baptized at Prenen Evangelical Lutheran Church. Married Emilie Mathilde **Peter**[1297]. Immigrated via New York, November 1951 aboard the U.S.S. *General Greeley*. Died 3 Sep 2001, Parma, Ohio. Interment at Lutheran Cemetery.

    1298. i. Alfred Schütz b. 20 Sep 1938. d. 26 Aug 2007. m. Gerda Irmgard **?**.

3 children:

1299.   ii. Helga Schütz b. 1942. m. John **Haller**.
    1 child:

1300.   iii. Ingrid Lilly Schütz b. 14 Aug 1994. d. 5 Mar 2022. m. Klaus Dieter **Kitzler**.
    2 children:

1316. Georg **SCHÜTZ** born 1861 in Degučiai. Son of Adam Schütz and Marianna **Budwasch**. Baptized and confirmed at Mariampol Evangelical Lutheran Church. Married Emilie **Rosekeit**[1317] (1866-1927) 1884 at Mariampol Evangelical Lutheran Church. Immigrated July 1910 via Baltimore aboard the S.S. *Main*. Died 3 Jan 1920. Interment at Lutheran Cemetery.

1318.   i. Marie Schütz b. 12 Dec 1887. d. 22 Aug 1975. m. Leopold **Gudat**[1311] 1886-1948.
    4 children:
        Karl[1312] 1909-1978
        Anna[1313] 1911-1984
        Otto[1314] 1918-2004
        Edward[1315] 1918-1997

1319.   ii. Emilie "Millie" "Mildred" Schütz b. 1889. d. 13 Oct 1951. m. Heinrich Friedrich **Schwenter** 1886-1950. m. Heinrich **Ponto** 1889-1979.
    1 child:
        Lewis 1912-????

1320.   iii. Anna Schütz b. 1888 d. ????

1321.   iv. Auguste Schütz b. 1897. d. 14 May 1928. m. Adolf **Hasenbein** 1889-????. m. Peter Paul **Schmidt** 1898-1951.

1322.   v. Karl Eduard Schütz b. 1899. d. 25 Sep 1965. m. Vera E. **Koszak** 1900-1985.
    2 children:
        Edward 1923-1994
        Charles Richard 1925-2010

1323.   vi. Emma Schütz b. 1906. d. ????. m. Kaspar **Kellat** 1895-????. m. ? **Dryer**.

1319. Emilie „Millie" „Mildred" **SCHÜTZ (SCHWENTER) (PONTO)** born 1889 in Pakusinė. Daughter of Georg Schütz[1316] (1861-1920) and Emilie **Rosekeit**[1317] (1866-1927). Baptized and confirmed at Mariampol Evangelical Lutheran Church. Immigrated July 1910 via Baltimore aboard the S.S. *Main*. Married Matthias **Gudat**[1324] 9 May 1909 at Zion Evangelical Lutheran Church. Divorced 20 Mar 1922. Married Heinrich Friedrich **Schwenter**[1326] (1886-1950) 30 Aug 1922 by a Justice of the Peace in Cleveland. Divorced 24 Jan 1933. Married Heinrich **Ponto** (1889-1979) 18 Feb 1933 by a Justice of the Peace in Cleveland. Died 13 Oct 1951. Interment at Lutheran Cemetery. For list of children, see husband Matthias Gudat.

uio

1327. Auguste **SCHÜTZ (HASEBEIN) (SCHMIDT)** born 1897 in Trakėnai. Daughter of Georg Schütz[1316] (1861-1920) and Emilie **Rosekeit**[1317] (1866-1927). Baptized at Mariampol Evangelical Lutheran Church. Immigrated July 1910 via Baltimore aboard the S.S. *Main*. Married Adolf **Haseben** (1889-????) 18 Apr 1914 at Zion Evangelical Lutheran Church. Divorced 18 Apr 1916. Married Peter Paul **Schmidt** (1898-1951) 24 Jun 1916 at St. Paul's Evangelical Lutheran Church. Died 14 May 1928. Interment at Lutheran Cemetery.

1341. Anna Marie **SCHÜTZ (SCHMIDT)** born 14 Feb 1913 in Igliškėliai. Daughter of August Schütz and Marie **Kristeleit**. Baptized and confirmed at Mariampol Evangelical Lutheran Church. Married Adolf Franz **Schmidt**[1340] (1904-1977). Immigrated April 1952 via New York aboard the U.S.S. *General R. M. Blatchford*. Died 14 Mar 1995 in Largo, Florida. Interment at Lutheran Cemetery. For list of children, see husband Adolf Franz Schmidt.

SCHWANDT / SCHWAND

134. Gustav **SCHWANDT** (*SCHWAND*) born 3 Dec 1890 in Didiej Šelviai. Son of Friedrich Schwandt and Anna **Wels**. Baptized and confirmed at Wischtiten Evangelical Lutheran Church. Immigrated August 1911 via Philadelphia aboard the S.S. *Prinz Oskar*. Married Helene "Lena" **Fischer**[136] (1895-1947) 27 Dec 1921 at St. Johannes Independent Evangelical Church. Died 28 June 1956. Interment at Knollwood Cemetery, Mayfield Heights, Ohio.

    135.   i. Raymond Schwandt b. 8 Oct 1922. d. 22 Jan 1977. m. Gertrude F. **Henry** 1924-1999.
              1 child:
                      Linda Kay 1947-2001

SCHWED / SZWED / SCHWEDAS

1206. Anna **SCHWED (BUMBLIS)** born about 1837 likely near Senoji Radiškė. Daughter of Martin Schwed and Catherine **Grausch**. Married Johann **Bumblis**[1205] (1835-1920) 1861 at Mariampol Evangelical Lutheran Church. Immigrated August 1902 via Baltimore aboard the S.S. *Brandenburg*. Died 29 July 1921. Interment at Lutheran Cemetery. For list of children, see husband Johann Bumblis.

1464. Helene Marianna **SCHWED (PECK)** born 1883 in Obelija. Daughter of Adolf Schwed (1855-1917) and Marianna **Reder** (1860-1929). Baptized at Serey Reformed Lutheran Church. Married Harold Lyle **Peck** (1892-1963) 4 Sep 1923 at St. Paul Evangelical Lutheran Church. Died 30 Jan 1964 in Lake County, Ohio. Interment at Crown Hill Cemetery and Mausoleum, Twinsburg, Ohio.

    1465. i. Harold Peck Jr. b. 23 Oct 1914. d. 26 Dec 1973. m. Elsie Alberta **Werman** 1924-2008.
           1 child:
                James E. Peck 1941-1988

    1466. ii. Ethel Eleanor Peck b. 23 Oct 1916. d. 13 Dec 1992. m. Frank **Hogya** 1918-????.
           1 child:
                Ilene 1936-

    1467. iii. Wilbert James Peck b. 18 Dec 1932. d. 4 Jan 2010. m. Gladys Mae **Smith** 1933-.
           5 children:
                Patricia
                David
                Richard
                Wilbert Jr.
                Donna

1468. Marianna Anna **SCHWED (WELLNER)** born 1885 in Obelija. Daughter of Adolf Schwed (1855-1917) and Marianna **Reder** (1860-1929). Baptized at Serey Reformed Lutheran Church. Married Paul August **Wellner** (1880-1936) 19 Oct 1903 at Zion Evangelical Lutheran Church. Died 20 Jan 1977. Interment at Crown Hill Cemetery and Mausoleum in Twinsburg, Ohio.

    1469. i. Ruth Wellner b. 13 Oct 1904. d. 25 May 1998. m. Norman **DuPerow** 1896-1976.

    1470. ii. Florence D. Wellner b. 1 Jul 1906. d. 25 Jul 1983. m. Louis Anthony **Fodor** 1901-????.

1 child:
>
> Donald Edward 1929-2009

1471. iii. August Wellner b. 23 Sep 1908. d. 23 Sep 1908.

1472. iv. Walter Wellner b. 30 Jul 1910. d. 15 Dec 1971. m. Louise **Aslaksen** 1912-1969.
> 2 children:
>> Paul Patrick 1941-2021
>> Walter T. 1943-

1473. v. Lucille Bernice Wellner b. 29 Oct 1912. d. 17 Oct 1994. m. Arthur **Miller** ????-????.
> 3 children:
>> Dana
>> Michelle
>> Arthur

1474. vi. Alberta Hartel Wellner b. 15 Nov 1914. d. Jul 1979.

1475. vii. Kenneth Wellner b. 26 Dec 1917. d. 1 Jan 1970. m. Florence M. **Pelgar** 1920-2004.
> 1 child:
>> Barbara

1476. Anna **SCHWED** born 1887 in Obelija. Daughter of Adolf Schwed (1855-1917) and Marianna **Reder** (1860-1929). Baptized at Serey Reformed Lutheran Church. Died 22 Jun 1961 in East Cleveland. Interment at Lutheran Cemetery.

1486. Karl "Charles" **SCHWED** born 1877 in Jukneliškė. Son of Ludwig Schwed (1842-1906) and Anna **Zaam** (sp?). Baptized at Mariampol Evangelical Lutheran Church. Married Louise **Wenicke** (1893-1982) 24 Apr 1912 at Bethlehem Evangelical Lutheran Church. Died 4 Sep 1947. Interment at Knollwood Cemetery, Mayfield Heights, Ohio.

1487. i. Rose Schwed b. 10 Feb 1913. d. 28 Feb 2004. m. Glen Oren **Wray** 1912-1979.
> 1 child:
>> Barbara 1943-

1488. ii. Clarence Herman Schwed b. 13 Aug 1914. d. 20 May 1980. m. Maethorne **Palmer** 1918-????.
> 2 children:
>> Karen L 1947-
>> Gary D. 1950-

1489. iii. Margaret Schwed b. 20 Feb 1921. d. 25 May 2021. m. John M. **Soltis** 1921-2008.
> 2 children:
>> Gail D. 1947-
>> Lynn S. 1949-

1490. iv. Charles William Schwed b. 11 Apr 1926. d. 11 Jan 2020. m. Lois Jean **Grapatin** 1930-2016.
> 3 children:
>> Cheri
>> Maureen
>> Charles Keith

1491. Heinrich **SCHWED** born 15 May 1889 in Ringdaudai. Son of Friedrich Albert Schwed (1844-1911) and Anna **Reder** (1858-1924). Baptized at Goddlau Evangelical Lutheran Church. Immigrated July 1909 via New York aboard the S.S. *George Washington*. Married Amelia **Lehmann**[87] (1893-1960) 18 Feb 1912 at Zion Evangelical Lutheran Church. Died 28 Jun 1942. Interment at Lutheran Cemetery.

> 88. i. William Julius Schwed b. 1 Dec 1912. d. 21 Apr 1988. m. Emma **Lang** 1914-2004.
>> 1 child:
>>> Donald 1937-2009.
>>> m. Helen **Roll** 1918-1995.

> 89. ii. Emma Schwed b. 22 Jun 1914. d. 24 Jun 1914.

> 90. iii. Lydia Amelia Schwed b. 23 Sep 1915. d. 23 Jun 1994. m. Wilber A. **Beal**.
>> 1 child:
>>> Janice

1492. Helene Emma "Lena" **SCHWED (WOLF)** born 1893 in Kineryszki (no longer exists; near Aleksotas). Daughter of Friedrich Albert Schwed (1844-1911) and Anna **Reder** (1858-1924). Baptized at Goddlau Evangelical Lutheran Church. Immigrated July 1909 via New York aboard the S.S. *George Washington*. Married Oswald Walter **Wolf** (1891-1972) 13 Sep 1913 at Zion Evangelical Lutheran Church. Died 1982. Interment at Lutheran Cemetery.

> 1493. i. Emma Wolf b. 18 Jul 1914. d. 1 Jan 1990. m. James Colmer **Beall** 1911-1970.
>> 2 children:
>>> Laura L. 1933
>>> Jacqueline 1938-

1494. ii. Lena Wolf b. 23 Sep 1915. d. 13 Oct 2002. m. John Albert **Mikulitz** 1911-2004. m. Robert S. **Bohr** 1925-2005.
> 3 children:
>> June Lee 1938-2001
>> Janet 1938-
>> JoAnne 1948-

1495. iii. Walter Henry Wolf b. 3 Feb 1918. d. 28 Jan 1998. m. Alma **Brauer**[901] 1919-2018.

1496. iv. Lillian Wolf b. 19 Jun 1921. d. 4 Feb 2007. m. Allen Hugh **Sackmann** 1921-1991.
> 1 child:
>> Allen Hugh Jr. 1940-

1497. Julius Gustav **SCHWED** born 28 Jul 1896 in Poderiškiai. Son of Friedrich Albert Schwed (1844-1911) and Anna **Reder** (1858-1924). Baptized at Goddlau Evangelical Lutheran Church. Married Louise **Lehmann**[93] (1898-1982) 27 Oct 1917 at Zion Evangelical Lutheran Church. Died 15 Jan 1966. Interment at Lutheran Cemetery.

94. i. Alma L. Schwed b. 6 Jul 1918. d. 6 Jun 2008. m. John Walter **Dutchcot**[101] 1913-2006.
> 1 child:
>> Judy A 1947-

95. ii. Arthur W Schwed b. 1920. d. 10 Feb 1964. m. Irene E. 1921-1988.

SCHWELGIN

369. Adolf "Edward" **SCHWELGIN** born 8 January 1892 in Šilavotas. Baptized and confirmed at Mariampol Evangelical Lutheran Church. Son of Anna **Schwelgin**. Immigrated August 1909 via Baltimore aboard the S.S. *Breslau*. Married Albine **Lang**[368] (1891-1981) 22 Aug 1914 at St. Paul's Evangelical Lutheran Church. Divorced 1925. Married Rosalia ? Died 14 Aug 1948, Mayview, Pennsylvania. Interment at Greenwood Cemetery, Sharpsburg, Pennsylvania.

    370.   i. Arthur Schwelgin b. 22 Jul 1915. d. 26 Aug 1968. m. Beatrice **Bellock** 1918-1975.
            1 child:
                Arthur Anthony 1944-2009

1368. Johann **SCHWELGIN** born 9 Dec 1876 in Šilavotas. Son of Ludwing Schwelgin and Elisabeth **Nurnat**. Baptized and confirmed at Mariampol Evangelical Lutheran Church. Immigrated July 1900 via Baltimore Married Helene **Baltronat**[1368] (1885-1942) 18 Feb 1906 at Zion Evangelical Lutheran Church. Died 30 Oct 1936. Interment at Lutheran Cemetery.

    1370.   i. Carl Wilhelm Schwelgin b. 28 Jun 1907. d. 5 Jan 1980. m. Adeline **Krause** 1906-1999.
            3 children:
                Nancy 1935-2002
                Robert C. 1941-
                Sally R. 1948-

    1371.   ii. Emma Emilie Schwelgin b. 15 May 1909. d. ????.

    1372.   iii. Adolf Ludwig Schwelgin b. 26 Nov 1910. d. 23 Apr 1988. m. Lydia Amelia **Pekrul** 1917-2007.
            3 children:
                Emily Henriette 1937-2001
                Lydia 1939-
                Adolph Ludwig Jr. 1946-

    1373.   iv. Walter Gustav Schwelgin b. 5 Oct 1912. d. 16 Jan 1994. m. Agnes **Rowerstein** 1910-1999.

    1374.   v. Johann Martin Schwelgin b. 31 Oct 1914. d. 1 Jun 1917.

    1375.   vi. Helen Lydia Schwelgin b. 19 Oct 1916. d. 23 Jul 1997.

    1376.   vii. Albert Frederick Schwelgin b. 15 Sep 1918. d. 20 Oct 1978.

1377. viii. Marie Augusta Schwelgin b. 15 Feb 1920. d. 26 Nov 1999. m. Charles Kirkwood **Meese** 1903-1984.
       2 children:
            Norman Charles 1946-2021
            Charlene 1950-

1378. ix. Harry Herman Schwelgin b. 7 Mar 1924. d. 2 Nov 1966. m. Helen **Farson** 1921-2011.

SCHWENTER / SCHWENTOR

1326. Heinrich Friedrich **SCHWENTER** born 16 Sep 1886 in Vainatrakis. Son of Julius Ludwig Schwenter and Wilhelmine Julia **Hazengeitz** (sp?). Baptized and confirmed at Mariampol Evangelical Lutheran Church. Immigrated November of 1909 via Baltimore aboard the *S.S. Brandenburg*. Married Emilie "Millie" **Schütz**[1319] 30 Aug 1922 by a Justice of the Peace in Cleveland. Divorced 24 Jan 1933. Died 13 Dec 1950. Interment at Lutheran Cemetery.

SEMLER

464. Karl Adam **SEMLER** born 1866 in Balbieriškis. Son of August Semler and Karoline **Lang**. Baptized at Prenen Evangelical Lutheran Church. Married Johanna **Samuel** (1873-1957) 2 Nov 1892. Died 24 Mar 1950. Interment at Lutheran Cemetery.

    465.   i. William Adolph Semler b. 10 Sep 1893. d. 27 Sep 1958. m. Virginia **Rose** 1913-1975.

    466.   ii. Elsie Semler b. 4 May 1895. d. 20 Oct 1990. m. George Henry **Starke** 1896-1967.
>
> 2 children:
> Raymond George 1919-2001
> Ralph 1930-

    467.   iii. Bertha Semler b. 21 Apr 1898. d. 7 Jun 1976. m. Matthew John **Lamont** 1889-1940.
>
> 1 child:
> Norma Louise 1920-2001

    468.   iv. Mildred E. Semler b. 27 Oct 1902. d. 5 Mar 1999. m. Frank Everett **Robinson** 1894-1985.
>
> 1 child:
> Thomas A.

    469.   v. Katherine Semler b. 17 Feb 1906. d. ????. m. Stanley G. **Powell** 1905-????.

SIMON / SIEMON / SEAMAN / SEAMON / SIMONAT / SIMONEIT

562. Marianna "Marie" **SIMON** (*SEAMAN*) (**WACHHAUS**) born 1875 (village unidentifiable; somewhere near Kalvarija). Daughter of Johann Simon and Christine **Jekel**. Baptized at Kalwaria Evangelical Lutheran Church. Married Adolf "Adam" **Wachhaus**[555] (1876-1949). Died 13 May 1947. Interment at East Cleveland Township Cemetery. For list of children, see husband Adolf "Adam" Wachhaus.

563. Johann **SIMON** (*SEAMAN*) born 1864 in Zawody (current place name unknown). Son of Johann Simon and Christine **Jekel**. Baptized at Kalwaria Evangelical Lutheran Church. Married Anna **Niederstrasse** (1870-1939) 5 Oct 1893 at Christ Lutheran Church in Mahanoy City, Pennsylvania. Died 30 Apr 1943. Interment at Lutheran Cemetery.

    564.   i. Frederick Seaman b. 9 Aug 1893. d. 30 Oct 1951. m. Auguste Edith **Grossman** 1894-1956.
        2 children:
            Lillian 1918-1964
            Arthur James 1919-1964

    565.   ii. Carl "Charles" Seaman b. 1898. d. 4 Oct 1927.

    566.   iii. Harold Seaman b. 29 Dec 1902. d. 2 May 1983. m. Elizabeth **Meier** b. 1906. d. ????.

    567.   iv. Edward Seaman b. 11 Sep 1905. d. 4 Apr 1970. m. Mildred **Zgajnar Ganner** 1907-1963.
        2 children:
            Edward G. 1937-
            Dale D. 1939-

    568.   v. Emma Seaman b. 12 Mar 1909. d. 23 Apr 1998. m. Frank A. **Bratton** 1904-1987.
        1 child:
            Wayne 1935-

SOKOLEK / SOKOLIK

1043. Adolf **SOKOLEK** born 1883 in Miklausė. Son of Adam Sokolek and Karoline **Worm**. Baptized at Serey Evangelical Lutheran Church. Immigrated September 1903 via Baltimore aboard the S.S. *Neckar*. Married Marianna **Reinke**[1042] (1886-1956) 6 Aug 1905 at Zion Evangelical Lutheran Church. Died 1934. Interment at Lutheran Cemetery.

    1044. i. Helene W. Sokolik b. 10 Sep 1906. d. 29 Jul 1985. m. Adolf Georg **Neitzel**[791] 1901-1986.
        2 children:
            Mildred Loretta 1924-2015
            Eleanore Louise 1925-2013

    1045. ii. Marie Regina Sokolik b. 7 Sep 1908. d. 20 Nov 1989. m. Emil W. **Drachenberg** 1905-1973.
        2 children:
            Robert Carl 1926-1998
            Dorothy 1930-

    1046. iii. Adolph Carl Sokolik b. 29 Apr 1911. d. 14 Mar 1978. m. Bertha **Worm**[1071] 1910-1938. m. Winifred **?**
        2 children:
            Arlene 1932-2015
            Charles 1935-

    1047. iv. Emil Rudolph Sokolik b. 27 Aug 1913. d. 25 Apr 1990. m. Agnes Anna **Ineman** 1914-2013.
        3 children:
            Lois J. 1933-2021
            Alan 1938-
            Ronald 1943-2023

    1048. v. Gustave W. Sokolik b. 20 Jul 1916. d. 24 Apr 1995. m. Florence Mary **Ineman** 1916-1994.
        3 children:
            Joan 1928-
            Janct 1939-
            Jean

SPEI

417. August **SPEI** born 3 Apr 1874 in Vištytis. Son of Julius Spei and Anna **Richtat**. Baptized and confirmed at Wischtiten Evangelical Lutheran Church. Immigrated January 1909 via New York aboard the S.S. *Samland*. Married Emma **Parry**[410] (1893-1964) 4 Sep 1915 at Bethlehem Evangelical Lutheran Church. Died 26 May 1971 in Lakeland, Florida. Interment unknown.

    418.   i. Herbert Harry Spei b. 30 Apr 1918. d. 20 Jun 2000.

    419.   ii. Howard Perry Spei b. 24 Nov 1923. d. 13 Dec 2010. M. Shirley M. **Tavernier** 1922-2011.
          2 children:
              David L.
              Sharon L.

SPURGAT / SPORGAT

1303. Jakob **SPURGAT** born 2 Jul 1890 in Grygaliszki (near Wiżajny, Poland). Baptized at Wischainy Evangelical Lutheran Church. Son of Andreas "Heinrich" Spurgat (1835-????) and Christine **Wagner**. Married Henriette **Erzthaler**[1261] (1886-1969) 7 Aug 1926 at St. John's Lutheran Church. WWI Veteran. Died 29 Oct 1967. Interment at Lutheran Cemetery.

STASSUN / STASUN / STOSSUN

1130. Friedrich **STASSUN** born May 1872 in Grzybina (Poland). Son of Josef Stossun and Karoline **Oberüber**. Baptized at Wischainy Evangelical Lutheran Church. Married Marie **Widra** (1883-1949) 4 Oct 1902 at Immanual Lutheran Church, Braddock, Pennsylvania. Died 16 Mar 1925. Interment at Lutheran Cemetery.

    1131. i. Martha Stassun b. 22 Oct 1904. d. 4 May 1989. m. Ferdinand Johann **Eder** 1896-1937. m. William H. **Dull** 1906-1978. m. John Milton **Schockley** 1905-1966.
          4 children:
               Marie Martha 1922-2006
               Walter F. 1924-
               Edna H. 1926-
               June F. 1929-

    1132. ii. Heinrich Stassun b. 8 Aug 1906. d. 1 Oct 1974. m. Martha Bertha **Portofe** 1913-2003.
          2 children:
               Carolyn Marie 1944-
               Norma J. 1947-

    1133. iii. Anna Stassun b. 8 Aug 1909. d. 23 May 1995. m. ? **Moore** 1905-????.

    1134. iv. August Stassun b. 8 Aug 1909. d. ????.

    1135. v. Otto Friedrich Stossun b. 25 Jun 1912. d. 16 Sep 1982. m. Anna **Nastiuk** 1916-1963.
          1 child:
               Bernice 1942-

1136. Marie **STOSSUN (KLAMER)** born 20 Aug 1879 in Grzybina (Poland.) Daughter of Josef Stossun and Karoline **Oberüber**. Baptized at Wischainy Evangelical Lutheran Church. Married Friedrich **Klamer** (1879-1971) 19 Nov 1905 at Zion Evangelical Lutheran Church. Died 6 May 1965. Interment at St. John Lutheran Cemetery in South Euclid, Ohio.

    1137. i. Henry W. Klamer b. 7 May 1907. d. 27 Jul 1986. m. Dorothy M. **Hyser** 1909-1996.
          2 children:
               Keith Broughton 1934-1987
               Ruth J. 1940-

1138. ii. Vandaline Marie Klamer b. 27 Feb 1916. d. 24 Nov 1993. m. Helmer Henry **Hein** 1913-1999.
    2 children:
        Carol Jane 1942-
        Diane S. 1949-

1139. Heinrich **STOSSUN** born 11 Sep 1886 in Grzybina (Poland). Son of Josef Stossun and Karoline **Oberüber**. Baptized at Wischainy Evangelical Lutheran Church. Married Emma **Weber** (1875-1945) 9 Dec 1905 at Zion Lutheran Church in Pittsburg, Pennsylvania. Died 16 Jul 1935 in South Euclid, Ohio. Interment at St. John Lutheran Cemetery, South Euclid, Ohio.

  1140. i. Ludwig August Stasun b. 23 Jul 1908. d. 28 Apr 1991. m. Iva L. **Detering** 1913-1988.
    2 children:
        June 1939-
        Kenneth 1945-

  1141. ii. Baby Boy Stassun b. 7 Jun 1910. d. 7 Jun 1910.

1258. Gustav **STOSSUN** born 1866 in Grzybina (Poland). Son of Josef Stossun and Karoline **Oberüber**. Baptized at Wischainy Evangelical Lutheran Church. Married Marie Emma **Erzthaler**[1259] (1873-1966) 31 Dec 1896 at Zion Evangelical Lutheran Church. Died 29 Nov 1926 in Pittsburg, Pennsylvania. Interment at Woodlawn Cemetery, Aliquippa, Pennsylvania.

  1260. i. Emma Marie Stassun b. 9 Oct 1897. d. 21 May 1995. m. Robert **Schmidt** 1891-1957.
    3 children:
        Norton Robert 1917-1954
        Jermone Norton 1921-1944
        Romelda Emma 1933-1978

1498. Gustav Josef **STOSSUN** born May 1877 in Leszkiemie (Poland). Son of Antoni Stossun and Luise **Ostrowski**. Baptized at Wischainy Evangelical Lutheran Church. Died 6 Mar 1903. Interment at Woodland Cemetery.

TENNEBOR / TENNEBAR

996. Emilie „Milly" **TENNEBOR** (**PETERS**) born 1895 in Wiżajny (Poland). Daughter of Georg Tennebor (1862-1926) and Helene **Kausch**[998] (1863-1925.) Baptized at Wischainy Evangelical Lutheran Church. Immigrated February 1902 via New York aboard the S.S. *Southwark*. Married Adolf **Peters**[887] (1891-1973) 16 Jun 1923 at Zion Evangelical Lutheran Church. Died Jun 1952. Interment at Lutheran Cemetery. For list of children, see husband Adolf Peters.

997. Georg **TENNEBOR** born 1862 in Wiżajny (Poland). Son of Friedrich Tennebor and Elisabeth **Reinke**. Baptized at Wischainy Evangelical Lutheran Church. Married Helene **Kausch**[998] (1863-1925) 1883 at Wischainy Evangelical Lutheran Church. Died 28 Apr 1926. Interment at Lutheran Cemetery.

    999.   i. Friedrich Tennebor b. 23 April 1886. d. ????. Twin of Georg.

    1000.   ii. Georg Tennebor b. 23 April 1886. d. 27 Sep 1963. m. Auguste **Schiemann** 1885-1963. Twin of Friedrich.
        2 children:
            Edith 1910-1983
            Howard George 1912-1946

    1001.   iii. August Tennebor b. 1887. d. ????.

    1002.   iv. Auguste Tennebor b.16 September 1889. d. ????. Twin of Karoline

    1003.   v. Karoline "Lena" Tennebor b. 16 September 1889. d. 12 Oct 1955. m. Gustav **Polenschat** 1883-1948. Twin of Auguste.
        7 children:
            Arthur 1909-1909
            Albert 1910-1966
            Lillian Ruth 1912-1991
            Emil 1916-1916
            Howard 1916-1916
            Raymond Leonard 1918-1988
            Gertrude 1922-

    1004.   vi. Anna Tennebor b. 1892. d. ????.

    996.   vii. Emilie "Milly" Tennebor b. 1895. d. Jun 1952. m. Adolf **Peters**[887] 1891-1973.
        1 child:
            Ralph 1927-

    1005.   viii. Bertha Tennebor b. 1901. d. ????.

1006. ix. Tillie Tennebor b. 27 Oct 1906. d. 1980. m. Joseph E. **Bard** 1900-1973.

1000. Georg **TENNEBOR** born 1886 in Wiżajny (Poland). Son of Georg Tennebor[997] (1862-1926) and Helene **Kausch**[998] (1863-1925). Twin of Friedrich Tennebor[999] (1886-????). Baptized at Wischainy Evangelical Lutheran Church. Immigrated March 1902 via New York aboard the S.S. *Vaterland*. Married Auguste **Schiemann** (1885-1963) 27 Feb 1910 at St. Paul's Evangelical Lutheran Church. Died 27 Sep 1963. Interment at Lutheran Cemetery.

    1007. i. Edith Tennebar b. 7 Oct 1910. d. 25 Jan 1983. m. Adolph Heinrich **Gottlieb** 1907-1979.
        1 child:
            Robert Henry 1943-

    1008. ii. Howard George Tennebar b. 10 Nov 1912. d. 27 Jul 1946.

1003. Karoline "Lena" **TENNEBOR (POLENSCHAT)** born 1889 in Wiżajny (Poland). Daughter of George Tennebor[997] (1862-1926) and Helene **Kausch**[998] (1863-1925). Twin of Auguste Tennebor[1001] (1889-????). Baptized at Wischainy Evangelical Lutheran Church. Immigrated February 1902 via New York aboard the S.S. *Southwark*. Married Gustav **Polenschat** (1883-1948) 4 Sep 1908 in Cleveland by a Justice of the Peace. Died 12 Oct 1955. Interment at Lutheran Cemetery.

    1009. i. Arthur Polenschat b. 24 Jun 1909. d. 11 Aug 1909.

    1010. ii. Albert Gustave Polenschat b. 2 Sep 1910. d. 7 Jun 1966. m. Lydia **Bumblis** 1912-2005.
        2 children:
            Jeanette 1934-
            Joa C. 1941-2017

    1011. iii. Lillian Ruth Polenschat b. 15 Jun 1912. d. 15 Jan 1991. m. Adolph **Renke**[171] 1904-1990.

    1012. iv. Emil Polenschat b. 9 Nov 1916. d. 9 Nov 1916. Twin of Howard Polenschat.[1013]

    1013. v. Howard Polenschat b. 9 Nov 1916. d. 2 Dec 1916. Twin of Emil Polenschat.[1012]

    1014. vi. Raymond Leonard Polenschat b. 2 Nov 1918. d. 10 Jul 1988. m. Wilda Marcellea **Wonders** 1921-1992.

1015. vii. Gertrude Jean Polenschat b. 9 Aug 1921. d. 3 Nov 2011. m. Alvin Woodrow **Evans** 1917-2009.
      1 child:
           Linda 1947-

TETMEIER / TETMEYER / TETTMEIER

848. Ferdinand Christof **TETMEIER** born 11 May 1857 in Rėčiūnai. Son of Friedrich Tetmeier and Marie **Ewald**. Baptized and confirmed at Wischtiten Evangelical Lutheran Church. Married Henriette **Lindhammer**[863] (1853-1935) 1877 at Wischtiten Evangelical Lutheran Church. Died 19 Oct 1935. Interment at Lutheran Cemetery.

    849.   i. Anna Tetmeier b. 27 Nov 1879. d. 17 Apr 1958. m. August **Gehrke** 1878-1903. m. Matthias **Reiter** 1869-1956.
        1 child:
            Clarence Walter 1902-1981

    850.   ii. Wilhelmine Tetmeier b. 21 Mar 1882. d. 23 Nov 1946. m. Henry Theodore **Gehrke** 1880-1958. m. William H. **Kindra** 1859-1923 m. Claude Mason **Brownwell** 1882-1929. m. Frederick C. Irons 1891-1960.
        1 child:
            Lillian Dorothy 1904-1990

    851.   iii. Adeline "Lena" Tetmeier b. 23 Jul 1887. d. 04 Feb 1907.

    852.   iv. Emma Bertha Tetmeyer b. 18 Feb 1893. d. 29 Apr 1977. m. Edward C. **Newman** 1888-1979.
        2 children:
            Eleanor 1915-2002
            Dorothy 1923-2004

    853.   v. Ella Edna Tetmeyer b. 22 Mar 1896. d. 23 Mar 1986. m. Leslie Frank **Linn** 1894-1981.
        1 child:
            Leslie Frank 1922-1998

849. Anna **TETMEIER (GEHRKE) (REITER)** born 27 Nov 1879 in Liukiai. Daughter of Ferdinand Christof Tetmeier[848] (1857-1958) and Henriette **Lindhammer**[863] (1853-1935). Baptized and confirmed at Wischtiten Evangelical Lutheran Church. Married August **Gehrke** (1878-1903) 1 Aug 1901 at Zion Evangelical Lutheran Church. Married Matthias **Reiter**[847] (1869-1956) October 1905. Died 17 Apr 1958. Interment at Lutheran Cemetery.

    854.   i. Clarence Walter Gehrke b. 4 May 1902. d. 6 Jul 1981. m. Ursula Elva **Fox** 1901-1984.
        1 child:
            Clarence Harlan 1926-1984

850. Wilhelmine **TETMEIER (GEHRKE) (BROWNELL) (KINDRA) (IRONS)** born 21 Mar 1882 likely in Liukiai. Daughter of Ferdinand Christof Tetmeier[848] (1857-1958) and Henriette **Lindhammer**[863] (1853-1935). Likely baptized at Wischtiten Evangelical Lutheran Church. Confirmed at Zion Evangelical Lutheran Church. Married Henry Theodore **Gehrke** (1880-1958) in Lorain, Ohio, by a Justice of the Peace. Divorced 24 Apr 1914. Married Claude Mason **Brownell** (1882-1929) 6 May 1916 in Cleveland by a Justice of the Peace. Divorced. Married ? **Tomko**. Divorced 7 Apr 1923. Married William H. **Kindra** (1859-1923) 5 May 1923 at Sixth Presbyterian Church. Married Frederick C. **Irons** (1891-1960) 14 May 1927 at Zion Evangelical Lutheran Church. Died 23 Nov 1946. Interment at Lutheran Cemetery.

    855.   i. Lilian Dorothy Gehrke b. 19 Jul 1904. d. 21 Oct 1990. m. Walter E. **Limpert** 1903-1988.

851. Adeline "Lena" **TETMEIER** born 23 Jul 1887 likely in Liukiai. Daughter of Ferdinand Christof Tetmeier[848] (1857-1958) and Henriette **Lindhammer**[863] (1853-1935). Likely baptized at Wischtiten Evangelical Lutheran Church. Confirmed at Zion Evangelical Lutheran Church. Died 4 Feb 1907. Interment at Lutheran Cemetery.

TIEDMANN

420. Julius **TIEDMANN** born 1859 in Milastonys. Son of Ferdinand Tiedmann and Karoline Kuczynski. Baptized at Serey Reformed Evangelical Church. Married Mathilde Pauline **Franulewicz**[481] (1857-1905) 1882 at Serey Reformed Evangelical Church. Married Pauline **Ratz** (1876-1956) 11 Aug 1906 in Cleveland by a Justice of the Peace. Died 14 Mar 1918. Interment at Lutheran Cemetery.

    421.   i. Julius Tiedmann b. 1883. d. 7 Jan 1944. m. Leokadia "Catherine" **Ackermann** 1887-1968.
9 children:
- Mathilde[433] 1905-1990
- William[434] 1907-1985
- Julius[435] 1909-1980
- Ruth[436] 1911-2002
- Helen L.[437] 1912-1999
- Irene[438] 1915-2006
- Arnold[439] 1916-1999
- Earl Howard[440] 1919-2008
- Evelyn[441] 1922-

    422.   ii. Adolf Eduard Tiedmann b. 15 Aug 1885. d. 21 Sep 1963. m. Eva **Hausrath** 1884-1942. m. Christine **Schultz**[1239] 1890-1989.
10 children:
- Edward 1909-1996[442]
- Gustav 1911-1965[443]
- Watler 1912-1975[444]
- Arthur 1913-1932[445]
- Carl 1915-1994[446]
- Oscar Oswald 1915-1994[447]
- Clarence 1919-1999[448]
- Violet 1921-1995[449]
- Lillian Ruth 1922-2004[450]
- Irene 1923-1927[451]

    423.   iii. Angelika Tiedmann b. 1888. d. 1888.

    424.   iv. Marianna „Marie" Tiedmann b. 1890. d. 20 Feb 1981. m. Johann Kramer 1890-????.
3 children:
- Clarence 1911-2002[452]
- Evelyn 1917-1996[453]
- June 1920-2002[454]

425. v. August John Tiedmann b. 24 Mar 1893. d. 24 Jun 1964. m. Julia **Potuk** 1913-2015.
   1 child:

426. vi. Olga Tiedmann b. 23 Feb 1901. d. 31 Oct 1995. m. Frank Donald **Kenat** 1906-1976.
   2 children:
   Virgina Lee 1939-1999
   Franklyn Donald 1941-2003

427. vii. Henry Tiedmann b. 11 Aug 1907. d. 11 Mar 1975. m. Anna Catherine **Kosiorek** 1916-1995.

428. viii. Lillian Tiedmann b. 5 Mar 1909. d. 7 Sep 1968. m. Francis William **Shemansky** 1913-1999.

429. ix. Josephine Tiedmann b. 17 Dec 1910. d. 7 Sep 1941. m. John L **Miller** 1914-1995.
   1 child:
   Judith 1938-

430. x. Ruth Tiedmann b. 1 Jan 1913. d. 10 Apr 1972.

431. xi. Elsie Tiedmann b. 15 Aug 1914. d. 7 Aug 2006. m. John **Motel** 1909-1978.
   2 children:
   Lawrence 1937-
   Elise J. 1940-1940

432. xii. Elmer William Tiedmann b. 14 Feb 1917. d. 20 May 1983. M. Helen **Motel** 1923-1999.
   2 children:
   Maureen 1945-
   Sally 1948-

421. Julius **TIEDMANN** born 1883 in Obelija. Son of Julius Tiedmann[420] (1859-1918) and Mathilde **Franulewicz**[481](1857-1905). Baptized at Serey Reformed Lutheran Church. Immigrated March 1897 via New York. Married Leokadia Emilie "Catherine" **Ackermann**[190] (1885-1936) 23 Jan 1904 at Zion Evangelical Lutheran Church. Died 7 Jan 1944. Interment at Lake View Cemetery.

433. i. Mathilde Tiedman b. 26 Mar 1905. d. 28 Nov 1990. m. Thomas **Lanese** 1901-1978.
   2 children:
   Thomas 1928-

Robert Albert 1933-2005

434. ii. William Tiedman b. 21 Feb 1907. d. 20 Jun 1985. m. Edna **Buildt** 1909-1998.
  1 child:
  William J. 1932-2023

435. iii. Julius Tiedman b. 29 Jul 1909. d. 7 Dec 1980. m. LaVerne Ruth **Buchman** 1914-1970.
  3 children:
  Richard 1937-
  Ronald Wayne 1938-1953
  Randall Keith 1949-2012

436. iv. Ruth Tiedman b. 1 Jan 1911. d. 22 Jan 2002. m. Maurice L **Jacobs** 1911-1957. m. Carl E. **Fix** 1912-????. m. Frank C. **Tomasello** 1908-1978.
  3 children:
  Ruth
  William
  Sharon Betty 1945-2014

437. v. Helen Louise Tiedman b. 16 Sep 1912. d. 23 Oct 1999. m. Edward William **Henkel** 1906-1988.
  2 children:
  Lilliam L. 1933-
  Kenneth Elmer 1935-2021

438. vi. Irene Tiedman b. 24 Aug 1915. d. 2 Mar 2006. m. Joe Frank **Spudick** 1910-1984.
  3 children:
  Irene 1946-2017
  Gloria 1947-
  Allen 1949-

439. Arnold Tiedman b. 7 Nov 1916. d. 2 Jul 1999. m. **?**

440. vii. Earl Howard Tiedman b. 10 Mar 1919. d. 2 May 2008. m. Anna Marie **Belus** 1922-2008.
  2 children:
  Shirley A 1943-
  Dennis Howard 1948-2003

441. viii. Evelyn Tiedman b. 14 Jun 1921. d. 13 Mar 2014. m. Joseph **Lopresti** 1919-2010.
  1 child:

Rose Marie 1950-

422. Adolf Eduard **TIEDMANN** born 15 August 1885 near Liškiava (his place of birth is listed as „Piliakalnis"). Son of Julius Tiedmann[420] (1859-1918) and Mathilde **Franulewicz**[481] (1857-1905). Baptized at Serey Reformed Lutheran Church. Immigrated July 1900 via New York aboard the S.S. *Matilda*. Married Eva **Hausrath** (1884-1942) 3 Oct 1907 in Cleveland by a Justice of the Peace. Married Christine **Schultz**[1239] (1890-1989) 23 Jun 1950. Died 21 Sep 1963. Interment at Lutheran Cemetery.

- 442. i. Edward Tiedman b. 12 Sep 1909. d. 25 Apr 1996. m. Leona **Burnard** 1907-????. m. Caroline **Diklich** 1919-1962. m. Madelyn **Harrison** 1906-2004.
    6 children:
    Edward Burnard 1931-1982
    Robert B. 1935-
    David B. 1938-
    Caroline Marie 1947-2020
    Raymond George 1943-2000
    Irene 1949-

- 443. ii. Gustav Tiedman b. 3 Feb 1911. d. 13 Nov 1965. m. Julia **Majercak** 1909-1998.
    1 child:
    Allan J. 1939-

- 444. iii. Walter Tiedman b. 18 Feb 1912. d. 9 Oct 1975. m. Mutia **Koki** (**Peni**?) 1935-1997.

- 445. iv. Arthur Tiedman b. 30 May 1913. d. 22 Apr 1932.

- 446. v. Carl Tiedman b. 12 Apr 1915. d. 6 Aug 1994. m. Frances **Planisek** 1915-1990.
    2 children:
    Linda F. 1945-
    Karen 1953-1972

- 447. vi. Oscar Oswald Tiedman b. 13 Apr 1916. d. 21 Jun 1994. m. Martha **Nieman**[1017] 1916-1999.
    1 child:
    Ronald O. 1937-

- 448. vii. Clarence Tiedman b. 26 Jul 1919. d. 10 Oct 1999. m. Pauline L. **Gerber** 1922-2007.

449. viii. Violet Tiedman b. 17 Aug 1920. d. 5 Jun 1995. m. Julius **Schneider** Jr. 1918-2004.
> 3 children:
>> Nancy Charlene 1939-2005
>> Kenneth M. 1942-
>> Gary B. 1947

450. ix. Lillian Ruth Tiedman b. 16 Feb 1922. d. 24 Oct 2004. m. Stanley Frank **Zaletel** 1912-1987. m. William Conrad **Neiding** 1904-1987.
> 1 child:
>> Dale Stanley 1948-

451. x. Irene Tiedman b. 7 Jul 1923. d. 15 Sep 1927.

424. Marianna "Marie" **TIEDMANN** born 1890 near Liškiava (place of birth listed as „Piliakalnis"). Daughter of Julius Tiedmann[420] (1859-1918) and Mathilde **Franulewicz**[482] (1857-1905). Baptized at Serey Reformed Lutheran Church. Immigrated June 1900 via New York abord the *S.S. Phönicia*. Married Johann "John" **Kramer** (1891-????) 10 Feb 1912 at St. Paul's Catholic Church in Cleveland. Died 20 Feb 1981 in Boca Raton, Florida. Interment unknown.

452. i. Clarence Kramer b. 9 Dec 1911. d. 18 Apr 2002. m. Olga **Greene** 1914-1992.
> 4 children:
>> Marilyn
>> Edward
>> Ginny
>> Larry

453. ii. Evelyn Kramer b. 1 Mar 1917. d. 20 Mar 1996. m. Eugene George **Getzien** 1912-1984.

454. iii. June Kramer b. 3 Feb 1920. d. 27 Aug 2002. m. Walter Arthur **Bell** 1916-1988. m. Robert B. **Baumwell** 1921-2009.
> 3 children:
>> John
>> Robert
>> Karen

425. August Johann **TIEDMANN** born 24 Mar 1893 in Seirijai. Son of Julius Tiedmann[420] (1859-1918) and Mathilde **Franulewicz**[481] (1857-1905). Baptized at Serey Reformed Lutheran Church. Immigrated June 1903 via New York aboard the S.S. *Batavia*. Married Julia **Potuck** (1913-2015). WWI Navy veteran and Merchant Marine Captain for 34 years. Died 24 Jun 1964, Philadelphia, Pennsylvania. Interment at Beverly National Cemetery, Beverly, New Jersey.

962. Pauline **TIEDEMANN (ERNST)** born 1861 in Seiliūnai. Daughter of Karl Tiedemann and Karoline **Gutknecht**. Baptized at the Serey Evangelical Lutheran Church. Married Karl **Ernst** (????-1895) 1888 at Serey Reformed Lutheran Church. Died 6 Nov 1942. Interment at Lutheran Cemetery.

    963.   i. Adolf Tiedemann[1229] b. 1885. d. 16 Jan 1949.

    960.   ii. Emilie Ernst b. 1889. d. 3 Aug 1957. m. Julius **Weinschröder**[569] 1886-1964.
        5 children:
            Gustave Adolph 1909-1984
            Elma 1911-1915
            Walter 1915-1915
            Richard 1916-2001
            Elmer J. 1920-1996

    935.   iii. Albert Ernst b. 1896. d. 31 May 1981. m. Olga **Hirsch**[934] 1898-1954.
        2 children:
            Raymond 1917-2000
            Irene Olga 1919-1994

1229. Adolf **TIEDMANN (*TEDMAN*)** born 1885 in Serijai. Son of Pauline **Tiedemann**[962] (1861-1942). Baptized at Serey Reformed Evangelical Lutheran Church. Died 16 Jan 1949, Canton, Ohio. Interment at St. Jacob's Lutheran Cemetery, Lake Township, Ohio.

TIESLAU / TISLAU / TIESLAUK / TISLAUK / TISLAK / DYSLAK / TISCHLER

363. Emilie **TIESLAU** (**KEMERAIT**) born 15 Aug 1880 in Kūlokai. Daughter of Georg Tieslau and Emilie **Hirsch**. Baptized and confirmed at Mariampol Evangelical Lutheran Church. Married Adolf **Kemerait**[357] (1874-1938) 25 Nov 1902 at Mariampol Evangelical Lutheran Church. Immigrated April 1903 via Philadelphia aboard the S.S. *Victoria*. Died 27 Oct 1943. Interment at Knollwood Cemetery, Mayfield Heights, Ohio. For list of children, see husband Adolf Kemerait.

1542. Jakob **TIESLAUK** (*TISCHLER*) born 1872 in Kłajpeda (Poland). Son of Johann Tieslauk and Justine **Woitowicz**. Baptized at Wischainy Evangelical Lutheran Church. Immigrated March 1898 aboard the S.S. *Friedrich der Große*. Married Wilhelmine **Filier**[1543] (1878-1944) 6 Oct 1898 at Zion Evangelical Lutheran Church. Died 19 Dec 1932. Interment at Lutheran Cemetery.

    1544. i. John Tischler b. 8 Oct 1899. d. 26 Jul 1969. m. Lillian **Groom** 1891-1950.

    1545. ii. Emma Tischler b. 1901. d. 17 Sep 1971. m. James T. **Pekar** 1898-1958.
        4 children:
           Dorothy 1920-1986
           James 1922-1985
           Wilma Marie 1927-1989
           Shirley Ann 1935-1995

    1546. iii. Jacob Martin Tischler b. 5 Jan 1904. d. 22 Nov 1964.

    1547. iv. Mathilde Tischer b. 14 Sep 1908. d. 22 Apr 1991. m. William B. **Running** Jr. 1911-1996.
        1 child:
           Robert W. 1948-

    1548. v. Stelle Irene "Estelle" Tischler b. 31 Dec 1911. d. 22 Feb 1988. m. Kenneth E. **Hastings** 1905-1984.

1549. Johann **TIESLAUK** (*TISCHLER*)) born 1866 in Kłajpeda (Poland). Son of Johann Tieslauk and Justine **Woitowicz**. Baptized at Wischainy Evangelical Lutheran Church. Married Marie **Kobinski** (1870-1941). Died 26 May 1942. Interment at Elmhurst Park Cemetery, Avon, Ohio.

    1550.   i. John Tischler Jr. b. 30 Nov 1890. d. 24 Jan 1978. m. Mary **Hodous** 1893-????.
           1 child:
               Elroy John 1915-1980

    1551.   ii. Charles John Tischler b. 7 Mar 1892. d. 9 Nov 1966. m. Elizabeth **Smith** 1894-????.

    1552.   iii. Jacob J. Tischler b. 1893. d. ????.

    1553.   iv. Martin Tischler b. 28 Nov 1894. d. 8 Jun 1968.

    1554.   v. Frank James Tischler b. 28 Dec 1896. d. 31 May 1980. m. Mary **Evanaski** 1898-1965.
           2 children:
               John Joseph Sr. 1917-1992
               Edward Harry 1919-1980

    1555.   vi. Edward Tischler b. 7 Oct 1898. d. 9 Jun 1929.

    1556.   vii. Henry „Harry" Tischer b. 17 Mar 1901. d. 14 Dec 1947. m. Marie **Brown** 1903-????.
           1 child:
               James J. 1922-1997

    1557.   viii. Mamie E. Tischler b. 1909. d. 31 May 1961. m. Robert P. **Ledvina** 1907-????. m. Joseph **Klekotta** 1900-1950.

    1558.   ix. Anna Tischler b. 1915. d. ????. m. Francis **Kraft** 1913-1974.
           2 children:
               Francis 1944-
               Dasvid 1948-

1559. Ludwig **TIESLAUK** (*TISCHLER*) born 1879 in Mierkinie (Poland). Son of Johann Tieslauk and Julianna **Zimmermann**. Baptized at Wischainy Evangelical Lutheran Church. Married Marie Teresia **Skumat** (1885-1974) 7 Sep 1903 at Zion Evangelical Lutheran Church. Died 3 Nov 1946. Interment at Lutheran Cemetery.

1560. i. Louis Tischler Jr. b. 14 Jun 1904. d. 27 Dec 1975. m. Mildred **Wetzel** 1905-1996.
       3 children:
          Martha J. 1936-
          Beverly Ann 1938-
          Cindy Lou 1944-

1561. ii. Augusta Tischler b. 12 Aug 1906. d. 28 Aug 1992.

1562. iv. Edna Tischler b. 3 Nov 1908. d. 19 Feb 1977. m. George A. **Haines** 1895-????. m. Frank J. **Killraya** 1905-1964.

1563. iii. Henry Tischler b. 27 Jan 1911. d. 17 Jan 1990. m. Margaret **Murray** 1919-1990.
       5 children:
          Barbara L. 1942-
          Karen Margaret 1946-1995
          Thomas J. 1948-1969
          Dale Richard 1952-2021

1564. iv. Edward Tischler b. 1 Feb 1914. d. 7 Dec 1996.

1565. v. Mamie Tischler b. 27 Nov 1916. d. 28 Dec 1991. m. John **Matlack** 1914-1991.
       3 children:
          Sandra L. 1933-
          John R. 1946-
          William

1566. vi. William Tischler b. 8 Nov 1919. d. 10 Dec 1978. m. June **Goede** 1920-????.
       3 children:
          Sharyn 1950-
          Gayle
          Robert

UNTERBERGER

537. Friedrich **UNTERBERGER** born 1862 in Bukta. Son of Josef Friedrich Unterberger (1833-????) and Marianna **Galinat** (1830-????). Married Anna Dorothea **Heimert**[544] (1865-1925) 1887 at Kalwaria Evangelical Lutheran Church. Died 18 Nov 1950. Interment at Lutheran Cemetery.

> 538. i. Amelia Unterberger[538] b. 1 Oct 1889. d. 5 Oct 1963. m. Harold Scott **Gehringer** 1887-1947.
> 2 children:
> Myrtle A.[545] 1911-1929
> Harold F.[546] 1912-1960
>
> 539. ii. Emil Friedrich Unterberger b. 9 Nov 1893. d. 24 Feb 1938.
>
> 540. iii. Emma Unterberger b. 28 May 1899. d. 22 Apr 1979.
>
> 541. iv. Elma A. Unterberger b. 9 Aug 1902. d. 4 Sep 1983. m. Joseph Albert **Scheimann** 1895-1949.
> 5 children:
> Frederick Joseph 1923-1999
> Anthony George 1924-1989
> Anna Marie 1925-2007
> Elma D. 1927-1973
> William Franklin 1930-1981
>
> 542. v. Harry A. Unterberger b. 20 Oct 1906. d. 26 Sep 1971. m. Virginia E. **Gerlach** 1914-2006.
> 2 children:
> Lois Jean 1932-
>
> 543. vi. Raymond Oswald Unterberger b. 18 Apr 1908. d. 15 Oct 1978.

538. Amelia **UNTERBERGER (GEHRINGER)** born 1 October 1889 in Krosnėai (or Krasenka). Daughter of Friedrich Unterberger[537] (1862-1950) and Anna Dorothea **Heimert**[544] (1864-1925). Baptized at Kalwaria Evangelical Lutheran Church. Immigrated June 1892 via Baltimore aboard the S.S. *Braunschweig*. Married Harold Scott **Gehringer** (1887-1947) 24 Dec 1907 in Cleveland by a Justice of the Peace. Died 5 Oct 1963. Interment at Lutheran Cemetery.

> 545. i. Myrtle A. Gehringer b. 2 Jan 1911. d. 8 Feb 1929. m. James Frank **Castle** 1908-1940.
>
> 546. ii. Harold F. Gehringer b. 7 Aug 1912. d. 3 Sep 1960.

547. Ludwig „Louis" Gustav **UNTERBERGER** born 25 Mar 1871 in Krokialaukis. Son of Josef Friedrich Unterberger (1833-????) and Marianna **Galinat** (1830-????). Baptized and confirmed at Mariampol Evangelical Lutheran Church. Married Bertha **Petratz** (1878-1920) 25 Feb 1899 at Zion Evangelical Lutheran Church. Married Lydia **Steinbrenner** (1878-1962) 11 Dec 1924 at St. Paul's Methodist Church. Died 9 Nov 1953. Interment at West Park Cemetery.

    548.   i. Alvin Unterberger b. 8 Dec 1900. d. 10 May 1977. m. Mabel Mary **Bendinger** 1909-1934. m. Mary **Wogner** ????-1975.
            3 children:
                Alice Adele 1927-1998
                Marian L. 1928-2012
                Robert

    549.   ii. Elsie Unterberger b. 18 Aug 1902. d. ????. m. Robert E. **Gordon** 1899-????.
            2 children:
                Ralph Jr. 1928-
                Curtis L. 1937-

550. Anna **UNTERBERGER** (**JANTZ**) (**ZIELKE**) born 23 Maz 1875 in Ungurinė. Daughter of Josef Friedrich Unterberger (1833-????) and Marianna **Galinat** (1830-????). Baptized and confirmed at Mariampol Evangelical Lutheran Church. Immigrated January 1899 via New York aboard the S.S. *Oldenburg*. Married Adolf **Jantz** (1873-1913) 3 Dec 1899 at Zion Evangelical Lutheran Church. Married Julius **Zielke** (1879-1940). Died 4 Oct 1949 in Grafton, Ohio. Interment at Nesbett Cemetery, Grafton.

    551.   i. Arthur Adelheim Jantz b. 2 Nov 1900. d. 21 Jan 1971. m. Pauline **Grell** 1900-1991.
            2 children:
                Nadine 1930-
                Elaine 1938-

    552.   ii. Herbert Bernhard Jantz b. 13 Aug 1902. d. 2 Dec 1903.

    553.   iii. Ewald Herman Jantz b. 18 May 1905. d. 4 Mar 1984. m. Blanche **Wise** 1905-1981.
            2 children:
                Richard A. 1934-
                Marilyn R. 1938-

    554.   iv. Harold Jantz b. 23 Oct 1910. d. 27 Nov 1999. m. Vivian Twylah **Wheeler** 1914-2003.
            2 children:
                Harry Adolph 1934-2019
                Karely T. 1938-

WACHHAUS

555. Adolf „Adam" **WACHHAUS** born 1876 in Matuliškiai. Son of Matthias Wachhaus and Henriette **Krause**. Baptized and confirmed at Wilkowischken Evangelical Lutheran Church. Married Marianna **Simon**[562] (1875-1947) in Pennsylvania. Died 27 Jun 1949. Interment at East Cleveland Township Cemetery.

    556.   i. Edith Wachhaus. b. Jun 1899. d. 4 Mar 1908.

    557.   ii. Adam Gustave Wachhaus b. 14 Dec 1902. d. 3 Sep 1967. m. Louise **Ihle** 1899-1990.
        1 child:
            David 1933-

    558.   iii. Wanda M. Wachhaus b. 5 Jan 1905. d. 24 Feb 1987. m. Albert **Perry**[412] 1899-1973.
        2 children:
            Albert D. 1929-1929
            Ronald Lee 1932-2015

    559.   iv. Ottilie Wachhaus b. 2 Jul 1906. d. 27 Apr 1911.

    560.   v. Anna Wachhaus b. 23 Jan 1909. d. ????. m. Harold **Holland** 1906-1946.
        1 child:
            Janet A. 1947-

    561.   vi. Helen Wachhaus b. ????. d. ????.

WALINSKI / WOLINSKE

23. Georg "George" **WALINSKI** (*WOLINSKE*) born 6 Sep 1880 in Kreivukė. Son of Georg Walinsk and Eva **Kasperait**. Baptized at Kalwaria Evangelical Lutheran Church. Immigrated November 1900 via New York aboard S.S. *Prinz Friedrich Wilhelm*. Married Emilie Rosalia **Wilk**[28] (1886-1870) 4 Feb 1912 at Zion Evangelical Lutheran Church. Died 18 Feb 1962. Interment at Lutheran Cemetery.

24.   i. Elsie Wolinske b. 1912. d. 13 Dec 1915.

25.   ii. Lydia Wolinske b. 27 Dec 1914. d. 10 Nov 1915.

26.   iii. Ruth Walinske b. 13 Apr 1917. d. 6 Nov 2002. m. Herbert Hermann **Schmiel**.
        1 child:
            Nancy Carol 1944-1989

27.   iv. Lillian Walinske b. 11 Oct 1919. d. 17 Sep 1978. m. Raymond **Schmiel**.
        1 child:
            Margaret Schmiel

WEGNER / WAGNER

1262. Johann **WEGNER** born 1883 in Šilsodis. Son of Johann Wegner and Henriette **Kebbel**. Likely baptized at Wirballen Evangelical Lutheran Church. Married Henriette **Erzthaler**[1261] 3 Sep 1905 at Zion Evangelical Lutheran Church. Died 1921. Interment at Lutheran Cemetery.

    1263.   i. Walter Wegner b. 24 Aug 1906. d. 1922.

    1264.   ii. Edna Jean Wagner b. 18 Sep 1908. d. 6 Sep 1989. m. Peter **Weiss** 1902-1977.

    1265.   iii. Viola Wagner b. 1915. d. 13 Sep 1968.

WEIER / WIEHER

56. Pauline **WEIER (WITZKE)** born 18 Dec 1886, likely near Marijampolė. Daughter of August Weier and Eva **Nowiak**. Immigrated via New York May 1894 aboard S.S. *Dania*. Married Emil **Witzke** 23 June 1906 at Bethany Lutheran Church. Died 18 Aug 1953. Interred at Whitehaven Memorial Park, Mayfield, Ohio.

    63.   i. Beatrice Witzke b. 8 Aug 1906. d. 12 Apr 1983. m. Paul W. **Hoelting** 1906-1936. m. Vernon Bruce **Jones** 1907-1959.
        1 child:
            Paul William Hoelting 1930-2006

    64.   ii. Edith Witzke b. 2 Dec 1909. d. 7 Nov 1991.

    65.   iii. Lillian "Lydia" Martha Witzke b. 7 Apr 1912. d. 7 Sep 1988. m. Donald James Morrison.
        1 child:
            Leonard D 1943-

    66.   iv. Helen Mildred Witzke b. 7 Dec 1918. d. 12 Aug 1998. m. Ronald Wilson Thomson 1917-1990.

57. Helene Edna **WEIER (WALLACE)** born 1888 in Tarpučiai. Daughter of August Weier and Eva **Nowiak**. Baptized at Mariampol Evangelical Lutheran Church. Immigrated via New York May 1894 aboard S.S. *Dania*. Married ? **Wallace**. Death and interment unknown.

58. August Karl **WEIER** born 14 Dec 1889 in Tarpučiai. Son of August Weier and Eva **Nowiak**. Baptized at Mariampol Evangelical Lutheran Church. Immigrated via New York May 1894 aboard S.S. *Dania*. Married Marjory **Immel** (1893-1965). Died 15 Aug 1965. Interment unknown.

59. Albert C. **WEIER** born 1893 in Degučiai. Son of August Weier and Eva **Nowiak**. Baptized at Mariampol Evangelical Lutheran Church. Immigrated via New York May 1894 aboard S.S. *Dania*. WWI Veteran. Married Florence W. **Ackroyd** 2 July 1918 at Grace Congregational Church. Died 21 Mar 1976. Interment unknown.

WEINSCHRÖDER / WEINSCHREIDER

569. Julian "Julius" **WEINSCHRÖDER** born 1886 in Krokialaukis. Son of Friedrich Wilhelm Weinschröder and Marianna Julianna **Gräzer**. Baptized at Serey Reformed Lutheran Church. Immigrated August 1906 via Baltimore aboard the S.S. *Rhein*. Married Emilie **Ernst**[960] (1889-1957) 15 Jun 1907 at Zion Evangelical Lutheran Church. Died 16 Jun 1964. Interment at Lutheran Cemetery.

    570.   i. Elmer Weinschreider b. 19 Feb 1911. d. 10 Sep 1915.

    571.   ii. Walter Weinschreider b. 5 Apr 1915. d. 3 Oct 1915.

    572.   iii. Richard Weinschreider b. 6 Oct 1916. d. 29 Jun 2001. m. Mildred M. **Marshall** 1917-1974.
        1 child:
            Roger David 1945-2006

    573.   iv. Elmer Weinschreider b. 31 Mar 1920. d. 6 Mar 1996. m. Olga **?** 1922-2000.
        1 child:
            Dale L. 1946-

574. Leon „Leo" **WEINSCHRÖDER** born 1891 in Krokialaukis. Son of Friedrich Wilhelm Weinschröder and Marianna Julianna **Gräzer**. Baptized at Serey Reformed Lutheran Church. Immigrated June 1909 via New York aboard the S.S. *President Lincoln*. Married Albine **Hirsch**[956] (1895-1986) 23 May 1914 at Zion Evangelical Lutheran Church. Died 17 Dec 1969. Interment at Lutheran Cemetery.

575. Natalie **WEINSCHRÖDER (MUSCHINSKI)** born 1874 in Seirijai. Daughter of Friedrich Wilhelm Weinschröder and Marianna Julianna **Gräzer**. Baptized at Serey Reformed Lutheran Church. Married Gustav **Bender** in 1894 at Mariampol Evangelical Lutheran Church. Married Adolf **Muschinski**[576] (1883-1956) 1910 at Serey Reformed Lutheran Church. Immigrated December 1912 via New York aboard the S.S. *President Lincoln*. Died 22 Mar 1968. Interment at Lutheran Cemetery. For list of children, see husband Adolf Muschinski.

    580.   i. Malwine Bender b. 1901. d. 1908.

    955.   ii. Bertha Bender b. 1898. d. 1996. m. Wilhelm **Hirsch**[952] 1884-1960.
        2 children:
            Arthur Wilhelm[953] 1919-2011
            Gertrude[954] 1921-2022

581. Malwina „Malvina" **WEINSCHRÖDER (SCHÜTZ) (HUTH)** born 1882 in Seirijai. Daughter of Friedrich Wilhelm Weinschröder and Marianna Julianna **Gräzer**. Baptized at Serey Reformed Lutheran Church. Married Ferdinand **Schütz (Schultz)**. Immigrated June 1909 via New York aboard the S.S. *President Lincoln*. Divorced 26 May 1931. Married Philip **Huth** (1877-1948) 20 June 1941 in Cleveland by a Justice of the Peace. Died 5 Mar 1965. Interment at Lutheran Cemetery.

582. i. Adolf Schultz b. 26 Jun 1907. d. 21 Nov 1983. m. Pauline **Hodonowitz** (1912-1990).
> 2 children:
>> Richard Michael 1935-1997
>> Arlene Lillian 1940-2017

583. ii. Jennie Schultz b. 16 Aug 1908. d. 10 Apr 1986. m. Michael A. **Martino** (1901-????).

584. iii. Lillian Scheutz b. 2 Apr 1916. d. 20 Apr 2007. m. Edward **August** (1915-1999),
> 1 child:
>> Dorothy J. 1948-

585. iv. Lydia Schultz b. 15 Oct 1917. d. 23 Feb 2001. m. William Otto **Hartstock** (1917-2003).
> 2 children:
>> Joanne L. 1944-
>> Wesley O. 1948-

586. v. Ewald Schultz b. 19 May 1920. d. 21 Apr 2002. m. Elizabeth Natalia **?** 1916-2005.
> 2 children:
>> Pamela 1946-
>> Barbara Ann

587. vi. Bertha Schultz b. 12 Sep 1921. d. 9 Nov 1997. m. Carl **Weiss** 1919-????.
m. Andrew James **Horrick** 1907-1991.
> 2 children:
>> Clayton 1948-
>> Laraine 1949-

WIEMERT

21. Emilie **WIEMERT** (**SALEKER**) born 3 Mar 1872 near Kalvarija. Baptized at Mariampol Evangelical Lutheran Church. Daughter of Wilhelm Wiemer (1833-1876) and Anna Esther **Walinski** (1846-1922). Married Johann Andreas „Heinrich" **Saleker**[1] 21 May 1893 at Zion Evangelical Lutheran Church. Died 27 Apr 1943. Interment at Lutheran Cemetery. For list of children, see listing for Johann Andreas "Heinrich" Saleker,[1] Great-great-grandmother of IAGL co-founder Owen M. McCafferty II.

22. Friedrich **WIEMERT** (*WIEMMERT*) born 21 July 1873 in Kalvarija. Son of Wilhelm Wiemer (1833-1876) and Anna Esther **Walinski** (1846-1922). Immigrated July 1892 via Baltimore aboard S.S. *Karlsruhe*. Married Justine Auguste **Saleker**[14] 2 June 1904 at Zion Evangelical Lutheran Church. Died 5 July 1908. Interment at Woodland Cemetery. For list of children, see Justine Auguste Saleker[14].

23. Anna **WIEMERT** (**KLIMACH**) (*KLIMACK*) born 27 Jan 1875 in Kalvarija. Baptized at Kalwaria Evangelical Lutheran Church. Daughter of Wilhelm Wiemer (1833-1876) and Anna Esther **Walinski** (1846-1922). Confirmed at Mariampol Evangelical Lutheran Church. Immigrated April 1895 via Baltimore aboard S.S. *Weimar*. Married Wilhelm **Klimach** (1875-1908) 6 July 1897 at Zion Evangelical Lutheran Church. Died 4 Feb 1942. Interment at Lutheran Cemetery.

    24.   i. William Edward Klimack b. 4 Mar 1898. d. 24 Oct 1983. m. Irma **Bierfriend** 1906-1990.
            1 child:
                Phyllis Klimack 1936-

    25.   ii. Otto Oswald Klimack b. May 1899. d. 3 May 1899.

    26.   iii. Friedrich Arthur Klimack b. 13 Jun 1900. d. 26 Jun 1908.

    27.   iv. Ema Martha Klimack b. 15 May 1902. d. 25 Nov 1903.

    28.   v. Walter Oscar Klimack b. 15 May 1904. d. 26 Jun 1908.

    39.   vi. Ida Ottilie Klimack b. 14 Mar 1906. d. 26 Jun 1908.

    30.   vii. Harold Richard Klimack b. 28 Jul 1908. d. 25 Feb 1969. m. Catherine Suzanne **Harich**.
            2 children:
                Harold Richard Jr. 1934-2008
                Karen Katherine 1937-1967

311. August Martin **WIEMERT** born 22 Nov 1874 in Užbaliai. Son of Georg Wiemer and Pauline **Kremer**. Baptized at Prenen Evangelical Lutheran Church. Immigrated Nov 1896 via New York aboard S.S. *München*. Married Wilhelmine **Essel**[315] (1879-1965) 8 Apr 1901 at St. Paul's Evangelical Lutheran Church. Died 5 Dec 1963. Interment at Northfield Macedonia Cemetery, Macedonia, Ohio.

    312.   i. Natalie Wiemert b. 15 Jul 1901. d. 26 Apr 1969. m. Harvey F. **Stark** 1904-1931.
            1 child:
                Jean Natalie 1928-1929

    313.   ii. Sophia Wiemert b. 1 Jul 1903. d. Jun 1980. m. George **Krauss** 1897-1951.
            1 child:
                Allen George 1929-2003

    314.   iii. Helen Wiemert b. 9 Aug 1907. d. 16 Sep 1992. m. Ernest H. **Dietrich** 1907-1975.
            2 children:
                Verner Ernest 1927-2000
                Sterling Trayver 1932-2008

WILK / WILCZINSKI / WOLF

28. Emilie Rosalia **WILK** (*WALINSKI*) born 9 Oct 1886 in Bakšiškiai. Daughter of Matthias Wilk (1857-1943) and Rosine **Rudat** (1865-1945.) Married Georg **Walinski**[23] 4 Feb 1912 at Zion Evangelical Lutheran Church. Died 27 Jan 1970. Interment at Lutheran Cemetery. For list of children, see husband Georg Walinski.[23]

29. Gustav **WILK** born 4 Jan 1889 in Bakšiškiai. Son of Matthias Wilk (1857-1943) and Rosine **Rudat** (1865-1945.) Married Florence **Guyner** 31 Dec 1935 in Saginaw, Michigan. Immigrated August 1923 via New York aboard the S.S. *George Washington*. Died 20 Dec 1973. Interment at Lutheran Cemetery.

30. Auguste **WILK** (**VIDRA**) born 22 Jun 1891 in Vaitkabaliai. Daughter of Matthias Wilk (1857-1943) and Rosine Rudat (1865-1945). Immigrated Nov 1911 via Baltimore. Married John **Vidra** 3 Jul 1915 at Zion Evangelical Lutheran Church. Died 22 Aug 1978 in Munson Township, Ohio. Interment at Evergreen Cemetery, Painesville, Ohio.

    31.   i. Richard Vidra b. 7 Jan 1919.
  doi. 9 Apr 1987.

918. Gustav **WILK** (*WOLF*) (*WILCZINSKI*) born 1891 in Trakėnai. Son of Josef Wilk and Marie **Bauer**. Baptized at Kalwaria Evangelical Lutheran Church. Immigrated June 1911 via Baltimore aboard the S.S. *Cassel*. Married Olga **Baumann**[917] (1895-1978) 7 Oct 1916 at Zion Evangelical Lutheran Church. Died 2 Jun 1953. Interment at Lutheran Cemetery.

    919.   i. Emma Wilk b. 15 May 1917. d. 16 Feb 2009. m. Nick **Schenovitch** 1915-2010.
        1 child:
          Joan

    920.   ii. Helene "Lena" Wilk b. 14 Sep 1918. d. 26 Mar 1984. m. John J. **Sajetowski** 1913-1944. m. John C. **Spangler** 1919-1984.
        2 children:
          Richard

    921.   iii. Martha Wilk b. 18 Jun 1920. d. 23 Feb 1985. m. Frederick **Mieser** 1916-1993.
        2 children:
          Fred 1939-
          Nancy 1948-

    922.   iv. Edna G. Wilk b. 4 Apr 1922. d. 18 Jun 1992.

923.   v. Albert G. Wilk b. 20 May 1926. d. 29 Jun 1986. m. Laverne Marion **Hric** 1926-2005.
         3 children:
            Thomas

924.   vi. Lillian Helen Wilk b. 18 Apr 1931. d. 27 Mar 1999. m. Dedalo **Montali** 1927-2007.

925.   vii. Janet Eleanor Wilk b. 25 Jun 1936. d. 8 Sep 2013. m. Ernest L. **Jameson** 1925-1982.
         1 child:
            Kenneth C. 1964-1982

1083. Emilie **WILK (BAUER)** (*BARANOWICZ*) born 1884 in Bolcie (Poland). Daughter of Karl Wilk and Anna **Gerulat**. Baptized at Wischainy Evangelical Lutheran Church. Married August **BAUER** (*Baranowicz*) 7 Apr 1907 at Zion Evangelical Lutheran Church. Died April 1978. Interment at Lutheran Cemetery. For list of children, see husband August Bauer.

WISGIN

983. Richard **WISGIN** born 20 Oct 1884 in Liudvinavas. Son of August Wisgin and Marie **Gasner**. Baptized and confirmed at Mariampol Evangelical Lutheran Church. Immigrated July 1905 via New York aboard the S.S. *Patricia*. Married Bertha **Heinrich**[993] (1894-1991) 1 Dec 1917 at Zion Evangelical Lutheran Church. Died 19 Mar 1976. Interment at Knollwood Cemetery, Mayfield Heights, Ohio.

    984.   i. Edwin Richard Wisgin b. 4 May 1919. d. 13 Sep 2020. m. Marguerite Emily **Maxwell** 1921-1977. m. Natalie **Schultz** 1920-2020.
            2 children:
                Lynella 1946
                Sandra 1949-

    985.   ii. Norma Bertha Wisgin b. 15 Jun 1921. d. 20 Dec 2013. m. Edward Robert **Schultz**[372] 1920-2000.

986. Emilie **WISGIN (GRIBNER)** born 27 May 1877 in Liudvinavas. Daughter of August Wisgin and Marie **Gasner**. Baptized and confirmed at Mariampol Evangelical Lutheran Church. Married August **Gribner**[987] (1877-1937) 13 Aug 1904 at Schifflein Christi Evangelical Lutheran Church. Died 17 Aug 1926. Interment at Lutheran Cemetery. For list of children, see husband August Gribner.

WORM / WURM

614. Martin **WORM** born 1881 in Puńsk (Poland). Son of Martin Worm and Anna **Podzis**. Baptized at Seine Evangelical Lutheran Church. Immigrated April 1902 aboard the S.S. *Kaiserin Auguste Viktoria*. Married Amelia "Mollie" **Basenau**[609] (1891-1937) 29 Sep 1907 at Zion Evangelical Lutheran Church. Divorced about 1934. Died 17 Oct 1949. Interment at Lutheran Cemetery.

    615.   i. Florence Worm b. 10 Dec 1911. d. 15 Nov 1967. m. Leon B. **Pallerin** 1905-1982.

    616.   ii. Edna Worm b. 8 May 1913. d. 11 May 1914.

    617.   iii. Ruth Worm b. 15 Jul 1917. d. 28 May 2002. m. Pasquale **Felix** 1905-1970.
              5 children:
                    Shriley 1935-
                    Carol 1937-
                    Patrick 1942-
                    Anthony M. 1944-
                    Gloria 1949-

    618.   iv. Walter Worm b. 17 Jan 1918. d. 29 Feb 1980. m. Valeria Wanda **Will** 1915-1997.
              3 children:
                    Dale W. 1939-2009

    619.   v. Elizabeth "Bettie" Worm b. 14 Jul 1925. d. 23 May 1976. m. Vincent **Sesek** 1913-1978.

620. Rosalia "Rose" **WORM (EVANS)** born 1888 in Puńsk (Poland). Daughter of Martin Worm and Anna **Podzis**. Baptized at Seine Evangelical Lutheran Church. Immigrated August 1907 via New York aboard the S.S. *Amerika*. Married Julius **Evans**. Divorced. Death and interment details unknown.

    621.   i. Edna Evans b. 19 Mar 1910. d. 26 Feb 2009. m. Harold **Pekrul** 1908-1993.

1066. Karl **WORM** born 1870 in Przystawańce (Poland). Son of Matthias Worm and Christine **Wesłowski**. Baptized at Seine Evangelical Lutheran Church. Married Auguste **Mittag**[1067] (1873-1941) 1894 at Kalwaria Evangelical Lutheran Church.
Immigrated 1896 via New York. Died 18 Dec 1934. Interment at Lutheran Cemetery.

    1068. i. Adolf Worm b. 1895. d. bef. 1900.

1069. ii. Oswald Fred Worm b. 25 May 1901. d. 14 Jan 1988. m. Viola **Leinarth** 1905-1985.

1070. iii. Gustave Carl Worm b. 26 Dec 1904. d. 2 Jan 1960. m. Mary Olive **Whyte** 1897-1968.

1071. iv. Bertha Worm b. 31 Oct 1910. d. 24 Jun 1938. m. Adolph Carl **Sokolik**[1046] 1911-1978.
    2 children:
        Arlene 1932-2015
        Charles 1935-

APPENDIX A – CLEVELAND LUTHERAN CEMETERY

Although many cemeteries throughout Ohio are the final resting place of many of Cleveland's *Deutsche aus Litauen*, there is one cemetery that stands out for the sheer number of members that are laid to rest there: the Lutheran Cemetery of Cleveland. Therefore, it is fitting that it receives its own place in this book due to the importance of genealogical research and the continuing legacy of this mostly unknown Cleveland community.

Before 1894, there was no dedicated Lutheran cemetery to serve the Evangelical Lutheran churches on the west and near west sides of Cleveland. Cleveland was home to many beautiful cemeteries, and in those early days, many of the *Deutsche aus Litauen* of Cleveland were buried in various cemeteries – Erie Street, Monroe Street, Woodland, Lakeview, Riverside, and others. For those who lived farther east – Euclid, for example – there were also a significant number of Germans from Lithuania. St. John's Lutheran Cemetery later became a popular resting place for those who attended that large congregation.

By the 1890s however, Cleveland continued to grow as did the large Evangelical Lutheran congregations. The need became greater for a dedicated place for Lutherans to bury their deceased. In 1893, four of the west side Evangelical Lutheran churches — most of which were German-speaking congregations – began discussions on how such a cemetery could come into being. The four churches – St. Matthew's, Immanuel, Christus Kirche, and Trinity Lutheran – created a committee and presented a report to a union meeting in December of that year. Shortly after, the report was accepted, and a committee was created to find a suitable location for the cemetery in March 1894.

Laymen Charles Koch and Louis Hundertmark were chosen as the site selection committee (the two are both laid to rest in the cemetery). By late spring of 1894, two sites had been selected: a property on Linndale Road and a property on Pearl Street (now Pearl Road) in Brooklyn, Ohio. Eventually, the site on Pearl Street was selected, and the sale of the land was conducted on 11 September 1894.

The tract of land, which was adorned with numerous large and historic trees, was owned by Wilhelm Karl Huy (1840-1903), a German-speaking immigrant from Romansweiler near Strasbourg, France. The tract of land was sold for $18,000, roughly $644,000 in 2023 dollars. Ironically, Herr Huy was not buried in the cemetery when he died in 1903 — his final resting place is at Brookmere Cemetery, farther up the road on Pearl.

The Evangelical Lutheran Cemetery Association, formed by pastors of the four churches, dedicated the new cemetery on Sunday 2 December 1894. Herr Martin Schmidt (1871-1894) was the first to be interred there having died in October of that year as a result of lockjaw from an accidental bullet injury during a hunting expedition. Though he was originally interred at Monroe Street, he was later laid to rest at Lutheran Cemetery. His large, black granite marker is located in Section M, under one of the cemetery's most impressive and oldest trees.

This book lists 240 *Deutsche aus Litauen* who have been laid to rest at the Lutheran Cemetery on Pearl Road. The earliest confirmed burial for a *Deutsche aus Litauen* is Fraülein Adeline Tetmeier[851] born on 28 July 1887, likely in Liukiai, and died in Cleveland 4 February 1907. She was the daughter of Ferdinand Christof Tetmeier and Henriette Lindhammer. The Tetmeiers were neighbors of my Saleker family who were also from Liukiai.

I have been unable to locate any *Deutsche aus Litauen* who were buried in the Lutheran Cemetery earlier than 1907. This may be due to the fact that the vast majority of the *Deutsche aus Litauen* community lived further east during this time and there were closer cemeteries. Another possible reason could be the rules of the cemetery during its early years. An 1894 newspaper article — just as the Evangelical Lutheran Cemetery Association was being founded — stated that those buried there will be only from the four managing churches. If this was the case, perhaps sometime around 1907, that requirement was lifted.

After 130 years, the Lutheran Cemetery is still active and well maintained. Though many of the large trees that adorned the park have since been removed (mainly due to damage and age), the Moses Cleaveland tree is still standing in section M among some of the largest and most ornate graves in the cemetery. The tree was part of a program begun in 1946 to celebrate Moses Cleaveland's (the namesake of the city) landing in the area in 1796. The tree would have been standing at that time. Indeed, there are several *Deutsche aus Litauen* graves that enjoy the shade of that tree as does the grave of Martin Schmidt — the first burial at the cemetery.

If you have any doubt that this cemetery was founded by German-speaking Lutherans, simply take a walk in any direction and you will be certain. Many of the oldest headstones are etched in German with phrases like "*Ruhe in Frieden*" and "*Mutter*" and "*Vater*" along with other Bible verses in German. Naturally, the surnames on many of these stones are German though interlaced with them, you will find stones etched in Polish and other Slavic languages.

Given the number of burials of the *Deutsche aus Litauen* in the Lutheran Cemetery in Cleveland, it is safe to say that the grounds are one of the most significant sites in the US for the *Deutsche aus Litauen* community and perhaps the only such cemetery of its kind in the country. Nearly everyone in the *Deutsche aus Litauen* community will likely find a connection to someone buried there. Stones are presented in the order that they were photographed.

I have tried my best to photograph all the headstones of the *Deutsche aus Litauen* in this book that were erected at the Lutheran Cemetery. Some burials do not have headstones — others have yet to be identified or who could not be verified with birth, marriage, or death records in the Suwałki Governorate. For descendants of those who do not have a headstone, it is still possible to purchase a new stone and have it set in the plot. The Lutheran Cemetery Association will advise you on the setting fee as well as the style and size of the marker that can be placed in the plot.

APPENDIX B – PHOTOGRAPHS OF LUTHERAN CEMETERY

Author's Note: To see digital similar colored images and transcriptions of each stone, go to FindaGrave.com.

PHOTOGRAPHS OF HEADSTONES

EMILIA BIRKOBEIN

EDWARD & LYDIA ESSEL
TILLIE PERRY

CLARA POHL

HELENE A. SEIDMAN

JOHN J. POHL

CLARA POHL

ERICH REITER

FANNIE KLOTZOBER

BERTHA KLOTZOBER

ELSIE & LYDIA WOLINSKE

JOSEPH, BERTHA, & BERTHA T. PERRY

EDWARD, NELLIE, & GUSTAV LUKAT

EDWIN & HELEN KOKOSKY

EMMA M. & BABY KALWEIT

FRED & ALBINA KOKOSKY

ANNA KOKOSKY

JOSEPH & MARIE HAUSRATH

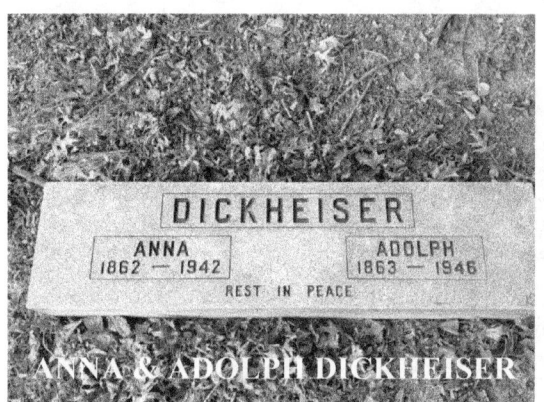
ANNA & ADOLPH DICKHEISER

HUGO NOWJACK

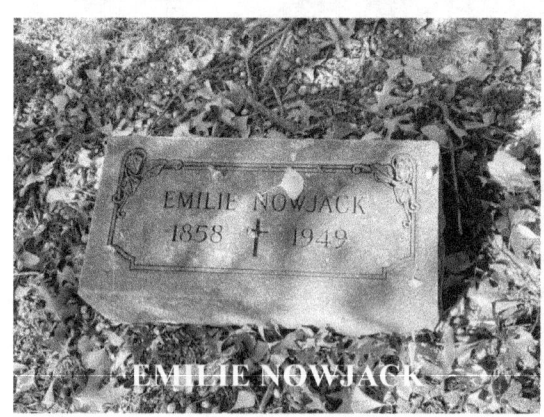
EMILIE NOWJACK

AUGUSTA, CARL & OTTILIE LOGIES

MARIE STASUN

EMMA M. UNTERBERGER

CHRIST & ANNA MISSUN

MARTHA KROSNOSKI

ANNA WEBER MISSUN

OSWALD G. & CARL O. MISSUN

EMILIE POLTER

FRANK A. & ALBINA SALEWSKI

GUSTAV WILK

AMELIA BAUER

AUGUST BAUER

LORETTA J. AUKSCHUN

GEORGE & EMILIE WOLINSKE

MILLY PETERS

JULIUS WEINSCHREIDER

ADOLPH PETERS

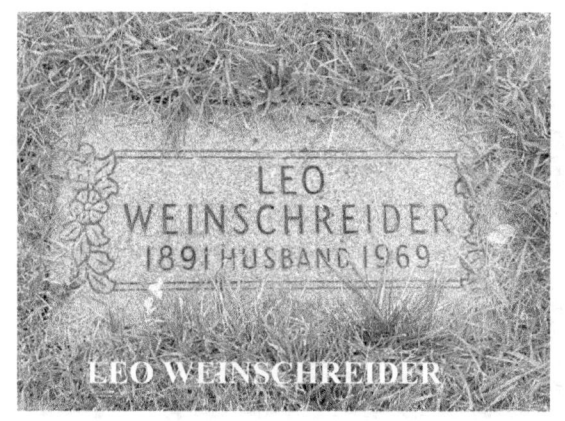

LEO WEINSCHREIDER

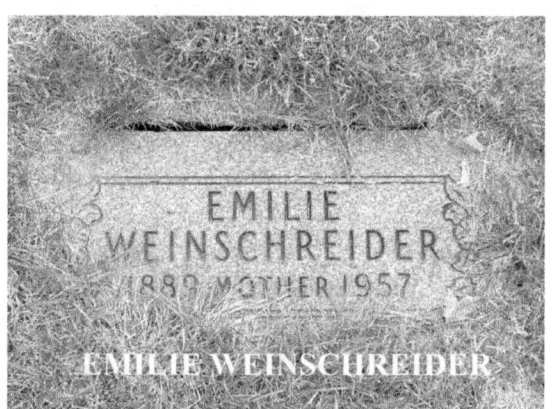

EMILIE WEINSCHREIDER

ALBINA WEINSCHREIDER

CAROLINE SALEWSKY

OLGA WILK

GUST WILK

EMILIA & AUGUST HEINRICH

LEOPOLD & AUGUSTA AUKSCHUN

AMELIA & CARL R. ESSEL

ANNA D. UNTERBERGER

FREDERICK W. UNTERBERGER

ADAM & CHRISTINA MELCHEREIT

BERTHA WELZ

RICHARD L. WISGIN

EDWARD GERLAT

GUSTAV E. NEUBACHER

ADOLPH & JULIA ESSEL

HELENA & GUSTAV SCHWAND

MARIE EMMA STASUN

AUGUST, WILHELMINA & GUSTAV R. BUSHER

GEORGE, AUGUSTA, & AUGUSTA BUSCHER

HENRY PUDIMAT

CARL & AMELIA ANDEXLER

HELENA BERWING

PAULINE PUDIMAT

JULIUS BERWING

HELENA JOHANNA WAGNER
AUGUST H. SCHACK
ANNA SCHACK
EDWARD SCHAK

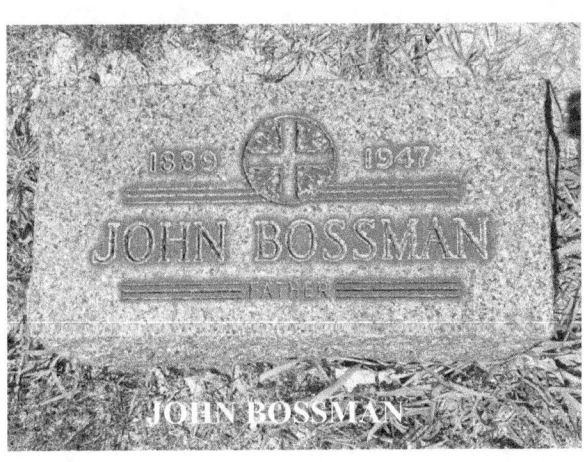

JOHN BOSSMAN

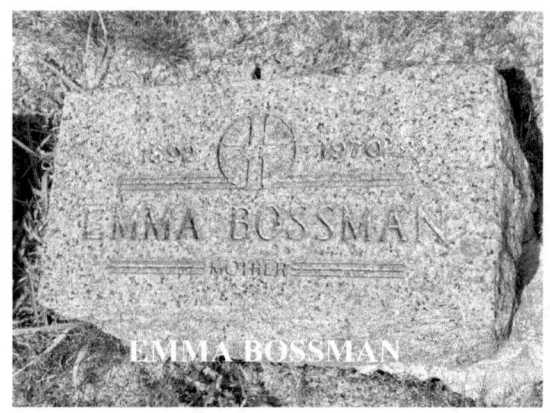
EMMA BOSSMAN

CARL & PAULINE BERWING

HELEN & AUGUST RIMKUS

CARL & HELENA BALTRUNAT

GEORGE TENNEBAR

GEORGE A. & MARY SCHEDAT

GEORGE SCHUTZ

MAX & ANNA REITER

CHRISTIAN & HENRIETTA TETMEYER

LENA & AUGUST POLENSCHAT

MARIE & FREDERICK STASSUN

ANNA, JOHN, JOHN, & CHARLES SEAMAN

JOHN & PAULINE KELLAT

HELENA & GEORGE DOCZKAT

EMILIE & KARL ROLOFF

ANNA & MICHAEL GERHART

CARL & PAULINE BOSSMAN

ADOLF NEITZEL

MARY & GERALDINE REINKE

ADOLF & ANNA SCHMIDT

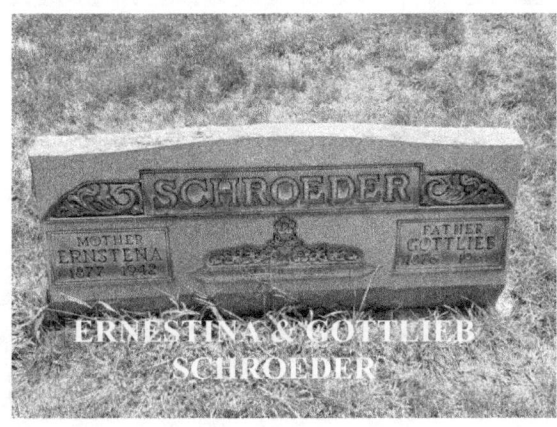
ERNESTINA & GOTTLIEB SCHROEDER

LUDWIG & MARIE FRIEDRICH

LENA & CARL FRIEDRICH

FRIEDRICH & HENRIETTE KIRSTEIN-GUENTHER

RUDOLF & META HEIN

CHRISTIAN, MINNA & WALTER KALWEIT

ANNA REITER

ANDREW REITER

AUGUSTA & GEORGE NOVACK

PAULINE LEHMAN

JOHN & HELEN SCHWELGIN

ANNA BUMBLIS

GUSTAVE BUMBLIS

ANNA MUSCHINSKY

ADELINE & CHRIST URGELEIT

MATT LEHMAN

MARTIN WORM

HENRY F. & MARIE BUMBLIS

ADOLPH & NATHALIA MUSCHINSKI

WILLIAM & BERTHA HIRSCH

CARL & EMILY NEUMANN

GEORGE SCHUTZ

AUGUST GRIBNER

FRED E. & MARY ALBRECHT

LOUIS & CHRISTINE CONRAD

AMELIA & ADOLPH SCHWED

EVA & ADOLPH TIEDMAN

AUGUSTA & CARL NIEDERSTRASSE

AMELIA & HENRY SCHWED

CHRIST, LILLIAN & ANNA KAIRAIT

JULIUS G. & LOUISE L. SCHWED

GUSTAV & ANNA PAMPUS

MINNIE & JOHN YURKSCHATT

FRANK G. & ANGELINE CONRAD

CHRISTINE, GEORGE, & CARL NIEDERSTRASSE

LEO HEIN

AUGUSTA KENAT & AUGUSTAS KINAITIS

EVA, AUGUST, LOUIS, & BERTHA KALCHERT

JOHN RENKE

JOHN & ANNA LANGMEYER

GUS & ELIZABETH BOSSMAN

EMILIE & HENRY FISCHER

AUGUST, MARY, & AUGUST SCHMIDT

JOSEPH METT

AUGUST & AMALIA HAASE

EMILIE GEHRINGER

MALVINA HUTH & ARLENE SCHULTZ

GUSTAVE BUMBLIS

KARL & AUGUSTA WORM

EVA WEIHER

MARTHA & JULIUS NIEDER

ALEX & JULIA MURANKE

CHRISTINA NEITZEL

AUGUST H. HEINRICH

OLGA ERNST

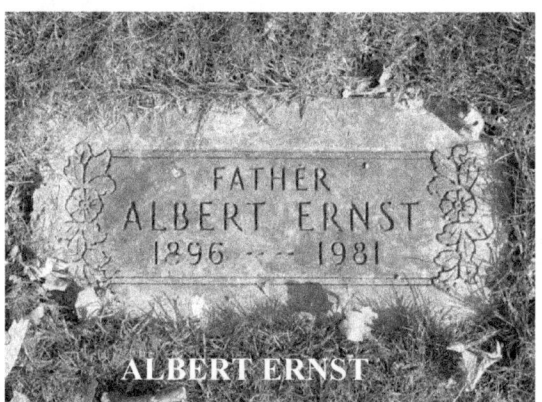

ALBERT ERNST

JOHN & ADELE PETERS

HENRIETTA & ADOLPH J. RENKE

MINNIE IRONS

ANNA & GEORGE MILLER

GUSTAV & ANNA PAMPUS

MILLIE PONTO

CARL A. & JOHANNA SEMLER

ANNA & THOMAS PARREY

AMELIA HEIN

GUSTAV WEBER

PAULINA ERENST

JACOB SPARGOT, HATTIE SPARGOT, WALTER & JOHN WAGNER

ALEX PODGIS

AMELIA & HENRY SALEKER

MAX & MARIE RAEDER

ADAM & CAROLINE PERRY

ADOLPH & MARIE SCHWED

ADOLPH ELMENTHALER

ANNA SCHWED

EMILIE ELMENTHALER

FERDINAND & MINNIE KIRSCHNICK

TINA PETERS

CARL PETERS

JUSTINA KENAT

JEANETTE J. & GUSTAV A. SALECKER

CARL BURKE, ANNA & EDWARD SCHULTZ

APPENDIX C – WORKS CONSULTED

The following works and collections were consulted during this research and serve as useful resources for researching the *Deutsche aus Litauen*.

Church Records of Baptisms, Marriages, Confirmations, and Deaths

- IAGL Online Index (index.germansfromlithuania.org)
- Missouri Synod, US, Lutheran Church records, 1851-1973 (ancestry.com collection 62265)
- Records of Schifflein Christi Lutheran Church (held at United Church of Christ archives, Cleveland)
- Records of Trinity Lutheran Church (FamilySearch.org collection 2115643)
- Records of Zion Evangelical Lutheran Church (held at the church rectory, Cleveland)
- U.S., Evangelical Lutheran Church in America Church Records, 1781-1969 (ancestry.com collection 60722)

Civil Records of Births, Marriages, and Deaths

- Ohio, County Births, 1841-2003 (familysearch.org collection 1932106)
- Ohio, Deaths, 1908-1953 (familysearch.org collection 1307272)
- Ohio, US, Birth Index, 1908-2003 (ancestry.com collection 3146)
- Ohio, US, County Marriage Records, 1774-1993 (ancestry.com collection 61378)
- US, Social Security Death Index, 1935-2014 (ancestry.com collection 3693)

Maps

- Historical maps: (https://www.lithuanianmaps.com/images/1859_Chrzan_13_Wilno_kpbc_mapywig_COMP.jpg)
- Locations with their modern Lithuanian names: (maps.google.com or maps.lt)

Naturalization & Immigration Records

- Baltimore, Maryland, U.S., Passenger Lists, 1820-1964 (ancestry.com collection 8679)
- Hamburg Passenger Lists, 1850-1934 (ancestry.com collection 1068)
- New York, U.S., Arriving Passenger and Crew Lists (including Castle Garden and Ellis Island,) 1820-1957 (ancestry.com collection 7488)
- Ohio, County Naturalization Records, 1800-1977 (familysearch.org collection 1987615)

- Ohio, US Naturalization Petition and Record Books, 1888-1946 (ancestry.com collection 2363)
- Pennsylvania, US, Arriving Passenger and Crew Lists, 1798-1962 (ancestry.com collection 8769)
- US, Border Crossings from Canada to U.S., 1895-1960 (ancestry.com collection 1075)
- US, Passport Applications, 1795-1925 (ancestry.com collection 1174)

Newspapers, Obituaries, & Cemeteries

- The Cleveland Necrology File and News Index (online via Cleveland Public Library)
- *The Cleveland Plain Dealer* (newspapers.com)
- *Cleveland Press* (newspapers.com)
- FindAGrave.com

Resources Abroad

- Records of the *Einwandererzentrallstelle* (invenio.bundersarchiv.de)
- Records of the International Tracing Service & the International Refugee Organization (arolsen-archives.org)

Telephone Directories

- US, City Directories, 1922-1995 (ancestry.com collection 2469)
- The White Pages (whitepages.com)

INDEX OF IMMIGRANTS

A

Ackermann, Adolf Franz 27
Ackermann, Albin "James" 30
Ackermann, Angelina 29
Ackermann, Berta 28
Ackermann, Edmund Eduard 28
Ackermann, Emilie *See* Nausner, Emilie
Ackermann, Heinrich 29
Ackermann, Leokadia Emilie "Catherine" 28
Ackermann, Lydia 30
Adler, Anna .... *See* Muschinski, Anna
Albrecht, Gustav 31
Andechser, Anna 36
Andechser, August 34
Andechser, Emilie. *See* Berwing, Emilie
Andechser, Emma 35
Andechser, Friedrich 35
Andechser, Karl 33
Augustat, Anna 37
Augustat, Josef 37
Aukschun, Adolf 40
Aukschun, Auguste .... *See* Baschar, Auguste
Aukschun, Gustav Leopold 40
Aukschun, Leopold 39
Aukschun, Martha 40
Aukschun, Oskar 39
Aukschun, Rudolf 40

B

Baltronat, Helene 42
Baltronat, Karl 41
Baltrunat, Auguste 42
Baltrunat, Helene Bertha 42
Baltrunat, Karl Wilhelm 42
Baltrunat, Magdalene Helene .... *See* Leichert, Magdalene Helene
Baranowicz, August 43
Baranowicz, Emilie .... *See* Wilk, Emilie
Bareig, Matthias Max .... *See* Perry, Matthias Max
Baschar, Auguste 49
Baschar, Gustav 49
Basenau, Adam "Edward" 46
Basenau, Adeline 45
Basenau, Amelia "Mollie" 46
Basenau, Elizabeth Emma. *See* Günther, Elizabeth Emma
Basenau, Eva "Evelyn" 46
Basenau, Gustav "Gust" 48
Basenau, Johann 45
Basenau, Karl 44
Basenau, Pauline *See* Jurkschat, Pauline
Batke, Emilie 50
Bauer, August. *See* Baranowicz, August
Bauer, Emilie .... *See* Wilk, Emilie
Baumann, Emilie 51
Baumann, Olga 52
Bender, Auguste 53
Bender, Bertha 53

347

Bender, Henriette 53

Berwing, Adolf Johann 55

Berwing, Auguste 55

Berwing, Emilie 56

Berwing, Johann Julius 56

Berwing, Karl Gustav 54

Berwing, Oskar Adolf 56

Berwing, Pauline Helene *See* Dikheiser, Pauline Helene

Birkoben, Albert 57

Birkoben, Auguste *See* Kausch, Auguste

Birkoben, Emilie ...... *See* Budnik, Emilie

Birkoben, Hugo Gustav 57

Birkoben, Karl 57

Blum, Gustav 58

Borchert, Eva 63

Bossman, Adam Edward ... *See* Basenau, Adam Edward

Bossman, Adeline *See* Basenau, Adeline

Bossman, Amelia Mollie .. *See* Basenau, Amelia Mollie

Bossman, Anna ..... *See* Jurkschat, Anna

Bossman, Elizabeth Emma *See* Günther, Elizabeth Emma

Bossman, Eva Evelyn *See* Basenau, Eva Evelyn

Bossman, Gustav Gust ...... *See* Basenau, Gustav Gust

Bossman, Johann .. *See* Basenau, Johann

Bossman, Karl .... *See* Basenau, Karl

Bossman, Pauline *See* Jurkschat, Pauline

Brauer, Gustav 64

Brownell, Wilhelmine ...... *See* Tetmeier, Wilhelmine

Budnik, Auguste . *See* Pushkat, Auguste

Budnik, Emilie 65

Buehrmann, Helene Bertha .... *See* Baltrunat, Helene Bertha

Buknat, Ludwig "Louis" 66

Bumblis, Adolf 59

Bumblis, Anna (1837) .... *See* Schwed, Anna

Bumblis, Anna (1886) ..... *See* Friedrich, Anna

Bumblis, August Gustav 59

Bumblis, Auguste 61

Bumblis, Johann (1835) 59

Bumblis, Johann (1876) 61

Bumblis, Marianna 61

Bumblis, Mathilde .... *See* Friedrich, Mathilde

Burke, Amelia Millie *See* Kinat, Amelia Millie

Burke, Anna .... *See* Kinat, Anna

Burke, Johanna 67

Burke, Karl Adolf 67

Burke, Karl Gustav 67

Buschar, Georg 69

Buschar, Julianna Auguste .. *See* Putnat, Julianna Auguste

C

Clark, Auguste .... *See* Berwing, Auguste

Conrad, Angelina .... *See* Ackermann, Angelina

Conrad, Ludwig Louis .... *See* Konrad, Ludwig Louis

Corban, Emilie .... *See* Kinat, Emilie

D

Dangelat, Anna 70

Dangelat, Ludwig "Louis" 70

Dangeleit, Albine... *See* Schultz, Albine

Degučiai
- Jessat, Gustav August 141
- Nowjak, Gustav Emil 218

Dengler, Olga .... *See* Nausner, Olga

Dick, Richard Emil .... *See* Dikschat, Richard Emil

Dickheiser, Marie .... *See* Muschinski, Marianna

Dikheiser, Adolf Luis 71

Dikheiser, Anna .... *See* Reinke, Anna

Dikheiser, Bertha 72

Dikheiser, Gustav Ferdinand 73

Dikheiser, Lydia 73

Dikheiser, Pauline Helene 71

Dikheiser, Wanda 73

Dikschat, Richard Emil 74

Dilewski, Johann .... *See* Dill, Johann

Dill, Alma 77

Dill, Angeline ..... *See* Reinke, Angeline

Dill, Erna 78

Dill, Erwin 77

Dill, Johann 75

Dill, Johann Jr 76

Dill, Julius 79

Dill, Karl 75

Dill, Karoline .... *See* Keller, Karoline

Dill, Walter 78

Dingfeld, Anna Helene 80

Dingfeld, Elizabeth 80

Dingfeld, Wilhelmine 80

Doczkat, Bertha .. *See* Klotzhber, Bertha

Doczkat, Emilie ..... *See* Doczkis, Emilie

Doczkat, Johann .... *See* Doczkis, Johann

Doczkis, Emilie 81

Doczkis, Georg 82

Doczkis, Helene *See* Klotzhober, Helene

Doczkis, Johann 81

Dork, Adele Emilie 83

Dorn, Eduard Martin 83

Dorn, Maria 84

Dörsch, Elizabeth .... *See* Dingfeld, Elizabeth

Dreitzler, Karoline .... *See* Nausner, Karoline

Drescher, Anna .... *See* Geschwandtner, Anna

Dutchcot, Georg ...... *See* Doczkis, Georg

E

Eckert, Berta Louise 110

Eckert, Johanna Karoline 86

Eckert, Ludwig "Louis" Rudolf 85

Eichelberger, Rudolf Oskar 87

Elmentahler, Johann Adolf 88

Ernst, Adolf 89

Ernst, Emilie 89

Ernst, Olga .... *See* Hirsch, Olga

Ernst, Pauline ... *See* Tiedemann, Pauline

Erzthaler, Henriette 90

Erzthaler, Karl Friedrich 90

Erzthaler, Marie Emma 90

Essel, Anna 94

Essel, Eduard 91

Essel, Eduard Adolf 92

Essel, Eduard Karl 93

Essel, Marie 94

Essel, Mathilde Tillie .... *See* Klein, Mathilde Tillie

Essel, Wilhelmine Henriette 91

Evans, Rosalia Rose *See* Worm, Rosalia Rose

Evenden, Martha *See* Aukschun, Martha

F

Fee, Emma .... *See* Andechser, Emma

Fieler, Wilhelmine Henriette . *See* Essel, Wilhelmine Henriette

Fife, Auguste ...... *See* Berwing, Auguste

Filier, Wilhelmine 95

Filler, Wilhelmine Henriette .. *See* Essel, Wilhelmine Henriette

Fischer, Emilie ...... *See* Doczkis, Emilie

Fischer, Heinrich 96

Fischer, Helene 96

Francis, Lydia ... *See* Ackermann, Lydia

Franulewich, Julius .... *See* Franulewicz, Julius

Franulewicz, Eduard 98

Franulewicz, Johanna Karoline .... *See* Eckert, Johanna Karoline

Franulewicz, Julius 97

Franulewicz, Mathilde Pauline 97

Franulewicz, Olga 98

Franulewicz, Pauline Bertha 97

Frenkel, Malwine 99

Fretke, August .... *See* Friedke, August

Fretke, Marianna .*See* Reinke, Marianna

Friedke, August 100

Friedrich, Amalia *See* Schröder, Amelia

Friedrich, Anna 103

Friedrich, Ernestine 102

Friedrich, Gottlieb Ludwig 101

Friedrich, Helene Lena .... *See* Schröder, Helene Lena

Friedrich, Karl 102

Friedrich, Marie .... *See* Gleid, Marie

Friedrich, Mathilde 102

Furst, Anna .... *See* Augustat, Anna

G

Gall, Anna .... *See* Haase, Anna

Gehringer, Amelia .... *See* Unterberger, Amelia

Gehrke, Anna .... *See* Tetmeier, Anna

Gehrke, Wilhelmine .... *See* Tetmeier, Wilhelmine

Gergely, Anna .... *See* Peter, Anna

Gerlat, Eduard .... *See* Gerulat, Eduard

Gerulat, Bertha 104

Gerulat, Eduard 104

Geschwandtner, Anna 105

Geschwandtner, Olga 105

Ginter, Bertha 108

Ginter, Elizabeth Emma ... *See* Günther, Elizabeth Emma

Ginter, Julius .... *See* Günther, Julius

Gleichforsch, Marie ... *See* Lauks, Marie

Gleichforsch, Olga 106

Gleichfrosch, Adolf 106

Gleid, Marie 107

Golon, Marie .... *See* Essel, Marie

Gottschalk, Marta ..... *See* Rebner, Marta

Gribner, August .... *See* Grübner, August

Gribner, Emilie .... *See* Wisgin, Emilie

Grigat, Berta Louise 110

Grigat, Emilie 110

Grigat, Marie 110

Grübner, August 112
Gudat, Emilie 113
Gudat, Leopold 113
Gudat, Matthias Leopold 114
Günther, August................................108
Günther, Elizabeth Emma................109
Günther, Henriette ....*See* Schröder, Henriette
Günther, Julius 108
Gutman, Pauline ....*See* Reinke, Pauline
Gutmann, Karl Johann 115

H

Haase, Amalie.........*See* Konrad, Amalie
Haase, Anna......................................117
Haase, August 116
Haase, Karl "Carl" August...............117
Habersat, Karl 118
Haller, Natalie-Martha .... *See* Nausner, Natalie-Martha
Hartig, Anna .... *See* Reichel, Anna
Hartig, Auguste Bertha 119
Hartig, Julius Karl.............................119
Hasebein, Auguste *See* Schütz, Auguste
Hasenheit, Ottilie "Tillie" 120
Hausrath, August 121
Hausrath, August Johann 124
Hausrath, Dorothea "Dora"..............122
Hausrath, Eva....................................121
Hausrath, Ferdinand.........................122
Hausrath, Josef..................................121
Hausrath, Karoline . *See* Kinat, Karoline
Hausrath, Maria ....*See* Dorn, Maria
Heimert, Anna Dorothea..................125

Hein, Adeline.......*See* Pudimat, Adeline
Hein, Adeline (1889)......... *See* Nausner, Adeline
Hein, Adeline (1891)............ *See* Podzis, Adeline
Hein, Adolf................................... 126
Hein, Amalia 128
Hein, Amelia 129
Hein, Andreas............................... 127
Hein, Andreas \Heinrich"\............... 127
Hein, Emilie................*See* Batke, Emilie
Hein, Josef 130
Hein, Julius................................... 128
Hein, Leopold............................... 128
Hein, Louis ....*See* Hein, Ludwig
Hein, Ludwig................................ 129
Hein, Marianna.......*See* Kinat, Marianna
Hein, Marie (1887) . *See* Pudimat, Marie
Hein, Pauline .... *See* Herr, Pauline
Hein, Rudolf................................. 129
Heinrich, Adolf Eduard 132
Heinrich, Albert............................. 131
Heinrich, August (1855).................. 131
Heinrich, August (1893).................. 133
Heinrich, August Hermann............. 132
Heinrich, Bertha 133
Heinrich, Edmund 132
Heinrich, Emilie .... *See* Nowiak, Emilie
Heinrich, Johann............................ 134
Heinrich, Justine Auguste...*See* Saleker, Justine Auguste
Heinrich, Karl................................ 133
Heinrich, Marie 132
Hempel, Alma ....*See* Dill, Alma

Hempel, Oswald 135
Henry, August ...... *See* Heinrich, August
Henry, Justine Auguste ...... *See* Saleker, Justine Auguste
Henry, Karl .... *See* Heinrich, Karl
Herr, Dorothea Dora .... *See* Hausrath, Dorothea Dora
Herr, Ferdinand 136
Herr, Pauline 136
Hess, Emilie .... *See* Kinat, Emilie
Hess, Johann 137
Hinz, Olga .... *See* Franulewicz, Olga
Hirsch, Albertine "Bertha" 138
Hirsch, Albine 139
Hirsch, Auguste 139
Hirsch, Auguste Bertha .... *See* Hartig, Auguste Bertha
Hirsch, Bertha .... *See* Bender, Bertha
Hirsch, Gottlieb 138
Hirsch, Julius 139
Hirsch, Olga 138
Hirsch, Wilhelm 139
Horacek, Eva Evelyn *See* Basenau, Eva Evelyn
Hubert, Anna Helene 140
Huth, Malwina Malvina .... *See* Weinschröder, Malwina Malvina

I

Irons, Wilhelmine .... *See* Tetmeier, Wilhelmine

J

Janssen, Emma ...... *See* Nausner, Emma
Jantz, Anna .... *See* Unterberger, Anna
Jessat, Anna .... *See* Andechser, Anna

Jessat, Gustav August 141
Jesset, Gustav August .... *See* Jessat, Gustav August
Jonat, Amalie Mollie *See* Lukat, Amalie Mollie
Jonat, Johann 142
Jurgeleit, Adeline *See* Basenau, Adeline
Jurgeleit, Christ 143
Jurgeleit, Christine 143
Jurgelewitz, Berta 145
Jurgelewitz, Emma 145
Jurkschat, Adolf 146
Jurkschat, Anna 146
Jurkschat, Johann 146
Jurkschat, Pauline 146

K

Kairat, Anna .... *See* Lehmann, Anna
Kalchert, Bertha .. *See* Dikheiser, Bertha
Kalchert, Eva .... *See* Borchert, Eva
Kalchert, Gustav Albert 148
Kalchert, Lydia .... *See* Dikheiser, Lydia
Kalweit, Christian 149
Kalweit, Emma .... *See* Lehmann, Emma
Kalweit, Wilhelmine .... *See* Dingfeld, Wilhelmine
Kaptein, Eduard "Emmanuel" 150
Kaptein, Emma 151
Kaptein, Gustav 150
Kaptein, Ottilie 151
Kausch, Auguste 152
Kausch, Helene 152
Keller, Karoline 153
Kemerait, Adolf 154

Kemerait, Emilie.....*See* Tieslau, Emilie

Kenat, Karoline Lena............ *See* Kless, Karoline Lena

Kennath, Karoline Lena........ *See* Kless, Karoline Lena

Kiesling, Auguste Bertha..... *See* Hartig, Auguste Bertha

Kiesling, Hedwig "Hattie" 155

Kinaitis, August Augustis..... *See* Kinat, August Augustis

Kinat, Adolf 158

Kinat, Albine.......... *See* Schultz, Albine

Kinat, Amelia "Millie".................... 160

Kinat, Anna.................................. 156

Kinat, August............................... 160

Kinat, August "Augustis" 156

Kinat, Eduard Karl........................ 160

Kinat, Emilie (1874) 159

Kinat, Emilie (1887) 160

Kinat, Ferdinand 156

Kinat, Justine ....*See* Klaus, Justine

Kinat, Karoline 159

Kinat, Marianna 160

Kindra, Wilhelmine .... *See* Tetmeier, Wilhelmine

Kinski, Anna Helene........ *See* Dingfeld, Anna Helene

Kirschner, Anna.............................. 163

Kirschner, Auguste 162

Kirschner, Emilie........................... 164

Kirschner, Jeanette Johanna............. 163

Kirschner, Pauline......................... 163

Kirschnick, Wilhelmine Henriette ... *See* Essel, Wilhelmine Henriette

Kirstein, Henriette............ *See* Schröder, Henriette

Klamer, Marie .... *See* Stossun, Marie

Klaus, Justine................................. 165

Klein, Mathilde "Tillie" 169

Kless, Adolf "Adam"....................... 167

Kless, Bertha 168

Kless, Friedrich 168

Kless, Gustav................................. 166

Kless, Karoline "Lena" 166

Kless, Marie.................................. 166

Klimach, Anna......... *See* Wiemert, Anna

Klimack, Anna......... *See* Wiemert, Anna

Klotzhober, Bertha 170

Klotzhober, Helene......................... 170

Klotzober, Bertha ......*See* Ginter, Bertha

Klotzober, Matthias Martin 170

Kokoschka, Albine ......*See* Lang, Albine

Kokoschka, Anna ..... *See* Schnell, Anna

Kokoschka, Friedrich 171

Konrad, Amalie 172

Konrad, Christine .... *See* Jurgeleit, Christine

Konrad, Ludwig "Louis" 172

Kraft, Olga..................... *See* Peter, Olga

Kramer, Ludwig "Louis" Friedrich . 173

Kroschnewski, Jeanette Johanna ....*See* Kirschner, Jeanette, Johanna

Krüger, Hildegard Erna ..*See* Reinecker, Hildegard Erna

Kurban, Emilie .... *See* Kinat, Emilie

L

Lackner, Anna .....*See* Neubacher, Anna

Lackner, Bertha 174

Lackner, Georg............................... 174

Lang, Adeline "Nellie" 175
Lang, Adolf Eduard 179
Lang, Albert 177
Lang, Albine 175
Lang, Amelia 179
Lang, August .... *See* Gustav Ludwig August
Lang, Auguste 176
Lang, Berta .... *See* Jurgelewitz, Berta
Lang, Bertha .... *See* Gerulat, Bertha
Lang, Edward .. *See* Lang, Adolf Eduard
Lang, Emma ..... *See* Jurgelewitz, Emma
Lang, Ferdinand 176
Lang, Gustav Ludwig August 178
Lang, Karl 175
Lang, Ludwig "Louis" 175
Lang, Wilhelmine .... *See* Metdorf, Wilhelmine
Lange, Heinrich Robert Karl 177
Langmeyer, Anna .. *See* Kirschner, Anna
Lauks, Marie 180
Laws, Auguste .... *See* Berwing, Auguste
Lear, Amelia .... *See* Hein, Amelia
Lear, August .... *See* Lier, August
Lehman, Pauline *See* Kirschner, Pauline
Lehmann, Anna 181
Lehmann, Auguste *See* Hirsch, Auguste
Lehmann, Berhardt 182
Lehmann, Emilie 181
Lehmann, Emma 182
Lehmann, Ernestine .. *See* Romanowski, Ernestine
Lehmann, Julius 181
Lehmann, Luise "Elizabeth" 182

Lehmann, Mathias 181
Leichert, Christine 183
Leichert, Magdalene Helene 183
Lier, Amalia .... *See* Hein, Amelia
Lier, August 184
Lindhammer, Henriette 186
Lockner, Anna ...... *See* Neubacher, Anna
Lockner, Georg .... *See* Lackner, Georg
Logies, Auguste ... *See* Pushkat, Auguste
Logies, Gustav 187
Logies, Karl Franz 187
Logies, Ottilie .... *See* Kaptein, Ottilie
Lukat, Adeline Nellie *See* Lang, Adeline Nellie
Lukat, Albine 189
Lukat, Amalie "Mollie" 190
Lukat, Eduard 189
Lukat, Gustav 189
Lukat, Johann 190
Lukat, Leopoldine "Tina" 189
Luther, Anna .... *See* Schmidt, Anna

M

Mai, Albertine Bertha .... *See* Hirsch, Albertine Bertha
Mai, Alexander 191
Mauruschat, Eduard 193
Mauruschat, Johanna .... *See* Burke, Johanna
May, Albertine Bertha .... *See* Hirsch, Albertine Bertha
May, Alexander .... *See* Mai, Alexander
May, Leopold Leo Witold .... *See* Mai, Leopold Leo Witold
Metdorf, Wilhelmine 195

Mett, Auguste Pauline 194
Mett, Eva 194
Mett, Josef 194
Mielke, Emilie ...... *See* Nausner, Emilie
Miller, Adolf .. *See* Millerskofski, Adolf
Miller, Anna ...... *See* Reinke, Anna
Miller, Olga ...*See* Geschwandtner, Olga
Miller, Wilhelm Albert ...... *See* Millerskofski, Wilhelm Albert
Millerskofski, Adolf 196
Millerskofski, Wilhelm Albert 196
Missun, Anna 198
Missun, Christian "Christ" 198
Mittag, Auguste 199
Moebius, Berta ... *See* Ackermann, Berta
Müller, Olga ..*See* Geschwandtner, Olga
Müllerszkowski, Ottilie Tillie ...... *See* Hasenheit, Ottilie Tillie
Muranke, Alexander ...... *See* Muranko, Alexander
Muranke, Julianna. *See* Podzis, Julianna
Muranko, Alexander 200
Muschinski, Adolf 201
Muschinski, Anna 201
Muschinski, Josef 201
Muschinski, Marianna 202
Muschinski, Marie ...... *See* Muschinski, Marianna
Muschinski, Natalie . *See* Weinschröder, Natalie

N

Nauruschat, Eduard ...... *See* Mauruschat, Eduard
Nausner, "Carl" Rudolf 204
Nausner, Adeline 205
Nausner, Alexander-Edmund "Edward 203
Nausner, Anna ...... *See* Pollak, Anna
Nausner, Bertha 203
Nausner, Emilie (1860) 206
Nausner, Emilie (1891) 203
Nausner, Emma 205
Nausner, Karoline 205
Nausner, Natalie-Martha 204
Nausner, Olga 204
Nausner, Reimund "Raymond" 206
Neiderstrass, Georg 214
Neiman, Anna ...... *See* Dangelat, Anna
Neiman, Gustav .. *See* Neumann, Gustav
Neitzel, Adolf Otto 207
Neitzel, Christine ...... *See* Leichert, Christine
Neitzel, Ferdinand Karl 207
Nemo, Martha .... *See* Aukschun, Martha
Netzel, Ernst Friedrich 208
Neubacher, Anna 209
Neubacher, Auguste ...... *See* Baltrunat, Auguste
Neubacher, Gustav Emil 209
Neubacher, Johann 209
Neubacher, Marie ...... *See* Grigat, Marie
Neubauer, Olga *See* Gleichforsch, Olga
Neumann, Auguste .. *See* Lang, Auguste
Neumann, Bertha 211
Neumann, Emilie ...... 211, *See* Gudat, Emilie
Neumann, Gustav 211
Neumann, Karl 211

Neumann, Karl Adolf 212
Nieder, Julius . See Niederstrasse, Julius
Nieder, Karl .... See Niederstrasse, Karl
Niederstrass, Christine .... See Schultz, Christine
Niederstrasse, Julius 214
Niederstrasse, Karl 215
Nieman, Bertha ... See Neumann, Bertha
Nieman, Emilie ... See Neumann, Emilie
Niess, Anna .... See Schulz, Anna
Niess, Gustav 216
Nos, Car Rudolf .... See Nausner, Carl Rudolf
Novack, Auguste .... See Kirschner, Auguste
Nowiak, Albin Alvin Friedrich Wilhelm .... See Nowjack, Albin Alvin Friedrich Wilhelm
Nowiak, Auguste .... See Kirschner, Auguste
Nowiak, Emilie 218
Nowiak, Eva 218
Nowiak, Georg 218
Nowiak, Gustav Emil .... See Nowjak, Gustav Emil
Nowiak, Hugo .... See Nowjack, Hugo
Nowiak, Irene .... See Nowjack, Irene
Nowiak, Ludwig Louis .... See Nowjack, Ludwig Louis
Nowiak, Richard See Nowjack, Richard
Nowjack, Albin "Alvin" Friedrich Wilhelm 220
Nowjack, Hugo 220
Nowjack, Irene 221
Nowjack, Ludwig "Louis" 221
Nowjack, Richard 219

Nowjak, Gustav Emil 219
Nowjak, Wanda .. See Dikheiser, Wanda

O

Ortman, Eva Evelyn .. See Basenau, Eva Evelyn
Otto, Anna .... See Saleker, Anna

P

Pampus, Anna .... See Jurkschat, Anna
Pampus, Gustav 223
Pasekel, Emilie .... See Grigat, Emilie
Pasekel, Ludwig "Louis" 222
Peck, Helene Marianna ...... See Schwed, Helene Marianna
Perrej, Adolf "Adam" 225
Perrey, Josef (1863) 228
Perrey, Josef (1866) 224
Perry, Adolf Adam ..... See Perrej, Adolf Adam
Perry, Anna Helene ... See Hubert, Anna Helene
Perry, Christof Adam "Christian" 227
Perry, Hedwig Hattie .... See Kiesling, Hedwig Hattie
Perry, Josef .... See Perrey, Josef
Perry, Matthias "Max" 226
Perry, Thomas 226
Peter, Adolf 230
Peter, Anna 230
Peter, Emilie Mathilde 232
Peter, Johann Josef 232
Peter, Karl Carl Charles See Peters, Karl Carl Charles
Peter, Olga 229
Peters, Adolf Ferdinand 231

Peters, Albert Ewald 231
Peters, Albertine *See* Schnell, Albertine
Peters, Anna .... *See* Reder, Anna
Peters, Auguste Pauline .... *See* Mett, Auguste Pauline
Peters, Emilie Milly .... *See* Tennebor, Emilie Milly
Peters, Johann Josef ... *See* Peter, Johann Josef
Peters, Karl "Carl" "Charles" 229
Peters, Leopoldine Tina .... *See* Lukat, Leopoldine Tina
Peters, Ludwig "Louis" 230
Podgis, Alexander 233
Podzis, Adeline 233
Podzis, Alexander .... *See* Podgis, Alexander
Podzis, Julianna 233
Pohl, Amelia .... *See* Lang, Amelia
Pohl, Johann 234
Polak, Amelia .... *See* Lang, Amelia
Polak, Johann .... *See* Pohl, Johann
Polenschat, Karoline Lena .... *See* Tennebor, Karoline Lena
Pollak, Anna 234
Ponto, Emilie Millie Mildred .... *See* Schütz, Emilie Millie Mildred
Pudim, Marie .... *See* Pudimat, Marie
Pudimat Adeline 235
Pudimat, Heinrich 235
Pudimat, Marie 235
Pudimat, Pauline Bertha .... *See* Franulewicz, Pauline Bertha
Puschkat, August 237
Pushkat, Auguste 237
Puskat, August .... *See* Puschkat, August

Puskat, Malwine . *See* Frenkel, Malwine
Putnat, Julianna Auguste 238

R

Rebner, Marta 239
Reder, Anna 240
Reder, Gustav 240
Reder, Marie .... *See* Heinrich, Marie
Reichel, Anna 241
Rein, Erna .... *See* Dill, Erna
Reinecker, Hildegard Erna 242
Reinecker, Ida Antonie *See* Schiller, Ida Antonie
Reinecker, Richard Johann.............. 242
Reinke, Adolf Julius 243
Reinke, Angeline 243
Reinke, Anna 243
Reinke, Henriette *See* Bender, Henriette
Reinke, Johann Karl 244
Reinke, Marianna 245
Reinke, Pauline................................ 245
Reiter, Andreas Heinrich 246
Reiter, Anna (1864) .. *See* Missun, Anna
Reiter, Anna (1879) *See* Tetmeier, Anna
Reiter, August 247
Reiter, Matthias "Max" 247
Renke, Adolf Julius .. *See* Reinke, Adolf Julius
Richter, Marie .... *See* Kless, Marie
Roloff, Adele Emilie ... *See* Dorn, Adele Emilie
Romanowski, Ernestine 248
Rosekeit, Emilie 249
Russ, Emma .... *See* Andechser, Emma

S

Saleker, Anna 250
Saleker, Emilie ...... *See* Wiemert, Emilie
Saleker, Gustav Adolph 251
Saleker, Henry .... *See* Saleker, Johann Andreas Heinrich
Saleker, Jeanette Johanna *See* Kirschern, Jeanette Johanna
Saleker, Johann Andreas "Heinrich" 250
Saleker, Justine Auguste 251
Salewski, Albine .... *See* Schultz, Albine
Schaak, Georg 253
Schaak, Josef 253
Schack, Georg .... *See* Schaak, Georg
Schack, Josef .... *See* Schaak, Josef
Scharfetter, Bertha ..... *See* Kless, Bertha
Scharfetter, Friedrich Wilhelm 254
Schiller, Ida Antonie 255
Schmidt, Adolf Franz 257
Schmidt, Anna 256
Schmidt, Anna Marie .*See* Schütz, Anna Marie
Schmidt, August 256
Schmidt, Auguste .. *See* Schütz, Auguste
Schmidt, Marianna .... *See* Bumblis, Marianna
Schneider, Adolf 258
Schneider, Bertha *See* Neumann, Bertha
Schneider, Emilie *See* Neumann, Emilie
Schneider, Julius 258
Schneider, Karl 259
Schnell, Albertine 260
Schnell, Anna 260
Schnell, Friedrich 260
Schönrank, Karl 261
Schröder, Amelia 263
Schröder, Ernestine .... *See* Friedrich, Ernestine
Schröder, Gottlieb 262
Schröder, Helene "Lena" 263
Schröder, Henriette 262
Schultz, Albine 264
Schultz, Anna .... *See* Kinat, Anna
Schultz, Christine 264
Schultz, Emilie Mathilde .... *See* Peter, Emilie Mathilde
Schultz, Johann .... *See* Schütz, Johann
Schulz, Anna 264
Schütz, Anna Marie 266
Schütz, Auguste 266
Schütz, Emilie ...... *See* Rosekeit, Emilie
Schütz, Emilie "Millie" "Mildred" .. 266
Schütz, Emilie Mathilde .... *See* Peter, Emilie Mathilde
Schütz, Georg 265
Schütz, Johann 264
Schütz, Malwina Malvina .... *See* Weinschröder, Malwina Malvina
Schwand, Gustav *See* Schwandt, Gustav
Schwand, Helene .... *See* Fischer, Helene
Schwandt, Gustav 267
Schwed, Anna 269
Schwed, Anna 268
Schwed, Emilie ... *See* Baumann, Emilie, *See* Lehmann, Emilie
Schwed, Heinrich 270
Schwed, Helene Emma 270
Schwed, Helene Marianna 268
Schwed, Julius Gustav 271

Schwed, Karl 269

Schwed, Luise Elizabeth. *See* Lehmann, Luise Elizabeth

Schwed, Marianna Anna 268

Schwelgin, Adolf "Edward" 272

Schwelgin, Albine ...... *See* Lang, Albine

Schwelgin, Helene .... *See* Baltronat, Helene

Schwelgin, Johann 272

Schwenter, Emilie Millie Mildred ... *See* Schütz, Emilie Millie Mildred

Schwenter, Heinrich Friedrich 274

Seaman, Johann .... *See* Simon, Johann

Seaman, Marianna Marie ..... *See* Simon, Marianna Marie

Semler, Karl Adam 275

Simon, Johann 276

Simon, Marianna "Marie" 276

Sliter, Bertha .... *See* Nausner, Bertha

Snyder, Auguste ... *See* Bender, Auguste

Sokolek, Adolf 277

Sokolek, Marianna .... *See* Reinke, Marianna

Spei, August 278

Springman, Marie .... *See* Essel, Marie

Spurgat, Henriette .... *See* Erzthaler, Henriette

Spurgat, Jakob 279

Stassun, Friedrich 280

Stasun, Amelia .... *See* Hein, Amelia

Stossun, Amelia .... *See* Hein, Amelia

Stossun, Gustav 281

Stossun, Heinrich 281

Stossun, Marie 280

Stossun, Marie Emma ...... *See* Erzthaler, Marie Emma

Strick, Auguste ... *See* Bumblis, Auguste

T

Tedman, Adolf ..... *See* Tiedmann, Adolf

Telatko, Anna .... *See* Muschinski, Anna

Tennebor, Emilie "Milly" 282

Tennebor, Georg b. 1862 282

Tennebor, Georg b. 1886 283

Tennebor, Helene .. *See* Kausch, Helene

Tennebor, Karoline "Lena" 283

Tetmeier, Adeline "Lena" 286

Tetmeier, Anna 285

Tetmeier, Ferdinand Christof 285

Tetmeier, Henriette .... *See* Lindhammer, Henriette

Tetmeier, Wilhelmine 286

Tiedemann, Pauline 292

Tiedman, Leokadia Emilie Catherine .... *See* Ackermann, Leokadia Emilie Catherine

Tiedmann, Adolf 292

Tiedmann, Adolf Eduard 290

Tiedmann, August Johann 291

Tiedmann, Christine .... *See* Schultz, Christine

Tiedmann, Eva .... *See* Hausrath, Eva

Tiedmann, Julius (1859) 287

Tiedmann, Julius (1883) 288

Tiedmann, Marianna "Marie" 291

Tiedmann, Mathilde Pauline .... *See* Franulewicz, Mathilde Pauline

Tieslau, Emilie 293

Tieslauk, Jakob 293

Tieslauk, Johann 294
Tieslauk, Ludwig 294
Tischler, Jakob .... *See* Tieslauk, Jakob
Tischler, Johann ... *See* Tieslauk, Johann
Tischler, Louis .... *See* Tieslauk, Ludwig
Tischler, Wilhelmine..............*See* Filier, Wilhelmine

U

Unterberger, Amelia 296
Unterberger, Anna............................297
Unterberger, Anna Dorothea............ *See* Heimert, Anna Dorothea
Unterberger, Friedrich.....................296
Unterberger, Ludwig "Louis" Gustav 297
Urgeleit, Christ......*See* Jurgeleit, Christ

V

Vidra, Auguste ....*See* Wilk, Auguste

W

Wachhaus, Adolf "Adam" 298
Wachhaus, Marianna Marie.*See* Simon, Marianna Marie
Wagner, Henriette............*See* Erzthaler, Henriette
Walinski, Emilie Rosalia .... *See* Wilk, Emilie Rosalia
Walinski, Georg "George" 299
Wallace, Helene Edna.......... *See* Weier, Helene Edna
Wegner, Johann...............................300
Weier, Albert C................................301
Weier, August Karl 301
Weier, Eva.................. *See* Nowiak, Eva

Weier, Helene Edna.........................301
Weier, Pauline 301
Weiher, Eva ....*See* Nowiak, Eva
Weinschröder, Albine........... *See* Hirsch, Albine
Weinschröder, Emilie.*See* Ernst, Emilie
Weinschröder, Julian "Julius"..........302
Weinschröder, Leon "Leo" 302
Weinschröder, Malwina "Malvina". 303
Weinschröder, Natalie 302
Wellner, Mary....*See* Schwed, Marianna Anna
Welz, Bertha ....*See* Lackner, Bertha
Westfal, Bertha ......*See* Nausner, Bertha
Wiemert, Anna .....304, *See* Essel, Anna
Wiemert, August Martin..................305
Wiemert, Emilie 304
Wiemert, Friedrich 304
Wiemert, Justine Auguste...*See* Saleker, Justine Auguste
Wiemmert, Friedrich ....*See* Wiemert, Friedrich
Wilczinski, Gustav .... *See* Wilk, Gustav
Wilk, Auguste..................................306
Wilk, Emilie 307
Wilk, Emilie Rosalia 306
Wilk, Gustav....................................306
Wilk, Olga ....*See* Baumann, Olga
Wimmert, Justine Auguste .*See* Saleker, Justine Auguste
Wisgin, Bertha.......*See* Heinrich, Bertha
Wisgin, Emilie................................308
Wisgin, Richard..............................308
Witlib, Emilie ....*See* Kirchner, Emilie
Witzke, Pauline........*See* Weier, Pauline

Wolf, Gustav .... *See* Wilk, Gustav

Wolf, Helene Emma Lena .*See* Schwed, Helene Emma

Wolinske, Georg George .*See* Walinski, Georg George

Worm, Amelia Mollie .... *See* Basenau, Amelia Mollie

Worm, Auguste ..... *See* Mittag, Auguste

Worm, Karl 309

Worm, Martin 309

Worm, Rosalia "Rose" 309

Y

Yurkschat, Johann .... *See* Jurkschat, Johann

Z

Zielke, Anna .... *See* Unterberger, Anna

Zigander, Albine .... *See* Lukat, Albine

Zorkis, Eva .... *See* Mett, Eva

INDEX OF PLACES WHERE IMMIGRANTS WERE BORN

A

Alytus
    Kiesling, Hedwig Hattie 155
Antakalnis
    Hasenheit, Ottilie Tillie 120
    Millerskofski, Adolf 196
Atesninkai
    Reder, Anna 240

B

Bakšiškai
    Pushkat, Auguste 237
Bakšiškiai
    Budnik, Emilie 65
    Wilk, Emilie Rosalia 306
    Wilk, Gustav 306
Balaikai
    Lukat, Albine 189
    Lukat, Amalie Mollie 190
    Lukat, Eduard 189
    Lukat, Gustav 189
    Lukat, Johann 190
    Lukat, Leopoldine Tina 189
Balbieriškis
    Ackermann, Albin James 30
    Ackermann, Angelina 29
    Ackermann, Berta 28
    Ackermann, Heinrich 29
    Ackermann, Leokadia Emilie
        Catherine 28
    Ackermann, Lydia 30
    Hartig, Julius Karl 119
    Mai, Alexander 191
    Mai, Leopold Leo Witold 191
    Nausner, Alexander-Edmund Edward
        203
    Nausner, Bertha 203
    Nausner, Carl Rudolf 204
    Nausner, Emilie 203, 206
    Nausner, Emma 205
    Nausner, Natalie-Martha 204
    Nausner, Olga 204
    Semler, Karl Adam 275
Bambiniai
    Kless, Marie 166
    Lang, Ludwig Louis 175
Bambininkai
    Lang, Ferdinand 176
Barkūniškis
    Muschinski, Josef 201
Bartninkai
    Aukschun, Leopold 39
Beržiniai
    Habersat, Karl 118
Bolcie (Poland)
    Birkoben, Albert 57
    Birkoben, Hugo Gustav 57
    Birkoben, Karl 57
    Reiter, Andreas Heinrich 246
    Reiter, August 247
    Reiter, Matthias Max 247
    Wilk, Emilie 307
Bukta
    Bumblis, Marianna 61
    Grigat, Berta Louise 110

Grigat, Marie 110
Gutmann, Karl Johann................115
Kemerait, Adolf...........................154
Lang, Albert.................................177
Lang, Auguste..............................176
Lang, Heinrich Robert Karl..........177
Schaak, Josef................................253
Unterberger, Friedrich 296

Bulotiškė
Burke, Johanna 67
Burke, Karl Gustav.........................67

Būriškės
Grübner, August 112

Butrimiškės
Hausrath, August 121
Hausrath, August Johann.............124
Nausner, Adeline 205
Nausner, Karoline........................205

C

Cigoniškiai
Hempel, Oswald 135

Čižiškiai
Dingfeld, Anna Helene 80
Dingfeld, Elizabeth........................80
Dingfeld, Wilhelmine 80

Cyrailė
Jurgeleit, Christ.............................143
Jurgeleit, Christine........................143

D

Deagučiai
Haase, Karl Carl August...............117

Degim (Panemunė)
Millerskofski, Wilhelmine Albert 196

Degučiai
Aukschun, Gustav Leopold 40

Aukschun, Martha........................ 40
Aukschun, Oskar.......................... 39
Aukschun, Rudolf 40
Baschar, Auguste 49
Basenau, Amalia Mollie................ 46
Berwing, Auguste.......................... 55
Berwing, Emilie 56
Berwing, Johann Julius 56
BErwing, Karl Gustav................... 54
Berwing, Oskar Adolf................... 56
Dikheiser, Adolf Luis.................... 71
Dikheiser, Lydia........................... 73
Dikheiser, Pauline Helene............. 71
Dikheiser, Wanda......................... 73
Haase, Anna 117
Heinrich, Adolf Eduard............... 132
Heinrich, Albert 131
Heinrich, August Hermann 132
Heinrich, Edmund 132
Konrad, Amalie.......................... 172
Konrad, Ludwig Louis 172
Nowjack, Albin Alvin Friedrich
  Wilhelm 220
Nowjack, Hugo 220
Schütz, Georg............................. 265
Weier, Albert C. 301

Derviniai
Haase, August 116

Didiej Šelviai
Schwandt, Gustav........................ 267

Didžioji Kirsna
Schmidt, August.......................... 256

Dotamai
Mittag, Auguste........................... 199

Dubiany (near Būdviečiai)
Neubacher, Gustav Emil 209

F

Folwark Sejny
    Keller, Karoline 153

G

Garliava
    Netzel, Ernst Friedrich 208

Gervėnai
    Hirsch, Gottlieb 138
    Hirsch, Olga 138

Gižai
    Lehmann, Anna 181
    Lehmann, Julius 181
    Rosekeit, Emilie 249

Griškabūdis (Nearby)
    Albrecht, Gustav 31

Grygaliszki (Poland)
    Spurgat, Jakob 279

Grzybina (Poland)
    Missun, Anna 198
    Stassun, Friedrich 280
    Stossun, Gustav 281
    Stossun, Heinrich 281
    Stossun, Marie 280

Gudinė
    Kirschner, Anna 163
    Kirschner, Emilie 164
    Kirschner, Jeanette Johanna 163

Gulbiniškiai
    Lehmann, Bernhardt 182

I

Igliškėliai
    Schütz, Anna Marie 266

Ivoniškio dvaras
    Schnell, Anna 260

J

Jackonys
    Polak, Johann 234

Javaravas
    Basenau, Adeline 45
    Jurkschat, Adolf 146
    Jurkschat, Anna 146
    Jurkschat, Pauline 146

Jiestrakis
    Pudimat, Marie 235

Jukneliškė
    Schwed, Karl 269

K

Kalvarija
    Augustat, Anna 37
    Baltronat, Helene 42
    Baltrunat, Auguste 42
    Baltrunat, Helene Bertha 42
    Baltrunat, Karl Wilhelm 42
    Bumblis, August Gustav 59
    Gudat, Leopold 113
    Reinke, Anna 243
    Simon, Marianna Marie 276
    Wiemert, Anna 304
    Wiemert, Emilie 304
    Wiemert, Friedrich 304

Kamičiai (Vilkaviškis)
    Augustat, Josef 37

Karklupėnai
    Hubert, Anna Helene 140

Kasteletiškė
    Hess, Johann 137

Kauniškiai
    Kinat, August 160

Kermušinė
    Peter, Emilie Mathilde 232

Kibyšiai
- Reinke, Pauline 245

Kineryszki
- Schwed, Helene Emma 270

Kineryszki (Aleksotas)
- Romanowski, Ernestine 248

Kłajpeda (Poland)
- Tieslauk, Jakob 293
- Tieslauk, Johann 294

Klėtkininkai
- Fischer, Heinrich 96
- Fischer, Helene 96

Krasenka
- Heimert, Anna Dorothea 125

Kregždžiai
- Doczkis, Emilie 81
- Doczkis, Georg 82
- Doczkis, Johanna 81
- Erzthaler, Henriette 90
- Erzthaler, Karl Friedrich 90
- Erzthaler, Marie Emma 90
- Klotzober, Matthias Martin 170

Kreivukė
- Walinski, Georg 299

Krejwiany (Poland)
- Schultz, Albine 264

Krikštonys
- Eckert, Johanna Karoline 86
- Elmentahler, Johann Adolf 88

Krokialaukis
- Schnell, Albertine 260
- Unterberger, Ludwig Louis Gustav 297
- Weinschröder, Julian Julius 302
- Weinschröder, Leon Leo 302

Krosna
- Bumblis, Johann 59
- Friedrich, Anna 103
- Friedrich, Mathilde 102
- Metdorf, Wilhelmine 195
- Niederstrass, Georg 214
- Niederstrasse, Julius 214
- Niederstrasse, Karl 215
- Schnell, Friedrich 260

Krosnėai
- Unterberger, Amelia 296

Kūlokai
- Tieslau, Emilie 293

Kumečiai
- Mett, Auguste Pauline 194
- Mett, Eva 194
- Mett, Josef 194

Kvietiškis
- Jurkschat, Johann 146
- Schneider, Julius 258

Kybartai
- Frenkel, Malwine 99
- Niess, Gustav 216
- Schulz, Anna 264

Kybartai (Lazdijai)
- Hein, Julius 128
- Hein, Leopold 128
- Kinat, Amelia Millie 160
- Kinat, Anna 156

L

Lankeliškiai
- Perrey, Josef 224

Lankupėnai
- Klotzhober, Bertha 170
- Klotzhober, Helene 170
- Missun, Christian Christ 198
- Neubacher, Anna 209
- Schröder, Amelia 263
- Schröder, Gottlieb 262

Schröder, Helene Lena 263
Schröder, Henriette 262
Lauckaimis
    Geschwandtner, Anna..................105
    Geschwandtner, Olga...................105
    Puschkat, August 237
Laukinčiai
    Hirsch, Albertine Bertha.............138
    Hirsch, Albine..............................139
    Hirsch, Auguste 139
    Hirsch, Julius 139
Leipalingis
    Muschinski, Adolf 201
Leszkiemie
    Stossun, Gustav 281
Liepajojai
    Pollak, Anna 234
Liškiava
    Franulewicz, Julius 97
    Franulewicz, Olga..........................98
    Franulewicz, Pauline Bertha..........97
Liudvinavas
    Andechser, Anna 36
    Andechser, Friedrich 35
    Buknat, Ludwig Louis 66
    Bumblis, Johann 61
    Wisgin, Emilie.............................308
    Wisgin, Richard 308
Liukiai
    Lindhammer, Henriette................186
    Saleker, Anna...............................250
    Saleker, Gustav Adolph...............251
    Saleker, Johann Andreas Heinrich 250
    Saleker, Justine Auguste..............251
    Tetmeier, Adeline Lena 286
    Tetmeier, Anna 285
    Tetmeier, Wilhelmine..................286
Lucyanow? (sp)

Nowiak, Georg.............................218
Ludvinavas
    Andechser, August 34

M

Marijampolė
    Andechser, Emma 35
    Basenau, Adam Edward 46
    Basenau, Eva Evelyn.....................46
    Basenau, Gustav Gust 48
    Berwing, Adolf Johann 55
    Dikheiser, Bertha...........................72
    Dikheiser, Gustav Ferdinand..........73
    Dikschat, Richard Emil 74
    Friedrich, Gottlieb Ludwig...........101
    Gleid, Marie 107
    Grigat, Emilie..............................110
    Kirschner, Auguste......................162
    Kirschner, Pauline 163
    Lehmann, Mathias.......................181
    Neumann, Bertha.........................211
    Neumann, Emilie.........................211
    Nowjack, Irene 221
    Pampus, Gustav...........................223
    Schönrank, Karl...........................261
    Weier, Pauline 301
Maszymietischken
    Perrej, Adolf Adam 225
Matuliškiai
    Scharfetter, Friedrich Wilhelm.....254
    Wachhaus, Adolf Adam 298
Maude (Poland)
    Kausch, Auguste 152
Mėčiūnai
    Kokoschka, Friedrich 171
Metelytė
    Lang, Gustav Ludwig August 178
Mickai

Logies, Gustav 187
Logies, Karl Franz 187
Mierkinie (Poland)
Tieslauk, Ludwig 294
Mikabaliai
Ackermann, Adolf Franz 27
Miklausė
Dangelat, Anna 70
Dangelat, Ludwig Louis 70
Dorn, Adele Emilie 83
Dorn, Maria 84
Sokolek, Adolf 277
Miknaičiai
Schiller, Ida Antonie 255
Milastonys
Tiedmann, Julius 287
Miroslavas
Ackermann, Edmund Eduard 28
Mockai
Dill, Johann 75
Mostowo
Herr, Pauline 136
Mureikai
Kaptein, Eduard Emmanuel 150
Kaptein, Gustav 150
Kaptein, Ottilie 151

N

Noragėliai
Reinke, Adolf Julius 243
Reinke, Angeline 243
Nowopól (Danieliškiai)
Peter, Anna 230

O

Obelija
Reinke, Marianna 245

Schwed, Anna 269
Schwed, Helene Marianna 268
Schwed, Marianna Anna 268
Tiedmann, Julius 288
Okliny (Poland)
Kausch, Helene 152
Olendrai
Gleichforsch, Adolf 106
Olginiai (Near Vaitkabaliai)
Klaus, Justine 165

P

Pagerniavė
Schneider, Adolf 258
Schneider, Karl 259
Pakusinė
Schütz, Emilie Millie Mildred 266
Paserninkai
Bender, Auguste 53
Bender, Henriette 53
Patašinė
Eckert, Ludwig Louis Rudolf 85
Patilčiai
Leichert, Christine 183
Leichert, Magdalene Helene 183
Paužiškiai
Basenau, Karl 44
Paželsviai
Lang, Albine 175
Penkiniai
Burkc, Karl Adolf 67
Piliakalnis (Liškiava)
Tiedmann, Adolf Eduard 290
Tiedmann, Marianna Marie 291
Pilokalnie (Seirijai)
Reinke, Anna 243
Pilokalnis

Franulewicz, Mathilde Pauline 97
Pilviškiai
    Aukschun, Adolf 40
Poderiškiai
    Schwed, Julius Gustav 271
Pogorzałek (Poland)
    Filier, Wilhelmine 95
Polesie (Near Pagiriai)
    Friedrich, Ludwig Louis 173
Polućce (Poland)
    Dill, Karl 75
    Hein, Rudolf 129
    Mauruschat, Eduard 193
    Muranko, Alexander 200
    Neumann, Karl 211
    Podgis, Alexander 233
    Podzis, Adeline 233
    Podzis, Julianna 233
    Pudimat, Adeline 235
    Pudimat, Heinrich 235
Pošnia
    Hartig, Auguste Bertha 119
    Hirsch, Wihelm 139
Potilsch (Bartininkai)
    Pasekel, Ludwig Louis 222
Prapuntai
    Friedke, August 100
Prienai
    Reichel, Anna 241
Pryga
    Hausrath, Eva 121
Przystawańce (Poland)
    Hein, Adolf 126
    Hein, Amalia 128
    Hein, Andreas Heinrich 127
    Worm, Karl 309
Puńsk
    Hein, Amelia 129
    Hein, Ludwig 129
Puńsk (Poland)
    Hausrath, Dorothea Dora 122
    Hausrath, Ferdinand 122
    Hausrath, Josef 121
    Worm, Martin 309
    Worm, Rosalia Rose 309
Puszogród (Near Panemunė)
    Baumann, Emilie 51
    Baumann, Olga 52
Putriškiai
    Buschar, Georg 69

R

Ramanavas
    Gleichfrosch, Olga 106
    Lauks, Marie 180
Randiškė
    Lang, Adeline Nellie 175
    Lang, Adolf Eduard 179
    Lang, Amelia 179
Raželiai
    Brauer, Gustav 64
Rėčiūnai
    Kalweit, Christian 149
    Tetmeier, Ferdinand Christof 285
Resuras
    Kalchert, Gustav August 148
Ringdaudai
    Schwed, Heinrich 270
Romanowce (Poland)
    Essel, Anna 94
    Essel, Eduard 91
    Essel, Eduard Adolf 92
    Essel, Eduard Karl 93
    Essel, Marie 94

Essel, Wilhelmine Henriette 91
Romanowo (Near Marijampolė)
    Gudat, Emilie 113
Rūda
    Lehmann, Emilie 181
    Lehmann, Emma 182
    Lehmann, Luise Elizabeth 182
Rudwaliszki (Near Liudvinavas)
    Klein, Mathilde Tillie 169

S

Sakiai
    Rebner, Marta 239
Seiliūnai
    Tiedemann, Pauline 292
Seimeniškiai
    Friedrich, Ernestine 102
    Friedrich, Karl 102
    Schmidt, Anna 256
Seirijai
    Ernst, Albert 89
    Ernst, Emilie 89
    Franulewicz, Eduard 98
    Muschinski, Anna 201
    Muschinski, Marianna 202
    Nausner, Reimund 206
    Peters, Albert Ewald 231
    Reinke, Johann Karl 244
    Tiedmann, August Johann 291
    Weinschröder, Malwina Malvina .303
    Weinschröder, Natalie 302
Sejny (Poland)
    Borchert, Eva 63
Senoji Radiškė
    Batke, Emilie 50
    Schwed, Anna 268
Serijai

Tiedmann, Adolf 292
Šilavotas
    Schwelgin, Adolf Edward 272
    Schwelgin, Johann 272
Šilsodis
    Wegner, Johann 300
Skardupiai
    Lackner, Bertha 174
    Lackner, Georg 174
Skirptiškė
    Schütz, Johann 264
Slibinai
    Perrey, Josef 228
    Perry, Christof Adam 227
    Perry, Matthias Max 226
    Perry, Thomas 226
Sosnowo (Marijampolė)
    Neumann, Gustav 211
Sudargas
    Eichelberger, Rudolf Oskar 87
Svidiškiai
    Schultz, Christine 264

T

Tarpučiai
    Nowjack, Ludwig Louis 221
    Weier, August Karl 301
    Weier, Helene Edna 301
Trakėnai
    Gudat, Matthias Leopold 114
    Lang, Karl 175
    Schütz, Auguste 266
    Wilk, Gustav 306
Trakiškiai
    Putnat, Julianna Auguste 238
Tupikai (Near Aštriakalnis)
    Kless, Adolf Adam 167

Kless, Friedrich 168
Kless, Gustav 166
Kless, Karoline Lena 166

Tupikiai (Near Auštriakalnis)
Kless, Bertha 168

Turgalauks
Jonat, Johann 142

U

Ungurinė
Baschar, Gustav 49
Bumblis, Adolf 59
Bumblis, Auguste 61
Heinrich, August 131
Heinrich, Karl 133
Neumann, Karl Adolf 212
Nowiak, Eva 218
Schaak, Georg 253
Unterberger, Anna 297

Urbantai
Heinrich, August 133
Heinrich, Bertha 133
Heinrich, Johann 134
Heinrich, Marie 132

Užbaliai
Wiemert, August Martin 305

Užsieniai
Blum, Gustav 58

V

Vainatrakis
Schwenter, Heinrich Friedrich 274

Vaiponiškė
Dill, Alma 77
Dill, Erna 78
Dill, Erwin 77
Dill, Johann Jr. 76
Dill, Julius 79

Dill, Walter 78

Vaitkabaliai
Wilk, Auguste 306

Valavičiai
Schmidt, Adolf Franz 257

Varnupiai
Andechser, Karl 33

Vartai
Peter, Johann Josef 232
Peter, Olga 229
Peters, Adolf Ferdinand 231
Peters, Karl Carl Charles 229
Peters, Ludwig Louis 230

Vazniškiai
Gerulat, Bertha 104
Gerulat, Eduard 104

Vilkabaliai
Baltronat, Karl 41

Vilkaviškis
Bender, Bertha 53
Jurgelewitz, Berta 145
Jurgelewitz, Emma 145
Reinecker, Hildegard Erna 242
Reinecker, Richard Johann 242

Virbalis
Lier, August 184
Reder, Gustav 240

Vištytis
Spei, August 278

Vyžpiniai
Kaptein, Emma 151

W

Widugiery (Poland)
Dorn, Eduard Martin 83
Kinat, Adolf 158
Kinat, August Augustis 156

Kinat, Eduard Karl (1886)............160
Kinat, Emilie........................159, 160
Kinat, Ferdinand...........................156
Kinat, Karoline 159
Kinat, Marianna............................160

Wiłkopedzie
    Hein, Josef....................................130

Wiżajny (Poland)
    Baranowicz, August 43
    Ginter, Bertha 108
    Günther, August 108
    Günther, Elizabeth Emma 109
    Günther, Julius.............................108
    Tennebor, Emilie Milly 282
    Tennebor, Georg..................282, 283
    Tennebor, Karoline Lena 283

Wojtokiemie (Poland)
    Neitzel, Adolf Otto....................... 207
    Neitzel, Ferdinand Karl................ 207

Z

Zailiai
    Peter, Adolf................................. 230

Zawody
    Simon, Johann............................. 276

Żelazkowizna (Poland)
    Neubacher, Johann....................... 209

Zwirgzda (Poland)
    Herr, Ferdinand........................... 136

INDEX OF *DEUTSCHE AUS LITAUEN* INTERRED AT LUTHERAN CEMETERY

Women are listed by their birth names.

A

Ackermann, Berta 28
Ackermann, Lydia 30
Albrecht, Gustav 32
Andechser, August 35
Aukschun, Leopold 40

B

Baltronat, Helene 44
Baltronat, Karl 43
Baltrunat, Karl Wilhelm 44
Baranowicz, August 45
Baschar, Auguste 52
Baschar, Gustav 52
Basenau, Eva 48
Basenau, Gustav 50
Basenau, Johann 47
Basenau, Karl 46
Batke, Emilie 53
Baumann, Emilie 54
Baumann, Olga 55
Bender, Auguste 56
Bender, Bertha 56
Bender, Henriette 56
Berwing, Adolf Johann 58
Berwing, Auguste 58
Berwing, Emilie 59
Berwing, Johann Julius 59

Berwing, Karl Gustav 57
Birkoben, Albert 61
Birkoben, Hugo Gustav 61
Birkoben, Karl 61
Borchert, Eva 67
Brauer, Gustav 69
Budnik, Emilie 70
Bumblis, August Gustav 63
Bumblis, Johann 64
Bumblis, Marianna 65
Burke, Johanna 72
Burke, Karl Adolf 72
Buschar, Georg 74

D

Dangelat, Ludwig 75
Dikheiser, Adolf Luis 76
Dikheiser, Bertha 77
Dikheiser, Lydia 78
Dikheiser, Pauline Helene 76
Dikheiser, Wanda 78
Dill, Karl 80
Dingfeld, Anna Helene 86
Dingfeld, Elizabet 86
Dingfeld, Wilhelmine 86
Doczkis, Georg 88
Doczkis, Johann 88
Dorn, Adele Emilie 89
Dorn, Maria 90

E

Eckert, Johanna Karoline 92
Elmentahler, Johann Adolf 94
Ernst, Albert 95
Ernst, Emilie 95
Erzthaler, Henriette 96
Erzthaler, Karl Friedrich 96
Erzthaler, Marie Emma 96
Essel, Eduard 97
Essel, Eduard Karl 99
Essel, Marie 100
Essel, Wilhelmine Henriette 97

F

Filier, Wilhelmine 101
Fischer, Helene 102
Franulewicz, Eduard 105
Franulewicz, Julius 103
Franulewicz, Pauline Bertha 103
Friedke, August 107
Friedrich, Anna 110
Friedrich, Ernestine 109
Friedrich, Gottlieb Ludwig 108
Friedrich, Karl 109

G

Gerulat, Bertha 111
Ginter, Bertha 115
Gleid, Marie 114
Grübner, August 119
Gudat, Emilie 120
Günther, August 116
Günther, Elizabeth Emma 116
Günther, Julius 115

H

Haase, August 123
Habersat, Karl 126
Hartig, Auguste Bertha 127
Hausrath, Eva 130
Hausrath, Josef 130
Heimert, Anna Dorothea 134
Hein, Adolf 135
Hein, Julius 138
Hein, Leopold 137
Hein, Ludwig 138
Hein, Rudolf 138
Heinrich, Albert 140
Heinrich, August Hermann 141
Heinrich, Johann 143
Hirsch, Albertine 147
Hirsch, Albine 149
Hirsch, Auguste 148
Hirsch, Gottlieb 147
Hirsch, Julius 149
Hirsch, Olga 147
Hirsch, Wilhelm 148
Hubert, Anna Helene 150

J

Jurgeleit, Christ 154
Jurgeleit, Christine 154
Jurkschat, Adolf 157
Jurkschat, Anna 157
Jurkschat, Johanna 157
Jurkschat, Pauline 157

K

Kalchert, Gustav August ... 159
Kalweit, Christian ... 160
Kaptein, Emma ... 162
Kaptein, Ottilie ... 162
Kausch, Auguste ... 163
Kausch, Helene ... 163
Kiesling, Hedwig ... 166
Kinat, Amelia ... 171
Kinat, Anna ... 167
Kinat, August (1879) ... 167
Kinat, August (1895) ... 171
Kinat, Marianna ... 171
Kirschner, Anna ... 174
Kirschner, Auguste ... 173
Kirschner, Emilie ... 175
Kirschner, Jeanette Johanna ... 175
Kirschner, Pauline ... 174
Klaus, Justine ... 176
Klein, Mathilde ... 180
Klotzhober, Helene ... 181
Kokoschka, Friedrich ... 183
Konrad, Amalie ... 184
Konrad, Ludwig ... 184
Kramer, Ludwig Friedrich ... 185

L

Lang, Adeline ... 188
Lang, Albine ... 188
Lang, Amelia ... 192
Lang, Gustav Ludwig August ... 191
Lang, Karl ... 188
Lehmann, Anna ... 194
Lehmann, Emilie ... 194
Lehmann, Emma ... 195
Lehmann, Luise ... 195
Lehmann, Mathias ... 194
Leichert, Christine ... 196
Leichert, Magdalene Helene ... 196
Lindhammer, Henriette ... 199
Logies, Karl Franz ... 200
Lukat, Eduard ... 202
Lukat, Gustav ... 202
Lukat, Leopoldine ... 202

M

Mai, Alexander ... 205
Mauruschat, Eduard ... 207
Mett, Augustine Pauline ... 208
Mett, Josef ... 208
Missun, Anna ... 212
Missun, Christian ... 212
Mittag, Auguste ... 213
Muranko, Alexander ... 214
Muschinski, Adolf ... 215
Muschinski, Josef ... 215

N

Neitzel, Adolf Otto ... 223
Neitzel, Ferdinand Karl ... 222
Neubacher, Johann ... 224
Neumann, Karl ... 227
Niederstrass, Georg ... 229
Niederstrasse, Julius ... 229
Niederstrasse, Karl ... 230
Nowiak, Emilie ... 235

Nowiak, Eva 234
Nowiak, Georg 234
Nowjack, Hugo 236
Nowjack, Irene 237

P

Pampus, Gustav 239
Perrej, Adolf 241
Perrey, Josef 240, 244
Perry, Matthias 242
Perry, Thomas 242
Peter, Adolf 246
Peter, Anna 246
Peter, Emilie Mathilde 248
Peter, Johann Josef 248
Peters, Albert Ewald 248
Peters, Karl 245
Peters, Ludwig 246
Podgis, Alexander 250
Podzis, Adeline 250
Podzis, Julianna 250
Pohl, Johann 251
Pudimat, Adeline 252
Pudimat, Heinrich 252
Putnat, Julianna Auguste 255

R

Reinke, Adolf Julius 260
Reinke, Angeline 260
Reinke, Anna 260, 261
Reinke, Johann Karl 261
Reinke, Marianna 262
Reiter, Andreas Heinrich 263
Reiter, Matthias 264
Rosekeit, Emilie 266

S

Saleker, Gustav Adolph 269
Saleker, Johann Andreas 267
Schmidt, Adolf Franz 274
Schmidt, August 273
Schnell, Albertine 277
Schnell, Anna 277
Schröder, Gottlieb 279
Schröder, Helene 280
Schröder, Henriette 279
Schultz, Albine 281
Schultz, Christine 281
Schütz, Anna Marie 283
Schütz, Auguste 283
Schütz, Emilie 283
Schütz, Georg 282
Schwed, Anna 285, 286
Schwed, Heinrich 287
Schwed, Helene Emma 288
Schwed, Julius Gustav 288
Schwelgin, Johann 289
Schwenter, Heinrich Friedrich 291
Semler, Karl Adam 292
Simon, Johann 293
Sokolek, Adolf 294
Spurgat, Jacob 296
Stassun, Friedrich 297

T

Tennebor, Emilie 299

Tennebor, Georg 299, 300
Tennebor, Karoline 300
Tetmeier, Adeline 303
Tetmeier, Anna 302
Tetmeier, Ferdinand Christof 302
Tetmeier, Wilhelmine 303
Tiedmann, Adolf Eduard 307
Tiedmann, August Johann 309
Tiedmann, Julius 304
Tieslauk, Jakob 310
Tieslauk, Ludwig 312

U

Unterberger, Amelia 313
Unterberger, Friedrich 313

W

Walinski, Georg 317
Wegner, Johann 318
Weinschröder, Julian 320
Weinschröder, Leon 320
Weinschröder, Malwina 321
Weinschröder, Natalie 320
Wiemert, Anna 323
Wiemert, Emilie 323
Wilk, Emilie 326
Wilk, Emilie Rosalia 325
Wilk, Gustav 325
Wisgin, Emilie 327
Worm, Karl 329
Worm, Martin 328

www.ingramcontent.com/pod-product-compliance
Lightning Source LLC
Chambersburg PA
CBHW080724230426
43665CB00020B/2606